MW00443540

Algorithmic Composition

A Guide to Composing Music with Nyquist

Algorithmic Composition

A Guide to Composing Music with Nyquist

Mary Simoni and Roger B. Dannenberg

Rensselaer Polytechnic Institute
Troy, New York

Carnegie Mellon University
Pittsburgh, Pennsylvania

THE UNIVERSITY OF MICHIGAN PRESS

Ann Arbor

Copyright © 2008, 2013 by Mary Simoni and Roger B. Dannenberg
All rights reserved

This book may not be reproduced, in whole or in part, including illustrations, in any form (beyond that copying permitted by Sections 107 and 108 of the U.S. Copyright Law and except by reviewers for the public press), without written permission from the publisher.

Published in the United States of America by
The University of Michigan Press
Manufactured in the United States of America
⊚ Printed on acid-free paper

2016   2015   2014   2013   4   3   2   1

ISBN 978-0-472-11868-7 (cloth : alk. paper)
ISBN 978-0-472-03523-6 (pbk. : alk. paper)
ISBN 978-0-472-02905-1 (e-book)

The authors have used their best efforts in preparing this book. These efforts include the development of software. The authors make no warranty of any kind, expressed or implied, with regard to the software included or referenced in this book.

About the cover: Inspired by *Atlas Eclipticalis* by John Cage (see Chapter 12), in which musical staves were superimposed over a star chart, this design by Roger B. Dannenberg includes a NASA Hubble Space Telescope (HST) image of the center of globular cluster M15 (15th object in the Messier Catalog), located 30,000 light-years away in the constellation Pegasus. The star image is by the Space Telescope Science Institute (STScI) and available at http://hubblesite.org/newscenter/archive/releases/1993/13/image/a.

Dedicated to

Kevin, Shannon and Sarah

Frances and Richard

Contents

Preface

This book is about learning to compose music using the SAL programming language and the compositional environment Nyquist developed by Roger B. Dannenberg.

The motivation for writing this book comes from several years of teaching music and engineering students the fundamentals of algorithmic composition. Algorithmic composition, for the purposes of this book, is defined as the use of computers to implement procedures that result in the generation of music. The idea of applying algorithms during the composition of music is pervasive throughout music history. The intent of this book is to give the reader the fundamentals of SAL and Nyquist accompanied by examples of algorithmically based compositions. Although not every aspect of SAL and Nyquist is covered in this book, readers will be well equipped to develop their own algorithms for composition. The *Nyquist Reference Manual* (part of the open-source Nyquist system) provides in-depth documentation of the Nyquist system.

As we wrote this book, we kept the needs of several kinds of readers foremost in mind:

- Musicians—These readers know the fundamentals of tonal music theory and have had formal instruction in music performance and composition. They may or may not have studied a programming language.
- Engineers—These readers have significant experience in designing and implementing algorithms but not necessarily for music. They have some knowledge of tonal music theory but have not likely had formal instruction in music performance or composition.
- Researchers—These readers have experience in both music and engineering and are interested in quickly and efficiently learning the fundamentals of SAL as a composition language.

This book is organized into three sections. Section I, comprised of Chapters 1 through 4, introduces the fundamentals of programming in SAL and Nyquist. Section I also includes a historical survey of algorithmic composition. Section II, comprised of Chapters 5 through 12, is the core content of the book. These chapters contain detailed information on the integration of SAL and Nyquist with an emphasis on music composition. Some readers may choose to reverse their study of recursion (Chapter 11) and iteration (Chapter 12). Readers with less programming experience generally find it easier to understand recursion if they have first studied iteration. Chapter 11 and Chapter 12 have many parallel examples designed to help the reader understand the differences between iteration and recursion through direct comparison. Section III, comprised of Chapter 13 through Chapter 16, may be regarded as advanced topics in algorithmic composition.

The reader is expected to be familiar with computers in general, creating, moving, naming, and opening files, editing text, setting up a personal computer to play audio files, and using a web browser. Beginners may need the assistance of an instructor or additional guides to general computing and computer music.

Acknowledgments

This book began as an introduction to the use of Common Music and Common Lisp. Common Music was developed by Heinrich (Rick) Taube with the support of Tobias Kunze, and this book would not have been possible without them. Although the book is now completely independent of Common Music and Common Lisp, the language SAL was adapted to Nyquist from recent versions of Common Music, and the pattern system in Nyquist is based on a similar design in Common Music.

We also acknowledge the work of David S. Touretzky for his influential book, *Common LISP: A Gentle Introduction to Symbolic Computation*. Although this book is no longer in print, it has been an invaluable teaching tool and reference for us and for students. Touretzky's emphasis on simplicity has opened the door of algorithmic composition to many music composition students.

Paul Berg, a pioneer and proponent of algorithmic composition, not only influenced our work, but he kindly suggested additional work and references.

Joe Wieciek contributed to the second version of this book, specifically by updating the bibliography, listening examples, and website.

We would also like to thank students who carefully reviewed the first version of this book prior to publication: Todd Bauer, Nathaniel Cartier, Michael Chiaburu, Hiroko Fukudo, Matthew Gill, Colin Meek, Christopher Peck, Nathan Proulx, Jennifer Remington, Christopher Rozell, Stephen Alex Ruthmann, Michael Vartanian, and John Woodruff. Their thoughtful comments and contributions have increased the accessibility and relevance of the content.

We are very much in gratitude to the University of Michigan School of Music for their excellent music technology facilities, technical staff, and loyal support of the work of Mary Simoni. Similarly, Carnegie Mellon has supported Roger Dannenberg's research and the development of Nyquist, without which this book would not have been possible. Nyquist, in turn, reflects the work of many contributors. Please see the *Nyquist Reference Manual* for acknowledgments of the growing list of Nyquist developers and contributors.

Chapter 1   Introduction

This book describes techniques for algorithmic composition using Nyquist, a computer language for sound synthesis and composition. The purpose of the book is to assist readers who are interested in composing music using computers. The best way of learning about algorithmic composition is by doing, so this book includes numerous carefully documented examples. Accompanying electronic media (http://www.algocompbook.com) include a full implementation of the Nyquist system for several operating systems as well as files containing most of the program examples in this book. This material and a personal computer are all the reader will need to start making music. The authors assume that the reader has very little experience with Nyquist (or SAL, a language on which Nyquist is based). For this reason, SAL and Nyquist are explained in the first four chapters. The authors assume the reader has an understanding of tonal music theory. Readers may find knowledge of MIDI (The Musical Instrument Digital Interface) (International MIDI Association, 1983; Rothstein, 1992) to be helpful, although most of the examples use Nyquist to generate sound directly.

Many wonderful compositions have been written over the years using Nyquist. By making the concepts of algorithmic composition and the details of Nyquist more approachable, the authors hope more people will be enticed to explore the potential of composition by computer. Nyquist is not the only computer music language or system, and any programming language can be used for music composition. Just as the concepts of this book could be expressed in French or Mandarin, the programming concepts you learn here can be transferred to other programming languages. However, the examples in this book wil use one language: Nyquist.

Nyquist offers two programming languages, at least on the surface. The first of these languages, SAL, is related to popular programming languages such as Basic and Pascal, but underneath, the *semantics* of SAL are based on Lisp. Lisp is the second language available to Nyquist programmers. Proponents regard Lisp as simple, elegant, and powerful, while detractors claim that Lisp is confusing. For casual users and novice programmers, SAL is probably simpler, and this book uses SAL.

1.1   SAL

The SAL language used in Nyquist is based on, and almost identical to, the SAL implementation in Common Music (Taube 2005). Like

Nyquist, Common Music was originally based on Lisp, and SAL was designed and implemented to provide an alternative, perhaps more familiar and easy-to-use syntax for Common Music users. SAL is based on commands containing expressions. The expression "12 + 3" means "the sum of 12 and 3," and the command "print 12 + 3" means "print the value of the expression '12 + 3'."

1.2   Lisp

SAL programs and commands are translated automatically by Nyquist into Lisp, making it easy to mix Lisp programs with SAL programs. The programming language Lisp derives its name from List Processing (Winston, 1989). List processing was developed in 1956 by artificial intelligence researchers Allen Newell, J. C. Shaw, and Herbert Simon, and the Lisp language was invented by John McCarthy (Touretzky, 1990). Since the early days of Lisp, researchers have discovered the power of Lisp's processing capabilities for music. Music, a time-based art form, oftentimes is conceived as a succession of events. The events may be a series of pitches, articulation patterns, or a succession of rhythms. Figure 1.2.1 depicts a pitch series that is accompanied by a list representation of that series. Each item in the list representation is called an element.

Figure 1.2.1: Pitch series represented by (C E D F)

Once musical events are described as elements of a list, Lisp functions may be applied to each element of the list to transform the elements. One such example might be to transpose every element of the list in Figure 1.2.1 up a major second returning the list (D F-sharp E G).

1.3   Nyquist

Nyquist is an extensible programming environment for sound synthesis and computer-based composition. The development of Nyquist began in 1990 by Roger Dannenberg (1997), and it has evolved with contributions by many people. Nyquist is based on a small implementation of Lisp called XLISP, which was designed and implemented by David Betz in the 1980's. To support efficient sound synthesis, Nyquist includes some fundamental extensions to XLISP, and this modified XLISP is fully contained within the Nyquist system. For SAL users, an XLISP program translates SAL programs into XLISP. Nyquist runs on Macintosh, Windows, and Unix operating systems. The software and accompanying electronic documentation are available as free, open source software at SourceForge.net (Dannenberg, 2005) and also in the electronic material that accompanies this book. You may think of Figure 1.3.1 when conceptualizing the software layers used by Nyquist.

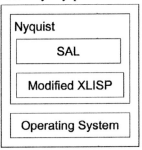

Figure 1.3.1: Software layers of Nyquist

The main task of Nyquist is to compute audio from programs. Normally, Nyquist can play audio immediately as it is computed, but Nyquist can also save sounds to sound files. It is also possible to use Standard MIDI Files for both input and output to Nyquist. Using MIDI Files, it is possible to output music to other programs such as Finale (Purse, 2005) and Sibelius (Rudolph and Leonard, 2007) that can display common music notation.

1.4 The Nyquist Integrated Development Environment

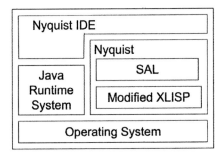

Figure 1.4.1: Software layers including Nyquist and the Nyquist IDE

While Nyquist can be run as a stand-alone program, it is much more convenient to use the Nyquist Integrated Development Environment (IDE) that supports program editing, on-line documentation, a sound browser, and graphical interfaces for some sound design tasks. The IDE is written in Java, yet another programming language. Java was created by James Gosling and his team at Sun Microsystems and first released in 1995. Java is a general purpose language with cross-platform support for graphical user interfaces, making it a good choice for the Nyquist IDE. The Java language is not normally visible to Nyquist users. Figure 1.4.1 elaborates on Figure 1.3.1 to include the Nyquist IDE. Note that the IDE uses Nyquist, but provides access to Nyquist only indirectly through the IDE interface.

1.5 Algorithmic Composition

An algorithm is defined as a set of rules or a sequence of operations designed to accomplish some task or solve a problem. Human beings are very good at designing and implementing algorithms. From getting dressed in the morning to cooking dinner, we are continuously developing algorithms to solve life's everyday problems.

Gareth Loy describes algorithms from a musical perspective. (Loy, 1989). An algorithm, by definition, must have a finite number of steps; have both input to and output from the algorithm; yield a result in a finite period of time; and have a precise definition for each step of the algorithm. Donald Knuth explains that there are also aesthetic criteria for the evaluation of an algorithm (Knuth, 1973). These aesthetic criteria include simplicity, parsimony, elegance, and tractability. Ideally, musical algorithms should strive to meet these criteria.

Composition is the process of creating a musical work (Apel, 1979). The term *composition* literally means to "put together" parts into a unified whole. The process of composing music is oftentimes characterized by trial and error. The composer tries something, listens, and determines if revisions are necessary. The composer is continually evaluating the effectiveness of a part in relation to the whole.

We combine the terms *algorithm* and *composition* to derive the term *algorithmic composition*. Algorithmic composition, in the simplest sense, occurs when a composer uses an algorithm to put together a piece of music. Since the mid-twentieth century, the computer has become a key partner in implementing algorithms that generate music. Because of the increased role of the computer in the compositional process, algorithmic composition has come to mean the use of computers to implement compositional procedures that result in the generation of music.

1.6   Additional References

Although this book provides the fundamentals of algorithmic composition using Nyquist, you may wish to augment your reading with additional references. This book focuses almost exclusively on the SAL language and syntax, but SAL is translated in a very direct way into the language Lisp. A knowledge of Lisp is useful to understanding SAL. Two excellent Lisp references include *LISP* by Patrick Henry Winston and Bertold Klaus Paul Horn (1989) and *Common LISP – The Language* by Guy L. Steele (1990). (Unfortunately, Common LISP is not fully compatible with XLISP, but the basic language concepts are the same, and if anything, XLISP is smaller and easier to master.) Nyquist is accompanied by volumous electronic documentation in HTML and printable PDF files. For detailed information on MIDI, consult the MIDI specification and supporting documents published by the International MIDI Association (1983) or a textbook on MIDI such as *MIDI: A Comprehensive Introduction* by Joseph Rothstein (1992). For additional information on strategies for algorithmic composition, refer to *Formalized Music* by Iannis Xenakis (1971, 1992), *Using the AC Toolbox: A Tutorial* by Paul Berg (2008), Chapter 19 of *The Computer Music Tutorial* by Curtis Roads (1996), Chapter 11 of *Computer Music: Synthesis, Composition, and Performance* by Charles Dodge and Thomas Jerse (1997), or *Notes from the Metalevel: An Introduction to Algorithmic Music Composition* by Heinrich Taube (2004).

The web site www.algorithmic.net by Chris Ariza is an excellent source for additional references, software, and discussion.

There are other automated compositional systems that use Lisp besides Nyquist. Among these are the AC Toolbox (Berg, 1996), Common Music, which also supports the SAL syntax (Taube, 1989), MIDI-LISP (Boynton, 1986), Lisp Kernel (Rahn, 1990), Patchwork (Laurson, 1989; Malt, 1993), Symbolic Composer (Tonality Systems, 1993), FORMES (Rodet, 1984), CompScheme (Döbereiner, 2008), and Impromptu (Sorenson, 2005).

Of course Lisp and SAL are not the only languages used for algorithmic composition. Chris Ariza's thesis (2005a) describes an approach using the language Python (Lutz, 2007). Another popular language and environment for algorithmic composition, especially in real-time interactive systems, is MAX, as described by Robert Rowe (1994) and Todd Winkler (2001). Other interesting languages and systems include Paul Hudak's Haskore system (2000) based on the language Haskel, and ChucK, a language and system for real-time music programs by Ge Wang and Perry Cook (2003).

Chapter 2 The History and Philosophy of Algorithmic Composition

In Chapter 1, we defined algorithmic composition as the use of a rule or procedure to put together a piece of music. This chapter will give you a broader understanding of algorithmic composition, how algorithms have been used throughout music history, and an introduction to the aesthetic issues of algorithmic composition.

2.1   The Process of Algorithmic Composition

A very simple example of using a procedure to generate a piece of music is to use a 12-sided die (numbered 1–12) to determine the order of pitches in a composition. An association, or mapping is made to correlate each pitch in a twelve-tone equal tempered scale with each number on the die. Figure 2.1.1 demonstrates the mapping of pitches to numbers.

Figure 2.1.1: Mapping between pitches and numbers

Say that we decide to roll the die six times. Our six tosses return the numbers 2, 5, 3, 9, 3, and 12. The music that results from our rolls of the die is found in Figure 2.1.2.

Figure 2.1.2: Random pitch sequence

Can such a simple algorithm produce interesting music? How do we determine the other aspects of the composition such as rhythm, timbre, loudness, register, etc.? Composers throughout music history have explored these questions.

2.2 A Brief History of Algorithmic Processes Applied to Music Composition

The Greek philosopher, mathematician, and music theorist Pythagoras (ca. 500 B.C.) documented the relationship between music and mathematics that laid the foundation for our modern study of music theory and acoustics. The Greeks believed that the understanding of numbers was key to understanding the universe. Their educational system, the quadrivium, was based on the study of music, arithmetic, geometry, and astronomy. Although we have numerous treatises on music theory dating from Greek antiquity, the Greeks left no clues as to whether they applied mathematical procedures to the composition of music.

Over a thousand years later, the work of music theorists such as Guido d'Arezzo established the framework for our conventional system of music notation. His system employed a staff accompanied by a clef making it possible for a composer to notate a score so that it could be performed by someone other than the composer. Prior to the development of the score, music was learned by rote and generally improvised and embellished by the performing musician. By the thirteenth century, formalized music composition began to replace improvisation and the roles of composer and performer became increasingly distinct.

The music theorist Franco of Cologne established rules for the time values of single notes, ligatures, and rests in his treatise *Arts canus mensurabilis* (ca. 1250). By the early fourteenth century, composers began to treat rhythm independently of pitch and text. French composers of the *ars nova*, such as Phillipe de Vitry and Guillaume de Machaut, used isorhythm as a means of unifying their compositions. Iso means "same" so isorhythm means literally "same rhythm." Isorhythm is the practice of mapping a rhythmic sequence, named the *talea*, onto a pitch sequence called the *color*. Figure 2.2.1 depicts the talea from the motet *De bon espoir-Puisque la douce-Speravi* by Guillaume de Machaut.

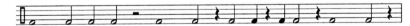

Figure 2.2.1: Talea of the isorhythmic motet *De bon espoir-Puisque la douce-Speravi* by Guillaume de Machaut

The next figure shows the color of the same motet.

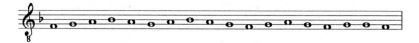

Figure 2.2.2: Color of the isorhythmic motet *De bon espoir-Puisque la douce-Speravi* by Guillaume de Machaut

The tenor of *De bon espoir-Puisque la douce-Speravi* was derived by mapping the color onto the talea as shown in Figure 2.2.3.

Figure 2.2.3: The tenor of *De bon espoir-Puisque la douce-Speravi* by Guillaume de Machaut

Phillipe de Vitry used a *palindrome* in the construction of the talea for his isorhythmic motet *Garrit gallus – In nova fert*. A palindrome is a pattern that reads the same forwards as it does backwards. Figure 2.2.4 shows the organization of the palindrome by measure. Measure 1 compares to measure 9, measure 2 compares to measure 8, etc.

Figure 2.2.4: The talea of *Garrit gallus – In nova fert* by Phillipe de Vitry

The Renaissance period witnessed the rise of polyphonic sacred and secular musical forms. By the Baroque period (1601–1750), highly developed contrapuntal forms such as the canon and fugue flourished. One of the great masters of contrapuntal forms was Johann Sebastian Bach. During the final years of his life, J.S. Bach composed such didactic contrapuntal works such as the *Musical Offering* and *The Art of the Fugue* (Bach, 1752). *The Art of the Fugue* is a brilliant pedagogical tool for the study of counterpoint that systematically documents the procedure of fugal and canonic composition.

The canon is a highly procedural contrapuntal form. The composer begins with a melody, called the leader, which is strictly followed at a delayed time interval by another voice, called the follower. Sometimes, the follower may present a variation of the leader through transposition, augmentation, or inversion. Figure 2.2.5 shows an excerpt from *The Art of the Fugue* by J.S. Bach that is a canon in both augmentation (note durations are stretched) and inversion (the up-down direction of intervals is reversed).

Figure 2.2.5: Canone I from *The Art of the Fugue* by J.S. Bach

In the final fugue of *The Art of the Fugue, Fuga XV*, J.S. Bach uses his own name, B-A-C-H, as the subject of the fugue: B-flat, A, C, and H. (H is the German letter for B.) His name is embedded in one of the most masterful contrapuntal works of all time.

Figure 2.2.6: Excerpt from *Fuga XV* from *The Art of the Fugue* by J.S. Bach

One of the most often cited examples of algorithmic music in the Classical period (1750–1827) is *Musikalisches Würfelspiel* by Wolfgang Amadeus Mozart (1756–1791). In this composition, Mozart (or perhaps someone using his name) composed discrete musical excerpts that could be combined to form a waltz. The order of musical excerpts was determined by rolling two six-sided dice. The person assembling the waltz would refer to a table created by Mozart that showed which music should be used for the values of 2–12 on the dice.

Romanticism pushed the harmonic vocabulary into the extreme use of chromaticism. After Richard Wagner (1813–1883), there was very little a composer could do that would be considered novel using tonal music theory. Arnold Schoenberg, and his pupils Anton Webern and Alban Berg, established new procedures for composition called *serial composition*.

In serial composition, the composer works with a series of twelve chromatic tones of equal importance. In strict serial composition, no tone may be repeated until all twelve have been used. The total number of twelve-note series is 479,001,600 (Brindle, 1969), which greatly expands the melodic and harmonic vocabulary of the late Romantic period. Because of the equal importance of the twelve chromatic tones, serial composition eroded tonality and gave rise to atonality.

Algorithmic procedures lend themselves well to serial composition. To introduce variation into a serial composition, the composer may use transformations of the tone row derived from transposition, inversion, retrograde, or retrograde inversion of the row. (This, however, leaves the composer with a mere 9,980,160 rows that are unique under these transformations.) Figure 2.2.7 shows the tone row used by Alban Berg in the *Lyric Suite* for string quartet composed in 1926.

Figure 2.2.7: The tone row for the *Lyric Suite* by Alban Berg

Figure 2.2.8 shows a matrix that was constructed based on the tone row from Alban Berg's *Lyric Suite*. The rows are numbered 1–12 and the columns are labeled A–L. The original form of the tone row is found in Row 1, Columns A–L, reading from left to right. The retrograde form of the tone row is found by reading Row 1, Columns A–L, reading from right to left. The inversion of the tone row is found in Column A reading Row 1 to Row 12 and the retrograde inversion is found in Column A reading from Row 12 to Row 1. Each Row and Column is further labeled with T followed by a value in the range 0–11. The T stands for transposition and the number is the level of transposition measured in half steps from the original tone row. For example, T5 means the tone row has been transposed up five half steps from the original form (e.g. a Perfect Fourth).

		A T0	B T11	C T7	D T4	E T2	F T9	G T3	H T8	I T10	J T1	K T5	L T6
1	T0	F	E	C	A	G	D	Ab	Db	Eb	Gb	Bb	B
2	T1	Gb	F	Db	Bb	Ab	Eb	A	D	E	G	B	C
3	T5	Bb	A	F	D	C	G	Db	Gb	Ab	B	Eb	E
4	T8	Db	C	Ab	F	Eb	Bb	E	A	B	D	Gb	G
5	T10	Eb	D	Bb	G	F	C	Gb	B	Db	E	Ab	A
6	T3	Ab	G	Eb	C	Bb	F	B	E	Gb	A	Db	D
7	T9	D	Db	A	Gb	E	B	F	Bb	C	Eb	G	Ab
8	T4	A	Ab	E	Db	B	Gb	C	F	G	Bb	D	Eb
9	T2	G	Gb	D	B	A	E	Bb	Eb	F	Ab	C	Db
10	T11	E	Eb	B	Ab	Gb	Db	G	C	D	F	A	Bb
11	T7	C	B	G	E	D	A	Eb	Ab	Bb	Db	F	Gb
12	T6	B	Bb	Gb	Eb	Db	Ab	D	G	A	C	E	F

Figure 2.2.8: Tone row matrix for Alban Berg's *Lyric Suite*

About the same time Alban Berg completed the *Lyric Suite*, Iannis Xenakis (1922–2001) began to make his way in the world. Xenakis received an engineering degree from the Athens Polytechnic School and studied music composition with Honegger, Milhaud, and Messiaen and architecture with Le Corbusier. Xenakis was keenly interested in the application of mathematics to music composition. In 1966, Xenakis founded the School of Mathematical and Automated Music in Paris. His music is described as *stochastic music,* meaning he uses probability theory in the selection of musical parameters. Xenakis exploited probability theory in his search for new musical form and structure. One of Xenakis' well-known works, *Pithoprakta* (1955–1956), creates dense sound masses determined by probabilistic methods.

The music of Karlheinz Stockhausen (1928–2007) stands in sharp contrast to that of Iannis Xenakis. Stockhausen developed serial composition to its extreme by applying serial methods not only to pitch, but also to rhythm, dynamics, timbre, and density. Stockhausen was influenced by the German philosopher Hegel and his doctrine on the unity of opposites. Stockhausen applied Hegelian philosophy by using calculations to pre-compose his music while integrating chance operations into the performance. A stunning example of his work is the *Klavierstück XI* (1956) composed for piano. The score, measuring about thirty-seven inches by twenty-one inches, consists of nineteen carefully composed segments that the pianist performs in whatever order his or her eye happens to fall upon the score. Stockhausen employed chance operations similar to those explored by Mozart in his *Musikalisches Würfelspiel* almost two hundred years earlier.

About the same time Stockhausen composed the *Klavierstück XI,* Lejaren Hiller and Leonard Isaacson were preparing to significantly alter the course of music history. Ada Augusta, Countess of Lovelace, worked with Charles Babbage on the development of a mechanical computer called the Analytical Engine. In 1842, she described the use of the computer in the creation of music and foretold the era of computer-assisted composition heralded by Hiller and Isaacson:

> The operating mechanism [of the Analytical Engine] ... might act upon other things ... whose mutual fundamental relations could be expressed by those of the abstract science of operations, and which should be also susceptible of adaptations to the action of the operating notation and mechanism of the Engine. Supposing, for instance, that the fun-

damental relations of pitched sounds in the science of harmony and of musical composition were susceptible of such expression and adaptations, the Engine might compose and elaborate scientific pieces of music of any degree of complexity or extent. (Roads, 1996)

It was 1957 when Lejaren Hiller and Leonard Isaacson programmed the ILLIAC computer at the University of Illinois to algorithmically generate music. The output of their software created *The ILLIAC Suite* scored for string quartet. The work of Hiller and Isaacson is documented in the book *Experimental Music* (Hiller, 1959). By 1962, Xenakis began to use the computer to assist in the calculations for his compositions *Amorsima-Morsima* and *Strategie, Jeu pour deux orchestres.*

John Cage (1912–1992) was a self-declared indeterminist. Cage integrated Eastern philosophies, especially Zen Buddhism, and the *I Ching Book of Changes,* into his compositions. A landmark collaboration between Cage and Hiller resulted in the multi-media composition *HPSCHD* (1967–1969). The composition uses computer printouts, excerpts of traditional music, and visual elements depicting space and rocket technology. The traditional music is derived from Mozart's *Musikalisches Würfelspiel* and his piano Sonatas. Cage's statement, "it is the machine that will help us to know whether we understand our own thinking processes," demonstrates his philosophical comradeship with Lejaren Hiller. *HPSCHD* requires up to seven harpsichords and fifty-one electronic tapes that are combined in any possible way to achieve unique performances. The composition received its world premiere before an audience of nine thousand at the University of Illinois on May 16, 1969. The performance included all seven harpsichords, fifty-one computer-generated tapes, eighty slide projectors, and seven film projectors.

For over two thousand years, composers have used algorithms to assist in the creation of new works. Algorithms for music composition have evolved into several categories: aleatoric (or chance) methods (e.g. Cage); determinacy (e.g. Schoenberg, Webern, and Berg); and stochastic (or probabilistic) methods (e.g. Xenakis and Hiller). Composers are applying not only mathematical models but also biological paradigms to the creation of music. Since almost any process may be modeled using a computer, almost any model may be used for music composition.

The principal questions facing composers who use algorithmic processes are rooted in aesthetics and philosophy. Why use algorithms in the composition of music? What is more important—the algorithm or the composition? How does a composer or listener decide if an algorithmic composition is successful?

2.3 Aesthetics of Algorithmic Composition

Aesthetics is a branch of philosophy that describes the theories and forms of beauty in the fine arts. It is our unique set of experiences, and our perception of those experiences, that shape our personal aesthetic. Our personal aesthetic is integrally intertwined with our personality as an artist. Each work of art is some manifestation of the artist's aesthetic.

In Chapter 1, we discussed Knuth's principles for determining the aesthetic merit of an algorithm. How do we decide if a composition that uses algorithms has aesthetic merit?

To answer this question, one must separate the process of composition from the product of composition, e.g. the music. Some algorithmic composers would argue that the aesthetic merit of an algorithmic composition should be based solely on the algorithm used to create the music. Other composers assert that both the algorithms used to create the composition and the composition itself should be assessed when determining aesthetic merit. There are still others who would argue that the algorithms used in algorithmic composition are simply a means to an end and for that reason, the algorithms themselves are not worthy of artistic scrutiny. These composers may believe that their success or failure as a composer is based on the listener's response, and therefore they have the right to throw away or modify the output of an algorithm to achieve their aesthetic goal.

All of these responses to the process and product of algorithmic composition are valid as each view is simply a manifestation of a personal aesthetic. Unfortunately, composers of algorithmic music have not been formally surveyed regarding their views on the aesthetics of algorithmic composition, so we do not know how many composers fall into which category at any given time or if there are more categories to consider.

In the absence of a formal survey, we let the repertoire of algorithmic composition speak for itself. In reviewing algorithmic processes throughout the twentieth century, the number of compositions that are supported by documented algorithms is dwarfed by those that are not. In fact, when asking composers to provide algorithms accompanied by software implementation for this book, many composers confided that their code is not up to Knuth's standards of simplicity, elegance, parsimony, and tractability. With rapid advances in automated music composition systems, and the tendency to embed the process in a technology, it is inherently more difficult to preserve the process than the product.

A group of visual and sonic artists developed their own criteria for determining the aesthetic merit of electronic art, including computer music (Mandelbrojt, 1999). These artists felt the criteria should be based on the poetic quality of the artist's vision; a successful relationship between the artist's idea and its realization, especially when the idea cannot be materialized through simpler traditional means; the efficiency with which the artist's idea is conveyed; and the originality of the idea or its realization. The evaluation of each of these criteria is not simply a "yes" or "no" as in the case of Knuth's criteria. On the contrary, the criteria summarized by Mandelbrojt require a graded continuum for each criterion to render an aesthetic judgment about a work. These criteria also presuppose that the person performing the evaluation knows something of the artist's intent. Unfortunately, such is not always the case.

Algorithmic composers need aesthetic criteria that are neither as limiting as Knuth's nor as assumptive as those described by Mandelbrojt. Composers of algorithmic music are obliged to carefully examine the quality of their artistic ideas and the efficiency with which their ideas are presented. Composers must create successful relationships between the artistic ideas and the technological media in which they work. The work must demonstrate originality or significant refinement of an existing idea and maintain the highest quality of technical production.

2.4 Suggested Listening

Garrit gallus – In nova fert by Phillipe de Vitry

Musical Offering and *The Art of the Fugue* by J.S. Bach

Musikalisches Würfelspiel by Wolfgang Amadeus Mozart

Lyric Suite by Alban Berg

Klavierstück XI by Karlheinz Stockhausen

The ILLIAC Suite by Lejaren Hiller and Leonard Isaacson

Amorsima-Morsima and *Strategie, Jeu pour deux orchestres* by Iannis Xenakis

HPSCHD by John Cage

Chapter 3   Introduction to SAL

Chapter 3 introduces you to the fundamentals of SAL and programming. You will learn about some of the various data types that SAL supports and many of its built-in functions called *primitives*. You will learn how to write your own functions and become familiar with typical error messages.

3.1   Data

Data means information. SAL supports many data types, including numbers, symbols, strings, and lists. Numbers include integers (or whole numbers) and floating point numbers. Floating point numbers are approximations of real numbers.

Example 3.1.1: Numbers

Integers:	−3, 0, 23, 8987
Floating Point Numbers:	−3.222, 3.1459, 0.0

Another data type in SAL is a symbol. Symbols look like words and may contain any combination of letters and numbers along with some special characters such as the hyphen (-), underscore (_), plus (+), and star (*).

Example 3.1.2: Symbols

Symbols: scale, f7-chord, b-flat_major, *transpose*

Two special symbols in SAL are #t and #f. #t represents *true* or *yes*, and #f represents *false*, *no*, or *nothing*. In XLISP, these values are usually named t and nil, and even within SAL, t and nil may be used in place of #t and #f. Except for a few built-in symbols such as #t and #f, the hash character (#) is not allowed in symbol names.

A string data type is a sequence of characters enclosed in double quotes.

Example 3.1.3: Strings

Strings: "A string: anything within double quotes!"
            "Is this a string?"

Another SAL data type is the list. A list is a collection of one or more things enclosed in braces. If the list includes more than one thing, they are separated by spaces. (Spaces include the space character, tab, and newline.) Each thing in the list is called an element. Therefore the list {c-major d-major f-major} has three elements, and the list {4.5 238 .0007 -23 glub} has 5 elements.

Lists are represented in the computer's memory as a chain of structures called *list cells*. You may think of a list cell as having two parts. The left part is referred to as the *first* and the right part is referred to as the *rest*. We often think of the cell as *containing* two things, the first part of a list and the rest of the list. It is more correct to realize that each of these two parts is really a pointer to (a memory address for) other locations in the computer's memory. The *first* pointer points to an element in a list and the *rest* points to the next cell in the list. Figure 3.1.1 is a list cell representation of the list {c-major d-major f-major}. Notice that the list cell chain ends in nil.

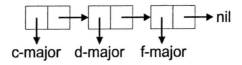

c-major   d-major   f-major

Figure 3.1.1: A list with three elements

Lists can be defined recursively: A list is either nil or a list cell whose *first* is an element and whose *rest* is a list. Often, algorithms that process lists have a similar recursive structure. For example, to play all notes in a list, play the first note (the *first* of the list), then apply the algorithm recursively to rest of the notes (the *rest* of the list). We will return to this idea in Chapter 11. You may recall that nil is a representation for *false*, so (curiously) a list with no elements can be written as nil, {}, or #f.

Lists that consist of one level of a list cell chain are called *flat lists*. When a list contains another list, it is referred to as a *nested list*. An example of a nested list is {c-major {c e g}}. The top-level of the chain of list cells contains two elements: the symbol c-major and the list {c e g}. This second top-level element contains three elements, namely the symbols c, e, and g. Figure 3.1.2 is a list cell representation of the nested list {c-major {c e g}}.

List expressions that have matching left and right braces are called *well-formed lists*. Both {c-major d-major f-major} and {c-major {c e g}} are well-formed lists.

SAL programs use braces to denote lists, and we generally use the same convention in this text; *however*, the Lisp programming language uses parentheses. For example, the Lisp print function prints the list {a b c} as (a b c). Occasionally, you may call a Lisp function from SAL that prints data using Lisp conventions, so do not be too surprised to see lists printed with parentheses.

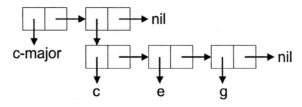

Figure 3.1.2: A nested list

3.2   Running Nyquist

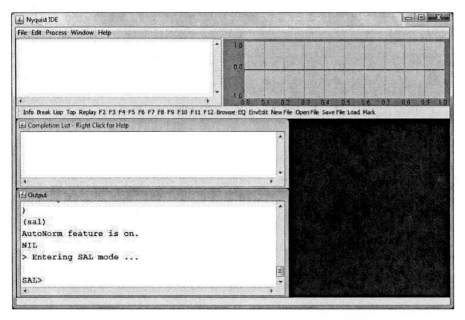

Figure 3.2.1: The Nyquist IDE

If you have not already done so, you should install Nyquist on your computer so that you can try out the examples that follow. Installation instructions and other electronic resources can be found at http://www.algocompbook.com. For most people, the preferred way to run Nyquist is to use the interactive development environment (IDE), a program written in Java named *jnyqide*. When you run *jnyqide*, you should see a screen similar to that in Figure 3.2.1. No-

Chapter 3 · Introduction to SAL

tice that the Output window shows output from Nyquist, which is running in a separate process controlled by *jnyqide*. To send input to Nyquist, type into the text area in the upper left region. When you type the ENTER key, the text is sent to Nyquist to be evaluated. Try typing play osc(c4) followed by the ENTER key. You should hear a 1-second-long sine tone.

In the following sections, continue typing examples into the text area followed by the ENTER key. The input you type will be echoed in the Output window followed by the output generated by Nyquist. Notice the row of labeled buttons just below the text input area. If you make an error, you can reset Nyquist for more input by clicking on the button named Top, which resets the system to Lisp mode, followed by clicking the button named SAL, which tells the system to accept SAL commands.

3.3 SAL Expressions

Expressions combine terms such as numbers, variables, and strings, using operators such as + and *, to denote computation. This section demonstrates how to form and evaluate SAL expressions. The next three sections describe how to use functions, which extend the range of computations you can write with expressions.

The best way to learn about how expressions and functions work in SAL is to use it. Follow along by typing these examples into Nyquist. *Before you start*, make sure that the output window in the lower left of the IDE has the prompt: "SAL>". If not, click on the SAL button on the row of buttons to switch to SAL mode.

Example 3.3.1: Printing expression values

The reader enters the bold text into the input window. The information following the bold text is the output generated by Nyquist. Some commentary appears in italics.

```
SAL> print 3 + 5.6
8.6

SAL> print 1 + 2 + 3
6

SAL> print 7 - 5
2
```

The quotient of two integers is an integer. Fractional parts are rounded toward zero:

```
SAL> print 23 / 8
2
```

Expressions can use parentheses:

```
SAL> print 3 + (3 - 2)
4
```

```
SAL> print 8 * 15 / 3 * (1 + 1)
80
```

In Example 3.3.1, each input to SAL is a print command, which tells SAL to evaluate one or more expressions and print the results. A general template for the print command is:

> print *expression, expression, ...*

Notice that *spaces around operators in expressions are required* in SAL. The expression "x + 2" means "the sum of the value of the variable named 'x' and two," but the expression "x+2" means "the value of the variable named 'x+2'"!

Table 3.3.1: Operators

Precedence	Operator Symbol	Operator Function
1	!	Not
2	@	Time shift
2	@@	Absolute time shift
2	~	Time stretch
2	~~	Absolute time stretch
3	^	Exponentiation
4	*	Multiplication
4	/	Division
5	+	Addition
5	-	Subtraction
5	%	Remainder (Modulus)
6	=	Equal
6	~=	General equality
6	!=	Not equal
6	<	Less than
6	>	Greater than
6	<=	Less than or equal
6	>=	Greater than or equal
7	&	And
8			Or

Chapter 3 · Introduction to SAL

With infix operators, evaluation order is not obvious. Does "1 + 2 * 3" mean "(1 + 2) * 3" or "1 + (2 * 3)"? To resolve the potential ambiguity, SAL uses two rules. First, operators have different priorities, so multiplication and division take precedence over addition and subtraction. Second, operators that share the same priority are evaluated left-to-right. When in doubt, it is always a good idea to use parentheses to make the evaluation order explicit.

The complete list of operators appears in Table 3.3.1 listed in order of their precedence.

3.4 Functions

Operators are convenient for common operations because we are in the habit of reading expressions such as "1 + 2," but there are many more operations than we have symbols for. We call these operations *functions*, give them symbolic names, and invoke them using a special syntax. The syntax for applying a function to data is illustrated by this template:

function(expression, expression, ...)

You may think of functions as procedures that (usually) operate on data and (usually) compute a result value. The template describes a *function call* where the expressions are evaluated from left to right, the resulting values are passed as inputs to the function, and the value returned by the function is the value of the overall expression. SAL functions may be categorized as either primitives or user-defined functions.

A *primitive* is a built-in function or simply put, a function that SAL already knows about. SAL has many primitives that operate on numbers, symbols, sounds, and lists. Example 3.4.1 illustrates some primitives that take numbers as inputs and produce numbers as results.

Example 3.4.1: Arithmetic primitives

The abs *function takes the absolute value of an integer or floating point number.*

```
SAL> print abs(-7.2)
7.2

SAL> print abs(14.5)
14.5
```

The sqrt *function takes the square root of a floating point number, but raises an error and quits if given an integer. The square root of a negative number is undefined and raises a different kind of error.*

```
SAL> print sqrt(25.0)
5
SAL> print sqrt(25)
error: bad integer operation
Call traceback:
     SAL top-level command interpreter

SAL> print sqrt(-25.0)
error: square root of a negative number
Call traceback:
     SAL top-level command interpreter
```

The primitive round *returns the integer nearest to its input. If the input is halfway between two integers (for example 3.5), round to the next higher integer.*

```
SAL> print round(3.5)
4

SAL> print round(2.49)
2

SAL> print round(2.875)
3
```

The primitive float *returns a floating-point number. Note that floating point numbers are printed without a decimal point if the digits to the right of the decimal point are all zeros.*

```
SAL> print float(4)
4
```

Trigonometric functions such as sin *(for sine) work with radians (not degrees) and do not accept integers.*

```
SAL> print sin(1.0)
0.841471
```

Function calls may be nested. SAL evaluates nested function calls by evaluating the innermost functions first to obtain values for more outer functions. To be more precise, function input *expressions* are evaluated from left to right, and then the function is applied to the re-sulting *values.* The result of this recursion is that the innermost ex-pressions are evaluated first. This rule applies to *functions.* In addition to functions and operators, some expressions look like functions but use a different rule for evaluation. We will see examples later.

Infix operators, such as "+" and "*," are just an alternate syntax for function calls. You can think of "1 + 2" as a convenient way to write "sum(1, 2)" after which the normal rule for function evaluation can be applied. Example 3.4.2 illustrates some nested function and operator expressions.

Example 3.4.2: Nested function calls

```
SAL> print sqrt(23.0 / 8)
1.69558

SAL> print sqrt(abs(-9.0))
3

SAL> print max(sin(float(1)), sqrt(1.0 / 2))
0.841471
```

SAL has many primitives that function on lists. A useful function is length, which returns the number of elements found on the top-level of a list.

Example 3.4.3: length

```
SAL> print length({16 2 5})
3

SAL> print length(
        {c-major {c e g} d-major {d f-sharp a}})
4
```

Notice the use of parentheses () and braces {}. The parentheses are an essential part of the function call syntax, and the braces are needed to denote a list value.

Also notice that commands can take more than one line of text. When you type commands into the Nyquist IDE, nothing is sent to Nyquist for evaluation until you complete a command followed by the ENTER key. For example, the second command in Example 3.4.3 is completed when you type the final closing parenthesis.

SAL may have a list of no elements. A list of no elements is referred to as the *empty list* or nil. Thus, nil is both a symbol and a list.

Example 3.4.4: length of empty lists

```
SAL> print length(nil)
0
```

```
SAL> print length({})
0
```

You may access different elements in a list. The primitive **first**
returns the first element of a list. (The function **car** is, for historical
reasons, another name for **first**.)

Example 3.4.5: first

```
SAL> print first(
        {c-major {c e g} d-major {d f-sharp a}})
C-MAJOR
```

Try entering some of the elements in the list using a combination
of upper-case and lower-case letters. You will notice that SAL is not
case sensitive.
The primitive **rest** returns all but the first element of a list as a
list. (And **cdr** is another name for **rest**.)

Example 3.4.6: rest

```
SAL> print rest(
        {c-major {c e g} d-major {d f-sharp a}})
{{C E G} D-MAJOR {D F-SHARP A}}
```

The first and rest of nil are defined as nil, but since nil also represents *false*, SAL prints nil as #f.

Example 3.4.7: first and rest of nil

```
SAL> print first(nil)
#f
```

```
SAL> print rest({})
#f
```

Other SAL primitives can be used to select other elements of a
list such as second, third, and fourth.

Example 3.4.8: second and third

```
SAL> print second(
        {c-major {c e g} d-major {d f-sharp a}})
{C E G}
```

```
SAL> print third(
        {c-major {c e g} d-major {d f-sharp a}})
D-MAJOR
```

SAL> print fourth({1 2})
#f
SAL> print fourth({1 2 3 4 5})
4

The primitive last returns the last element of a list as a list.

The primitive nth returns the nth element of a list, numbering from zero. The first input to nth is the number, and the second input is the list.

The primitive nthcdr returns all but the first n elements of a list. The first input to nthcdr is the number, and the second input is the list.

Example 3.4.9: last

```
SAL> print last({c e g})
{G}

SAL> print last(
        {c-major {c e g} d-major {d f-sharp a}})
{{D F-SHARP A}}
```

Example 3.4.10: nth and nthcdr

```
SAL> print nth(0, {c e g b-flat})
C

SAL> print nth(2, {c e g b-flat})
G

SAL> print nthcdr(0, {c e g b-flat})
{C E G B-FLAT}

SAL> print nthcdr(4,
        {c-major {c e g} d-major {d f-sharp a}})
#f
```

The primitive reverse reverses the elements in a list such that what was first is now last and vice-versa. reverse operates only on the top-level of the list.

Example 3.4.11: reverse

```
SAL> print reverse({c e g b-flat})
{B-FLAT G E C}

SAL> print reverse(
        {c-major {c e g} d-major {d f-sharp a}})
{{D F-SHARP A} D-MAJOR {C E G} C-MAJOR}
```

The cons primitive may be used to construct lists. The cons function creates a list cell. Often, list cells in Lisp are called *cons cells*. The cons function requires two inputs and returns a pointer to a new list cell whose first points to the first input and whose rest points to the second.

Example 3.4.12: cons

```
SAL> print cons(quote(a), {d e-flat})
{A D E-FLAT}
```

You might have expected the expression cons(a, {d e-flat}), but SAL would start the evaluation of this expression by evaluating **a**, which is assumed to be a variable. We will discuss variables later, but for now, the point is that we want the *symbol* **a** *to be used literally*. To prevent any interpretation of the expression **a** and to use it directly as a symbol, we must enclose it in the special form quote(). This is a *special form*, not a function, because it does not automatically evaluate its input expression.

Braces imply that the list elements are to be used literally, so no quote() is necessary for the second input to cons in Example 3.4.12. The cons function may be used to create lists by cons'ing a symbol to nil. If Example 3.4.13 is confusing, you should draw pictures as in Figure 3.1.1 and Figure 3.1.2, remembering that cons simply creates and returns one new list cell.

Example 3.4.13: cons with nil

```
SAL> print cons(quote(c-flat), nil)
{C-FLAT}

SAL> print cons({c e g}, nil)
{{C E G}}

SAL> print cons(nil, nil)
{#f}
```

The list primitive creates lists from inputs by making a list from them. list takes any number of inputs.

Example 3.4.14: list

```
SAL> print list(
        {c-major {c e g} d-major {d f-sharp a}})
{{C-MAJOR {C E G} D-MAJOR {D F-SHARP A}}}

SAL> print list(quote(a), {d e-flat})
{A {D E-FLAT}}

SAL> print list(quote(c-flat), nil)
{C-FLAT #f}
```

The primitive **append** accepts two (or more) inputs. When append is given two lists as its inputs, it returns a list that contains all of the elements of both lists as a list.

Example 3.4.15: append

```
SAL> print append({c e g}, {b-flat d})
{C E G B-FLAT D}
```

When append is given a list followed by a non-list, the result is not a well-formed list. This is printed with a warning as follows.

Example 3.4.16: append with ill-formed list

```
SAL> append({c e g}, quote(b-flat))
{C E G <list not well-formed> B-FLAT}
```

The list cell representation of this looks like Figure 3.4.1.

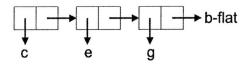

c   e   g   b-flat

Figure 3.4.1: The list formed in Example 3.4.16

Lists like this are rarely used and should be avoided. Now that you know what they are and how to recognize them, let us hope you never see them again.

The primitives **cons**, **list**, and **append** seem very similar. Let's carefully examine how Lisp evaluates these primitives when they are given two lists as input. Figure 3.4.2 shows list cell representations that serve as example inputs to cons, list, and append. Figure 3.4.3 shows the results of applying cons, list, and append to these same inputs. The SAL text output is followed by a list cell representation of the output.

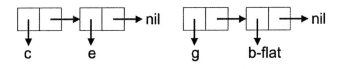

c   e   nil   g   b-flat   nil

Figure 3.4.2: List cell representation of inputs to cons, list, and append: {c e}, {g b-flat}

```
SAL> print cons({c e}, {g b-flat})
{{C E} G B-FLAT}
```

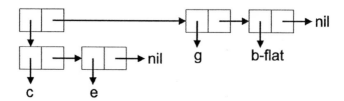

```
SAL> print list({c e}, {g b-flat})
{{C E} {G B-FLAT}}
```

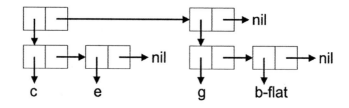

```
SAL> print append({c e}, {g b-flat})
{C E G B-FLAT}
```

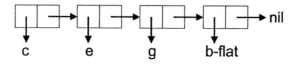

Figure 3.4.3: Compare and contrast cons, list, and append

The primitive random returns a random number. random expects an integer as its input. random returns a random integer between 0 (inclusive) and the value of its input (exclusive).

Example 3.4.17: random

```
SAL> print random(5)
0

SAL> print random(5)
2

SAL> print random(5)
3
```

Sometimes, we need a random real number as opposed to a random integer. rrandom returns a random real number between 0 and 1.

Example 3.4.18: rrandom

```
SAL> print rrandom()
0.583565

SAL> print rrandom()
0.808741
```

real-random returns a random floating point number uniformly distributed in the range given by the two inputs. The name of this function indicates the result is a real number (represented by a floating point value) as opposed to an integer. The result is not "really" random but pseudo-random. In fact, all of these random number generators will return exactly the same sequence of "random" values every time Nyquist is restarted.

Example 3.4.19: real-random

```
SAL> print real-random(1, 10)
6.26508

SAL> print real-random(1, 10)
5.31886

SAL> print real-random(0.1, 0.2)
0.135029
```

3.5   Predicates

Predicates are functions that return true or false. True in SAL is represented by the symbol #t and false in SAL is represented by the symbol #f.

An example of a simple predicate is symbolp. symbolp returns #t if the data passed to the function is a symbol and #f if it is not.

Example 3.5.1: symbolp

```
SAL> print symbolp(nil)
#t

SAL> print symbolp(.435)
#f
```

Another predicate is numberp. It returns #t if the data passed to it is a number and #f if it is not.

Example 3.5.2: numberp

```
SAL> print numberp(nil)
#f

SAL> print numberp(.435)
#t
```

The predicate floatp expects a number as input and returns #t if its input is a floating point number (called a FLONUM in SAL) and #f if it is not.

Example 3.5.3: floatp

```
SAL> print floatp(.324)
#t

SAL> print floatp(23)
#f
```

The predicate integerp expects any value as input and returns #t if its input is an integer and #f if it is not.

Example 3.5.4: integerp

```
SAL> print integerp(#t)
#f

SAL> print integerp(.324)
#f

SAL> print integerp(-7)
#t
```

Other predicates include oddp and evenp. These predicates expect an *integer* as input and return a #t or #f value if the input is an odd or even number.

Example 3.5.5: oddp

```
SAL> print oddp(5)
#t

SAL> print oddp(2)
#f

SAL> print evenp(5)
#f
```

```
SAL> print evenp(2.0)
error: bad floating point operation
```

The predicate zerop expects a number as input and returns a #t if its input is 0 and #f if its input is not zero.

Example 3.5.6: zerop

```
SAL> print zerop(5)
#f

SAL> print zerop(0)
#t
```

The predicate plusp expects a number as input and returns #t if the number is greater than zero and #f if the number is less than or equal to zero.

Example 3.5.7: plusp

```
SAL> print plusp(3.245)
#t

SAL> print plusp(0)
#f

SAL> print plusp(-76)
#f
```

The predicate minusp expects a number as input and returns #t if the number is less than zero.

Example 3.5.8: minusp

```
SAL> print minusp(3.245)
#f

SAL> print minusp(0)
#f

SAL> print minusp(-76)
#t
```

The relational operators <, >, <=, >=, =, != (not equal to) compare two or more numbers and return the result. Note that these are infix operators, so you write "1 < 2" rather than "<(1, 2)". Nevertheless, you should think of these operators as predicate functions that take values in and return true or false.

Example 3.5.9: Relational operators

```
SAL> print 67 < 34.5
#f

SAL> print 76 >= 68
#t

SAL> print 67 = 90
#f

SAL > print 4 != 5
#t
```

The operator "~=" should be used to compare strings or lists. Do not use the "=" operator to compare strings or lists.

Example 3.5.10: string comparison

```
SAL> print "a string" ~= "B String"
#f

SAL> print "a string" = "a string"
#f

SAL> print "a string" ~= "a string"
#t

SAL> print {{a b} c} = {{a b} c}
#f

SAL> print {{a b} c} ~= {{a b} c}
#t

SAL> print {a {b c}} ~= {{a b} c}
#f
```

The predicate listp returns #t if its input is a list and #f if its input is not a list.

Example 3.5.11: listp

```
SAL> print listp({c e g})
#t

SAL> print listp(nil)
#t
```

```
SAL> print listp(4)
#f
```

The predicate endp expects a list as input. endp returns #t if its input is the empty list and #f if its input is not an empty list.

Example 3.5.12: endp

```
SAL> print endp(nil)
#t

SAL> print endp({c e g})
#f

SAL> print endp(cons(quote(c), quote(d)))
#f
```

Notice that many of the predicates presented thus far have ended in the letter P. There are some predicates that do not follow this naming convention.

The predicate atom returns #t if its input is not a list cell. Otherwise, atom returns #f. Generally, anything that is not a list is an atom. The one exception is the empty list, which is both a list and an atom.

Example 3.5.13: atom

```
SAL> print atom(-4)
#t

SAL> print atom(quote(c))
#t

SAL> print atom({c e g})
#f

SAL> print atom(nil)
#t
```

The predicate null returns #t if its input is the empty list, otherwise null returns #f.

Example 3.5.14: null

```
SAL> print null(nil)
#t
```

```
SAL> print null(4)
#f

SAL> print null({c e g})
#f

SAL> print null({})
#t
```

null is similar to endp in that both predicates check for the empty list. The primary difference between the two predicates is that endp does not accept numbers as input.

Example 3.5.15: null vs. endp

```
SAL> print null(4)
#f

SAL> print endp(4)
error: bad argument type - 4
```

The value of an input is also called an *actual parameter* or an *argument*, so the error message in Example 3.5.15 means that the value (4) passed as an input is not valid for the function endp.

The logical operators & ("and") and | ("or") may be used to conjoin two or more forms. In SAL, when a logical value (true or false) is required, #f or nil is considered to mean false, and anything else (numbers, lists, symbols) is considered to mean true. Evaluation of & and | is based on the truth tables in Figure 3.5.1.

& (and)

Input 1	Input 2	Result
T	T	T
T	F	F
F	T	F
F	F	F

| (or)

Input 1	Input 2	Result
T	T	T
T	F	T
F	T	T
F	F	F

Figure 3.5.1: Truth tables for & and |

Unlike functions or operators, & and | are called *special forms* and do not evaluate their input expressions in the normal manner. The & ("and") form evaluates input expressions one-at-a-time from left to right until an expression evaluates to #f (false) at which point & returns #f. If both expressions evaluate to non-nil (true), & returns #t. Similarly, | ("or") evaluates input expressions one-at-a-time from left to right until an expression evaluates to #t (true) at which point | ("or") returns #t. If both expressions evaluate to #f (false), | ("or") returns #f.

Example 3.5.16: & and |

```
SAL> print numberp(quote(c-major)) &
            symbolp(quote(d-major))
#f

SAL> print numberp(quote(c-major)) |
            symbolp(quote(d-major))
#t
```

The predicates "!" (an operator) and NULL (a function) return the same results. NULL is generally used to check specifically for the symbol NIL, and ! is used to reverse a logical (true or false) value. Choosing the appropriate function name can help make your programs easier to understand. Note that "!" takes precedence over many other operators, so the expression "! 4 = 5" means the same as "(! 4) = 5", which might not be the intended computation! Also, notice that, while in some languages 0 (zero) means "false," in SAL, "0" is not nil (or false), so "! 0" is false. Finally, remember that even the ! operator needs to be separated from the following expression by at least one space.

Example 3.5.17: The ! operator

```
SAL> print ! 4 = 5
#f

SAL> print ! (4 = 5)
#t

SAL> print ! 1
#f

SAL> print ! 0
#f
```

```
SAL> print null(4 = 5)
#t

SAL> print null(1)
#f

SAL> print null(0)
#f

SAL> print null(nil)
#t
```

3.6   User-Defined Functions

To build programs that solve complex problems, it is necessary to write your own functions. User-defined functions may be used just like the SAL primitives.

The template to define a function is:

> define function *function-name*(*optional-inputs*)
>> begin
>>> *commands*
>> end

Note: the word define is optional, but we use it throughout this book to remind the reader that this is a function *definition*. To *call* or *invoke* a function, evaluate an expression based on this template:

> *function-name*(*optional-inputs*)

In Example 3.6.1, we define a function named my-c-chord that creates a list of the pitches C, E, and G.

Example 3.6.1: Defining a function

```
SAL> define function my-c-chord()
        begin
          return {c e g}
        end
```

Call the function.

```
SAL> print my-c-chord()
{C E G}
```

The function name is my-c-chord. The function does not expect any inputs, indicated by the empty input list "()". The function definition consists of a single command to return a list of the atoms c, e, and g. The return command causes an immediate exit from the containing function. After defining the function my-c-chord, we call it with no inputs. The value returned by the function is the list {C E G}.

In Example 3.6.2, we define a function that transposes a given key-number by a given interval. The function name is transpose-midi-note. The function expects two inputs, key-number and interval. The value returned by the function is the sum of these two inputs. Following the function definition, we call transpose-midi-note to transpose key-number 60 up by 12 half steps and down by 5 half steps.

Example 3.6.2: A transpose function

```
SAL> define function transpose-midi-note(
                      key-number, interval)
        begin
          return key-number + interval
        end
```

Transpose key-number 60 up 12 half steps.

```
SAL> print transpose-midi-note(60, 12)
72
```

Transpose key-number 60 down 5 half steps.

```
SAL> print transpose-midi-note(60, -5)
55
```

In Example 3.6.3, we define a predicate function rangep that determines if its input is a valid MIDI key number, e.g. an integer in the range 0–127.

Example 3.6.3: Definition and use of rangep

```
SAL> define function rangep(keynumber)
        begin
          return integerp(keynumber) &
                 (keynumber <= 127) &
                 (keynumber >= 0)
        end

SAL> print rangep(128)
#f

SAL> print rangep(-23.5)
#f

SAL> print rangep(64)
#t
```

The function rangep expects a number as input. The compare operators <= and >= will cause a run-time error if one of their inputs is not a number. Therefore, the first test is integerp(keynumber). If this is false, the remaining tests are not performed (recall that & evaluates expressions from left to right until false is encountered). The value returned by the function is #t or #f. In the example, rangep is tested with several inputs.

3.7 Getting Help

Lisp and Nyquist functions are all described in the Nyquist manual, which is installed along with the Nyquist programs and available in HTML, PDF, and ASCII text formats. Related functions tend to be grouped together in different chapters, and all functions are listed in the index.

3.8 Programming Errors

Beginning programmers soon discover that programs are much more likely to contain errors than not. There are many kinds of errors. *Syntax errors* occur when the program text does not express a valid program. For example, a string beginning with a quote (") but not ending in a matching quote is not valid. Also, a function call with extra commas, e.g. null(,,), is not valid. *Run-time errors* occur when a program tries to perform an operation that is not allowed, such as adding two values that are not numbers, or calling a function with the wrong number of input values. Finally, some programs run but produce the wrong answer. In some sense, this is the most difficult type of error because no problem is detected automatically.

3.9 Error Messages

Error messages are printed when a syntax error or run-time error occurs. Although it is annoying to discover that your program has an error, careful attention to error messages will help you to find and fix the problem.

When a syntax error occurs, the error output contains the line number where the problem was found, the line itself, and an indication of where to look for the problem. SAL cannot guess the intended meaning of the faulty program, so the error location is usually *the point at which the program stops being valid*. This may not be the exact location of the actual problem, but it is usually close.

Example 3.9.1: Unbound variable

```
SAL> print atom(b-flat)
error: unbound variable - B-FLAT
Call traceback:
    SAL top-level command interpreter
```

When a run-time error occurs, the error output contains an error description and a call traceback as shown in Example 3.9.1. The "Call traceback:" part of the error message describes the context of the error. In these examples, the context is obvious: the command you just typed, but later we will see more interesting cases.

We will also learn what variables are and what it means for them to be unbound. For now, if you see the error shown in Example 3.9.1, you probably forgot to quote a symbol or expression so that SAL will not try to evaluate it. A corrected version of the command is shown in Example 3.9.2.

Example 3.9.2: Quoting a symbol

```
SAL> print atom(quote(b-flat))
#t
```

Another common error is to pass the wrong data type to a function, as shown in the next example.

Example 3.9.3: Input is wrong data type

```
SAL> print zerop({c e g})
error: bad argument type - (C E G)
Call traceback:
    SAL top-level command interpreter

SAL> print first(4)
error: bad argument type - 4
Call traceback:
    SAL top-level command interpreter
```

Yet another common error is to pass the wrong number of inputs to a function.

Example 3.9.4: Passing the wrong number of inputs to a function

```
SAL> print cons(quote(a), quote(b), quote(c))
error: too many arguments
Call traceback:
    SAL top-level command interpreter
```

```
SAL> print transpose-midi-note(60)
error: too few arguments
Call traceback:
    SAL top-level command interpreter
```

3.10   Stack Traces

When expressions are nested and when user-defined functions are evaluated, the SAL evaluation process can be nested hundreds of levels deep. The top-level command can call a function, which calls another function, which calls another, and so on. Often, an error message has no immediate connection to the top-level expression you typed. The *traceback* facility lets you see exactly what the SAL evaluator was doing leading up to the error condition. Stack traces require careful study, but this can pay off handsomely when you need to know how an error occurred.

There are actually two traceback facilities offering different levels of detail. The first is the "SAL traceback" that we have already seen hints of. To illustrate the SAL traceback, consider the user-defined transpose-midi-note function and an expression that calls it with an incorrect input:

Example 3.10.1: Define and call transpose-midi-note

```
SAL> define function transpose-midi-note(
                         key-number, interval)
       begin
         return key-number + interval
       end

SAL> print transpose-midi-note(quote(c4), 4)
error: bad argument type - C4
Call traceback:
    TRANSPOSE-MIDI-NOTE(
        KEY-NUMBER = C4,
        INTERVAL = 4) at line 4
    SAL top-level command interpreter
```

At this point, it is pretty clear that C4 is a bad input (the values of input expressions are called *arguments*; notice the output text: "error: bad argument type - C4"), but what function generated the error message? Reading further, the Call traceback shows that the error occurred in transpose-midi-note, with inputs key-number = C4, and interval = 4. Furthermore, the error occurred at line 4 of the function (at the return statement). Why was transpose-midi-note called? The next line of the traceback says transpose-midi-note was called from the SAL top-level command interpreter. In other words, the user typed in a command.

The Call traceback tells you about SAL program evaluation, but sometimes more detail is useful. Recall that SAL works by translating programs into Lisp, so errors are actually detected in the process of Lisp evaluation. The Lisp evaluation system has its own stack trace mechanism. To enable this, set the "Print Stack Trace on Error" option in the Preferences dialog box (opened using the Preferences menu item). With this option, try the same call to transpose-midi-note:

Example 3.10.2: XLISP traceback

```
SAL> print transpose-midi-note(quote(c4), 4)
error: bad argument type - C4
Function: #<Subr-SND-OFFSET: #71c788>
Arguments:
  C4
  4
Function: #<FSubr-COND: #71fc50>
Arguments:
  ((NUMBERP S1) (COND ((NUMBERP S2) (+ S1 S2 …
  ((NUMBERP S2) (SND-OFFSET S1 S2))
  (T (LET ((S1SR (SND-SRATE S1)) …
Function: #<Closure-NYQ:ADD-2-SOUNDS: #736a50>
Arguments:
  C4
  4
Function: #<FSubr-COND: #71fc50>
Arguments:
  …
…many more function/argument pairs elided…
Function: #<Closure-SAL-COMPILE: #790864>
Arguments:
  "print transpose-midi-note(quote(c4), 4)"
  T
  NIL
  "<console>"
…more function/argument pairs elided…
1>
```

The full stack trace is over 100 lines long. It shows in detail how the program arrived at the error. A full understanding of the stack trace requires a good knowledge of Lisp, but a look at the stack trace can be helpful even without a complete understanding. The general format of the XLISP stack trace is just like the SAL stack trace: both give a list of functions and arguments (input values). Here, we see that the error occurred in SND-OFFSET, a Lisp primitive. (Lisp primitives are indicated by the "Subr-" prefix.) Looking down a bit further, we see that SND-OFFSET was called indirectly from NYQ:ADD-2-SOUNDS, which has inputs C4 and 4. This may seem a bit unrelated to the SAL program, but it should be clear that C4 and 4 come from the SAL command, and at least the word "ADD" should indicate that execution is related to the "+" in transpose-midi-note. Looking further down the stack trace, you can find a call to SAL-COMPILE, and one of the inputs is the SAL command represented as a string. This gives a bit of insight into how SAL programs are converted to Lisp and evaluated.

After the stack trace is printed, the prompt "1>" appears. The user can enter additional commands *in Lisp*, or return to SAL input mode. To resume working in SAL, click on the Top button of the IDE, then click on the SAL button. The output will look like this:

```
1> (top)
[ back to top level ]
> (sal)
Entering SAL mode ...
SAL>
```

To conclude, SAL automatically prints a stack trace that tells you where an error occurred, including the chain of calls from the command line to the function raising the error. If the nature of the error is still unclear, it can be helpful to take out the "magnifying glass" by enabling the "Print Stack Trace on Error" option and running the program again. The resulting stack trace has more detail, but the detail is expressed in terms of the underlying Lisp system, which may be less familiar. To resume work in SAL, push the Top and SAL buttons in the IDE.

3.11 Printing

The print command is also very useful for understanding and debugging programs. When functions and expressions are deeply nested, the print function allows you to insert check points and confirm that evaluation is proceeding as planned. In fact, print'ing is such a useful aid to debugging that SAL has a special command, display, that is especially designed for debugging. We will return to this topic after a discussion of programming concepts in the next chapter.

Chapter 4   Programming and Nyquist

In Chapter 3, we looked at data types (including numbers, symbols, and lists), expressions, and functions. In this chapter, we will learn how to write programs and make sounds.

4.1   Getting Started

The normal way to write a program is to type code into a file. The file is then *loaded* into Nyquist. Loading means that the expressions in the file are evaluated. Usually, most of the expressions in a file define functions. Files are convenient because, if there is an error, you can simply edit the file and reload it rather than retyping everything.

Using the jnyqide program, click on the New File button below the text input area. A new window will appear. Save the empty window to "simple.sal" so the editor will display the file using SAL syntax. Now, you can type a program into this window. Try typing the following text.

Example 4.1.1: simple.sal

```
;; a simple program
define function my-program()
  begin
    print "this is a test"
    play pluck(c4)
  end
```

Note: examples labeled with a filename as in Example 4.1.1 are included in the accompanying electronic media. (See page 1.)

This program begins with a *comment*. A comment is text that is not evaluated. Comments begin with a semicolon and extend to the end of the line. Sometimes, programmers use two or more semicolons to make comments stand out, but you could just as well write "; hey you! - a simple program" as long as the first character is a semicolon. Use comments to describe your programs, intentions, and details that you might forget when you (and others) read the program.

Following the comment is a function definition. The print command prints a line of text to the Nyquist output to confirm that

43

the function has been called. The pluck function generates a plucked string sound, and play plays the sound as audio. For now, do not worry about how pluck and play work because we just want to create and run any Nyquist program using files.

Notice that my-program has two commands (print and play). When a function definition has multiple expressions, they are evaluated sequentially.

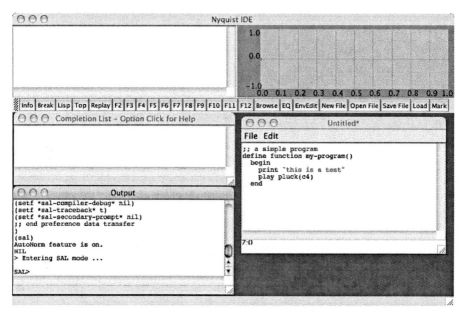

Figure 4.1.1: The Nyquist IDE (Macintosh version)

The screen should look something like Figure 4.1.1. When the program is ready, click on the Load button. Nyquist will then load the file and generate output similar to the following:

Example 4.1.2: Output from loading simple.sal

```
SAL> exec setdir("/Users/rbd/temp")

SAL> load "/Users/rbd/temp/simple.sal"

SAL>
```

Notice that you do not need to type anything to the text area. Instead, jnyqide automatically types a command to set Nyquist's current directory to wherever you saved the file and then a command to *load* the file.

After the file is loaded, my-program will be defined and available for use. To evaluate an expression (such as a function call), use the command exec as shown in Example 4.1.3.

Example 4.1.3: Using exec to call a function

```
SAL> exec my-program()
this is a test
Saving sound file to temp.wav

total samples: 44100
AutoNorm: peak was 1.24552,
    peak after normalization was 0.9,
    suggested normalization factor is 0.722587
SAL>
```

The print command in my-program generates the output line "this is a test". Next, the pluck sound is generated and played by the play function. Some information is printed by play. First, play normally saves a copy of the sound to a file, in this case "temp.wav." (You can replay the sound from this file by clicking on the Replay button in jnyqide.) Next, play tells us that it performed 44100 samples of audio. The line beginning with "Autonorm" tells us the peak audio level of the original sound was 1.24552. Normally, audio samples should be in the range from -1 to $+1$. If necessary, Nyquist tries to adjust the output level to avoid clipping. As indicated in the printout, the sound was scaled to achieve a peak of 0.9. Based on the final outcome, the "suggested" normalization factor of 0.722587 is the value that one might use to scale the sound manually. If you run my-program again, these numbers will change because the pluck sound is initialized with random numbers and produces different peak values each time.

Now go back to the program and change the c4 to f4. Add a new line at the end of the file to call my-program. The file should look like Example 4.1.4.

Now, click the Load button in jnyqide. The file is automatically saved and reloaded into Nyquist. Nyquist evaluates the expressions in the file one-by-one. The first expression *redefines* my-program. The next expression calls my-program. You should hear another plucked string sound on the new pitch f4.

Example 4.1.4: Using define function in simple2.sal

```
;; a simple program
define function my-program ()
  begin
    print "this is a test"
    play pluck(f4)
  end

exec my-program()
```

You have now been through two iterations of the standard cycle for program development:

1. create a text file defining functions and calling them

2. load the text file into Nyquist

3. observe and listen to the program behavior

4. edit the program to fix problems or add new features

5. jump to step 2

In the remainder of this chapter, we will first learn how to represent note lists, or *scores,* in Nyquist. Then we will learn how to turn scores into sounds.

4.2   Nyquist Instruments

Nyquist uses ordinary functions to define "instruments" that play notes in scores. Although the topic of sound synthesis could fill another book, we will look at the definition of note as an example of how instruments can be defined (see Example 4.2.1).

The next line uses the same define function as Section 3.6, but adds some new notation. The inputs list here is (pitch: 60, vel: 100). The trailing colons in the input names indicate that these are *keywords.* In previous functions, input values are associated with names in the function definition *by position,* that is, values are bound to symbols from left to right. With keywords, the expression that invokes the function lists keywords and associated values in pairs. The keywords in the calling expression end with a colon (:) to distinguish them from ordinary symbols. In the function *body,* the colons are omitted, so for example, pitch in the return command of Example 4.2.1 refers to the value associated with the pitch: keyword. We call these inputs *keyword parameters.*

Example 4.2.1: Defining an instrument in note.sal

```
load "pianosyn.lsp" ; load piano library

define function note(pitch: 60, vel: 100)
  begin
    return piano-note-2(pitch, vel)
  end
```

Keyword parameters are paired with default values, so pitch: 60 means the keyword pitch: can be used to provide a value for the pitch parameter, but if no such keyword is provided, the value will be 60.

In this example, the load "pianosyn" command is necessary to load the definition of piano-note-2 – it must be loaded before the first call to note. The load command has a similar effect to clicking on the Nyquist "Load" button. The value of note is computed by passing the pitch and vel parameters to piano-note-2, a Nyquist library function that makes a piano sound. You can try out note as follows.

Example 4.2.2: Using the note function

```
play note(pitch: 48) ; play a piano note
play note(pitch: 36) ~ 4 ; play a longer,
                         ; lower note
play note(pitch: 48, vel: 90) ; all
         ; parameters are specified
play note(vel: 90, pitch: 48) ; keyword
         ; parameters can be in any order
```

In fact, this note function is pre-defined in Nyquist. Rather than (re)defining note as in Example 4.2.1, you can simply use the built-in note function.

The next example defines another instrument based on Nyquist's pluck function. Because pluck uses positional parameters, we will not use it in scores but rather define a new function with keyword parameters. This new function will serve as a "wrapper," in other words just a bit of re-packaging, that calls pluck to do most of the work. Since we are defining a new function, we will add some new twists: an amplitude control based on the vel parameter and a low-pass filter with a variable cutoff frequency to control brightness.

The function plucked-string in Example 4.2.3 defines three keyword parameters, pitch, vel, and cutoff. The body of the function is just a return command that evaluates and returns a sound. The first line of the expression converts the "velocity" parameter vel, with a nominal range from 1 to 127, into a linear scale factor from 0.001 to 1.0. (We will revisit this in detail later.) This scale factor is multiplied by the next line, which computes a sound. The sound is just pluck processed by a low-pass filter (lp) tuned to the cutoff parameter. Frequencies above cutoff (in *Hertz*, or cycles-per-second) will be attenuated. Lower values of cutoff make the sound less bright.

Example 4.2.3: plucked-string.sal

```
define function plucked-string(pitch: 60,
                      vel: 100, cutoff: 10000)
  begin
    return ((0.00768553 * vel + 0.0239372) ^
           2) * lp(pluck(pitch), cutoff)
  end
```

4.3   Nyquist Scores

The examples above define a couple of functions, note and plucked-string, that produce sounds. How are these combined to make music? Nyquist uses lists to represent *scores* or *note lists*. A score is a list of notes or *sound events*, and a note is a list of three elements: a time, a duration, and a sound expression. Example 4.3.1 contains a score with 3 notes of the C-major scale.

Example 4.3.1: A score

```
{{0.0 1.0 {note pitch: 60 vel: 100}}
 {1.0 1.0 {note pitch: 62 vel: 110}}
 {2.0 1.0 {note pitch: 64 vel: 120}}}
```

Notice the overall form of this example. The score is a list of lists. The top-level list is a list of notes, or more generally, a list of *sound events*. The term *note* is often frowned upon in computer music circles because it implies many traditional assumptions about music. A *note* implies pitch, rhythm, and instrumentation, whereas a computer music score could just as well contain a recording of footsteps, a conversation, and a four-part chorale as three *sound events*. Since most of our examples in fact deal with notes, we will generally use that term when it is applicable. In this example, each line contains one note, expressed as a list.

Each list expressing a note starts with a starting time followed by a duration (or stretch factor). These notes start at times 0.0, 1.0, and 2.0. All have a duration of 1.0. Technically, the duration is really a time-scaling factor that "stretches" the normal duration of the note. Most notes have a nominal duration of 1, so the time-scaling factor, or *stretch factor*, becomes the duration, but it is possible for sound events to have any nominal duration.

The third element of each line is the sound expression, which tells how to create a sound. Notice that the sound expression does not follow the SAL syntax for function calls because the expression must be represented within a list structure, not as a textual program. To accomplish this, sound expressions within scores use *Lisp* syntax, which is convenient because SAL is implemented in Lisp and because Lisp programs are represented by lists. In Lisp notation, the first item in a list is a function name, and the remaining items are parameters to pass to the function. Thus, {note pitch: 60 vel: 100} is Lisp notation for note(pitch: 60, vel: 100). To complete the story, it should be mentioned that while lists in SAL are written with braces {}, lists in Lisp are written with parentheses (), and while keywords in SAL are written with a trailing colon (pitch:), keywords in Lisp are preceded with a colon (:pitch). If you stick to writing programs in SAL, these details should only rarely be visible.

Pitches are given by numbers consistent with MIDI: 60 is middle-C, 61 is C-sharp, and so on. In the example, pitches are middle-C, D, and E. Input values here are indicated by alternating *keywords* (pitch: and vel:) with *values* (e.g. 60 and 100).

As a slight extension to the score representation, scores can have an explicit starting time and ending time, indicated by a "pseudo-sound-expression" using the name score-begin-end.

Example 4.3.2: A score with begin and end times

```
{{0.0 0.0 {score-begin-end 0.0 4.0}}
 {0.0 1.0 {note pitch: 60 vel: 100}}
 {1.0 1.0 {note pitch: 62 vel: 110}}
 {2.0 1.0 {note pitch: 64 vel: 120}}}
```

In this case, the score begins at time 0.0 and ends at 4.0. If this score is spliced onto another one, the second score will start at time 4.0, even though the last note of the first score ends at time 3.

To convert a score into sound, use the score-play function. Notice that the play command requires an expression that results in a sound, so it cannot be used with a score. The score-play function converts a score to a sound, and since it also plays the sound, we do not want to invoke it with the play command. Instead, we simply evaluate (call) the score-play function using the exec command.

Example 4.3.3: Using score-play

```
exec score-play(
  {{0.0 0.0 {score-begin-end 0.0 4.0}}
   {0.0 1.0 {note pitch: 60 vel: 100}}
   {1.0 1.0 {note pitch: 62 vel: 110}}
   {2.0 1.0 {note pitch: 64 vel: 120}}})
```

When score-play interprets a score, it uses the score to determine the start time and duration of each note. For each note, at the appropriate time, Nyquist then evaluates the (Lisp syntax) expression to compute a sound. All resulting sounds are added together and played using the play command described earlier.

Nyquist has a special way to express chords. If the pitch: parameter is a list, the overall event expression is expanded into a set of expressions, one for each element of the pitch: list. Thus {0.0 1.0 {note pitch: {60 67}}} is equivalent to the two notes {0.0 1.0 {note pitch: 60}} and {0.0 1.0 {note pitch: 67}}.

It follows that if the pitch parameter is nil or the empty list, then this is a chord with zero notes and represents nothing (in musical terms, a rest).

Example 4.3.4: score-sort.sal

```
exec score-play(score-sort(
  {{0.0 0.5 {plucked-string pitch: 67 vel: 90 cutoff: 4000}}
   {0.5 0.5 {plucked-string pitch: 69 vel: 95 cutoff: 5000}}
   {1.0 0.5 {plucked-string pitch: 71 vel: 100 cutoff: 6000}}
   {1.5 0.5 {plucked-string pitch: 72 vel: 105 cutoff: 7000}}
   {2.0 0.5 {plucked-string pitch: 71 vel: 100 cutoff: 6000}}
   {2.5 0.5 {plucked-string pitch: 69 vel: 95 cutoff: 5000}}
   {3.0 1.0 {plucked-string pitch: 67 vel: 90 cutoff: 4000}}
   {0.0 1.0 {note pitch: 59 vel: 100}}
   {1.0 1.0 {note pitch: 55 vel: 100}}
   {2.0 1.0 {note pitch: 55 vel: 100}}
   {3.0 1.0 {note pitch: 59 vel: 100}}}))
```

Figure 4.3.1: Score from Example 4.3.4

Example 4.3.4 contains a short score with two instruments. score-play requires that scores be sorted, but in this case it is convenient to group the score notes by instrument. The notes are not sorted in time, but the score-sort function sorts the score into time order. Listen for the changes in the pluck sound due to the changing cutoff frequencies. The score in common music notation is shown in Figure 4.3.1.

4.4 Variables

Lisp symbols can be used to represent values. We have already seen in function definitions how symbols called *parameters* represent input values. It is also possible to associate any value with any symbol. The symbol is then called a *variable.*

Example 4.4.1: Variables

```
SAL> set a = 23 ; set variable A to value 23
SAL> print a ; print the value of A
23

SAL> print a + 5 ; use A in an expression
28

SAL> set a = 7 ; variables can be changed
SAL> print a
7

SAL> print a + 5
12
```

One use of variables is to represent scores. It is easier to type a variable name than to retype an entire score. Notice in Example 4.4.2 that the variable my-score is set once but used several times. (In this example, only user input is shown to save space.)

Variables and functions are different even though both are denoted by symbols. In fact the same symbol can represent both a variable *and* a function as shown in Example 4.4.3. To access the variable, just write the symbol's name. A symbol is an expression that evaluates to the current value of the variable denoted by the symbol. To denote the value returned by a call to a function, put a list of input expressions in parentheses after the symbol that names the function. This function call expression is evaluated as follows: First, the function associated with the symbol is found. Second, the input expressions are evaluated from left to right. Third, the resulting input values are passed to the function, the function body is evaluated, and a value is returned.

Example 4.4.2: Saving scores in variables in score-variables.sal

```
set my-score =
  {{0.0 0.5 {plucked-string pitch: 67
                     vel: 90 cutoff: 4000}}
   {0.5 0.5 {plucked-string pitch: 69
                     vel: 95 cutoff: 5000}}
   {1.0 0.5 {plucked-string pitch: 71
                     vel: 100 cutoff: 6000}}
   {1.5 0.5 {plucked-string pitch: 72
                     vel: 105 cutoff: 7000}}
   {2.0 0.5 {plucked-string pitch: 71
                     vel: 100 cutoff: 6000}}
   {2.5 0.5 {plucked-string pitch: 69
                     vel: 95 cutoff: 5000}}
   {3.0 1.0 {plucked-string pitch: 67
                     vel: 90 cutoff: 4000}}}
exec score-play(my-score)  ; play the score
exec score-print(my-score) ; neatly print score
; play at half speed
exec score-play(score-stretch(my-score, 2))
```

Example 4.4.3: Functions and Variables

```
SAL> define function foo()
       begin ; define foo as a function
         print "hi there"
         return "hi there"
       end
SAL> ; define foo as a variable:
     set foo = " goodbye "
SAL> exec foo() ; call foo as a function
hi there
SAL> print foo ; evaluate foo as a variable
 goodbye
SAL> ; concatenate strings:
     print strcat(foo(), foo, foo())
hi there
hi there
hi there goodbye hi there
```

4.5 Score Processing

SAL offers many functions for manipulating scores. Like score-sort in Example 4.3.4, all of these functions are named *score-something*, and all of these functions take a score as the first input.

Score functions do not modify the input score. Instead, they make a new score, so assign the result to a variable if you want to retain the changes.

Example 4.5.1: Using score-shift

```
SAL> set my-score = {{0.0 2.0 {note pitch: 60}}}
SAL> print score-shift(my-score, 3.0)
{{0 0 {SCORE-BEGIN-END 0 5}}
 {3 2 {NOTE pitch: 60}}}
```

The function score-shift adds a time offset to the times of notes. Notice that score-shift added a score-begin-end expression to the score. Almost all score functions add default begin and end times unless they are already specified. The main effect of the score-shift function is to change the starting time of the note from 0.0 to 3.

Most score functions can operate on a *range* of notes. The default range includes all notes, but keyword parameters can be used to specify a narrower range. The from-index: and to-index: keywords specify a range of notes by index. For example, to select only the 1st through 7th notes, you would use the keyword/value pairs from-index: 1, to-index: 7.

Another pair of keywords, from-time: and to-time:, can also be used to specify a range. For example, to select notes with start times greater than or equal to 5 seconds and less than 10 seconds, use from-time: 5, to-time: 10.

Example 4.5.2: Using score-shift

```
; add 3 seconds to all start times
print score-shift(my-score, 3.0)
; insert 3s rest at time 10
print score-shift(my-score, 3.0, from-time: 10)
```

The function score-transpose adds an offset to some parameter of every note. If the note does not have the parameter, the note is unchanged. To indicate which parameter to offset, the second parameter of score-transpose is a keyword symbol. You might expect to simply write a keyword symbol, e.g. pitch:, but when SAL sees a keyword (any symbol ending in a colon), it expects to see a following expression which is evaluated and passed as the value of a keyword parameter. Alternatively, you might think to write quote(pitch:), which is the normal way to write an expression that returns a symbol, but again, SAL looks for a following expression. For example, quote(pitch: c4) would satisfy the SAL compiler, but it does not express what we want *and* it would generate a run-time exception. The solution is a special form, keyword, that works something like quote, but converts an ordinary symbol into a keyword.

Example 4.5.3 uses the special keyword form to pass the symbols pitch: and cutoff: as inputs to score-transpose. Note that when using keyword, you *omit* the colon from the keyword symbol. Alternatively, one can write the symbol with a colon (:) prefix, e.g. :pitch, instead of keyword(pitch). The colon prefix receives no special treatment by the SAL compiler but in Lisp, it indicates a keyword. Lisp keywords (with colon prefix) are automatically initialized to their own symbol name, so you do not have to use quote. The value of :foo is quote(:foo)!

In Example 4.5.4, the function score-scale multiplies a selected parameter by some scaling. If the note does not have the parameter, the note is unchanged.

Example 4.5.3: Using score-transpose

```
; transpose pitch up one octave:
print score-transpose(my-score, keyword(pitch), 12)
; increase cutoff freq. by 1000:
print score-transpose(my-score, keyword(cutoff),
                                     1000)
```

Example 4.5.4: Increase cutoff frequencies by 50%

```
print score-scale(my-score, keyword(cutoff), 1.5)
```

The function score-sustain multiplies durations by a scale factor. The starting times of notes are not changed, so the effect is to make notes more *legato* or *staccato* without changing the rhythm or tempo.

Example 4.5.5: Using score-sustain

```
; increase durations by 25% in the time
; interval from 1 to 3 seconds
print score-sustain(my-score, 1.25,
                          from-time: 1, to-time: 3)
```

The function score-voice is used to change the *instrument,* or function symbol, in note expressions. The inputs are the score and a *replacement list.* The replacement list is of the form {{old_1 new_1} {old_2 new_2}}, where old_1, old_2, ... are existing instruments, and new_1, new_2, ... are the replacements.

Example 4.5.6: Using score-voice

```
; turn plucked-string into note and note into
; plucked-string
print score-voice(my-score,
                {{note plucked-string}
                {plucked-string note}})
```

The function score-merge combines any number of scores, preserving the notes and their times. score-merge accepts any number of scores as inputs. In Example 4.5.7, we combine a score with a copy of itself transposed up one octave. (Also known as octave doubling.) Then we produce an echo effect by copying the same score twice with slight delays, then combining the copies with the original.

score-append, illustrated in Example 4.5.8, joins scores sequentially – each score is started at the end of the previous score. If scores contain score-begin-end expressions, the begin time of each score is shifted to the end time of the previous score. If not, a score-begin-end expression is inserted with default start and end times based on the time of the first note and the time + duration of the last note. Like score-merge, score-append accepts and appends any number of scores.

Example 4.5.7: Using score-merge

```
; double every note an octave higher
print score-merge(my-score,
        score-transpose(my-score,
                        keyword(pitch), 12))
; make my-score with 2 echoes
print score-merge(my-score,
        score-shift(my-score, 0.1),
        score-shift(my-score, 0.2))
```

Example 4.5.8: Using score-append

```
; play my-score as is, then transposed
; up 1 step, then up another step
print score-append(my-score,
        score-transpose(my-score,
                        keyword(pitch), 2),
        score-transpose(my-score,
                        keyword(pitch), 4))
```

score-select is used to form a new score with only selected notes. To specify which notes are selected, you provide a predicate function with three inputs: the time, the duration, and the sound expression. These are the three elements of note or sound events in SAL scores. (You might expect the predicate to just accept a whole sound event as input, but since nearly every predicate would first extract the three elements from the event, score-select does that for you and passes the three values separately.)

In Example 4.5.9, a predicate is defined that is true when the pitch is less than 70. The predicate uses expr-get-attr, which searches for a keyword in the sound expression. If the keyword is found, the associated value is returned. If not, the third input (100) is returned as a default value. In this case, 100 was chosen to be greater than 70 so that the predicate will be false if no pitch is given. Notice that we need to pass a keyword symbol as the second input to expr-get-attr. As described for Example 4.5.3, we use keyword(pitch) to denote the value pitch:.

The following expression, beginning with score-select, then selects all notes in my-score that satisfy the predicate. Notice that we are passing a function (not-very-high) as a parameter. This is accomplished by passing the *name* of the function, which must be quoted; otherwise, SAL will evaluate not-very-high as a variable.

Example 4.5.9: Using score-select

```
; a predicate that returns true when pitch
; is less than 70
define function not-very-high(time, dur, expression)
  return expr-get-attr(expression, keyword(pitch),
                       100) < 70
; select all notes with pitch < 70 and time >= 2
print score-select(my-score, quote(not-very-high),
                   from-time: 2)
```

score-filter-length removes notes that extend beyond a given cut-off time. This is similar to using the to-time: parameter to limit the selected notes in a score function, but while to-time: compares note starting times, score-filter-length selects notes that *end* before the specified time. The *end* of a note is the start time plus duration.

Example 4.5.10: Using score-filter-length

```
; result will not extend beyond 2.4s
print score-filter-length(my-score, 2.4)
```

score-stretch-to-length stretches a score to a given length.

Example 4.5.11: Using score-stretch-to-length

```
print score-stretch-to-length(my-score, 5.0)
```

Chapter 4 · Programming and Nyquist

score-filter-overlap can be used to reduce a score to a mono-phonic texture. Wherever two notes overlap in time, the first note is kept, and the second is removed. As always, the original score is not modified, and a new monophonic score is returned.

Example 4.5.12: Using score-filter-overlap

```
print score-filter-overlap(my-score)
```

score-apply replaces each note by a function of the note. For example, you can add new keywords and values to each note in the score or you can change the duration of each note. In Example 4.5.13, the attribute/value pair accent: 100 is added to every note whose pitch is greater than 70. (Of course, this will only have an effect if the affected instruments define and use the accent: keyword parameter.) This example introduces the if command, which in its simplest form looks like
if expression then command
The if command first evaluates expression. If it is true, then command is performed. In this case the command sets sound to a new value with accent: 100. If expression is false, then command is skipped and the program continues with the next command (a return in this case). We consider the if command in greater depth in Chapter 8.

Example 4.5.13: Using score-apply in add-accents.sal

```
define function add-accents(time, dur, sound)
  begin
    ; if the pitch: attribute of the sound is
    ; greater than 70 ...
    ; ... then modify sound to have :accent 100
    if expr-get-attr(sound,
                     keyword(pitch), 70) > 70 then
      set sound =
      expr-set-attr(sound, keyword(accent), 100)
    ; whether or not sound was changed, form a
    ; new note to return by combining time, dur, and
    ; sound into a list
    return list(time, dur, sound)
  end

; now apply the function to a score
print score-apply(my-score, quote(add-accents))
```

Example 4.5.14 uses a longer form of the if command, which looks like this:
if expression then command-1 else command-2

This works just like the shorter form described above, except if *expression* is true, *command-1* is performed, but if *expression* is false, *command-2* is performed. The program normally continues with the command following the if. However, in this case, both *command-1* and *command-2* are return commands, which cause the function to return a value immediately. No further commands are performed (nor do any exist in this case).

score-adjacent-events is a general function that helps transform notes in context. For example, notes can be adjusted to eliminate intervals greater than an octave or to make each note extend to the start time of the next note. The specific process is defined by a function passed as a parameter. The function takes three inputs, the previous note, the current note, and the next note. The resulting score is the collection of all notes returned by the function.

So if the pitch is "not very high" (less than 72), a modified version of current is returned, otherwise; current is returned as is. To change the duration, one could use the list manipulation primitives first, rest, and list, but there are some predefined functions that make the job simpler. Here, event-set-dur is used to construct a copy of current with a modified duration. The duration is computed by taking the time difference between next and current. Although the time of a note is simply first(*note*), using the function event-time helps to make it clear to readers the intention of the expression.

Example 4.5.14: Using score-adjacent-events in adjust-dur.sal

```
; a predicate that returns true when pitch is
; less than 72
define function not-very-high(sound)
    return expr-get-attr(sound,
                         keyword(pitch), 100) < 72

; a function of 3 notes - extend duration of current
; note to the starting time of the next note
define function adjust-durations(
                         previous, current, next)
    begin
      if not-very-high(event-expression(current)) &
         next then
        return event-set-dur(current,
               event-time(next) - event-time(current))
      else return current
    end

exec score-play(score-adjacent-events(
                my-score, quote(adjust-durations)))
```

Not every note has a previous or a next note. When processing the first and last notes of a score, the previous and next values are #f. To prevent adjust-durations from trying to access the time of next, the if condition requires that next is not #f before accessing its time.

There are still more score functions available. Rather then continue with detailed explanations of each, we will offer just a brief synopsis and leave it to the reader to find details in the Nyquist manual.

- score-sort(*score, optional-copy-flag*) – sort elements of *score* into proper time order.
- score-repeat(*score, n*) – make a new score from *n* repetitions of *score*.
- score-index-of(*score, predicate*) – find the index of the first note that makes *predicate* true.
- score-last-index-of(*score, predicate*) – find the last note that makes *predicate* true.
- score-randomize-start(*score, amount*) – add or subtract random time offsets to notes.
- score-read-smf(*filename*) – read a standard MIDI file into a score.
- score-write-smf(*filename*) – write a standard MIDI file from a score.

There are also many helpful functions for accessing attributes of scores, note events, and expressions. By convention, the names of these functions are prefixed by an indicator of the data type that the function expects as the first input:

- score – functions operate on scores, which have the form {*event1 event2 ... eventn*}.
- event – functions operate on *events* which we also refer to as notes. Events have the form {*time duration expression*}.
- expr – functions operate on event expressions, which have the form {*instrument keyword$_1$: value$_1$ keyword$_2$: value$_2$ ... keyword$_n$: value$_n$*}.

A few of the score access functions are

- score-get-begin(*score*) – get the begin time of *score*.
- score-set-begin(*score, time*) – construct a copy of *score* with the begin time changed to *time*.
- score-get-end(*score*) – get the end time of *score*.
- score-set-end(*score, time*) – construct a copy of *score* with the end time changed to *time*.

Functions to access events include the following:

- event-time(*note*) – get the time of *note*.
- event-set-time(*note, time*) – construct a copy of *note* with a different start *time*.
- event-dur(*note*) – get the duration of *note*.
- event-set-dur(*note, dur*) – construct a copy of *note* with a different *dur*ation.
- event-expression(*note*) – get the expression from *note*.
- event-set-expression(*note, expr*) – construct a copy of *note* with a different *expr*ession.
- event-has-attr(*note, attribute*) – does the *note*'s expression have *attribute*?
- event-get-attr(*note, attribute, optional-default-value*) – get value of *attribute* from *note*.
- event-set-attr(*note, attribute, value*) – construct a copy of *note* with *attribute* changed or set to *value*.

Finally, we present access functions for sound expressions:

- expr-has-attr(*expression, attribute*) – test if *expression* has *attribute*.
- expr-get-attr(*expression, attribute, optional-default-value*) – get value of *attribute*.
- expr-set-attr(*expression, attribute, value*) – construct a copy of *expression* with *attribute* changed or set to *value*.

Chapter 5   Introduction to Algorithmic Composition

In Chapter 4, we learned how to use Nyquist to create, modify, and play scores. In principle, these functions can be used to create any score, but the work is tedious because so much must be specified by hand. In this chapter, we will learn new ways to create scores by writing programs. Programs can automate many tasks and allow the composer to focus on only the details that are of particular interest. Other details can be relegated to programs.

5.1   Getting Started

Since scores are just lists, it is perfectly possible to create them directly using SAL primitives including cons and list. However, a more structured and in many cases simpler approach is to use a special form called score-gen. Example 5.1.1 shows how you can write a program that uses score-gen to create a score with two notes.

Example 5.1.1: my-first-score.sal

```
set my-first-score =
    score-gen(score-len: 2,
              pitch: 60,
              vel: 100,
              ioi: 0.7,
              name: quote(note))
exec score-print(my-first-score)
exec score-play(my-first-score)
```

What does this code say? set is going to create and set the global variable my-first-score to the value of the score-gen expression. score-gen creates a score according to keyword parameters. Some of these parameters control the generation of notes, and some provide the actual contents of the note expressions. In this case, only score-len: controls the generation, saying to generate two notes. The rest of the parameters specify note contents.

To construct the notes, the pitch: and vel: parameters are entered directly into the note expression. The ioi: parameter specifies the inter-onset interval, the time between note start times. Since no time: parameter was specified, the default time of 0.0 is used for the first note. Since no dur: parameter was specified, the duration defaults to the inter-onset interval. The resulting note is {0 0.7 {note pitch: 60 vel: 100}}. The second note starts when the first note ends: {0.7 1.4 {note pitch: 60 vel: 100}}.

It may seem boring that all notes are alike. We will soon study many ways to achieve variation, but for now, we need to learn a little more about the mechanics of scores and score representation.

When you work by writing programs in files, your work is already saved as programs, but anything you compute exists only until you exit from Nyquist. Often, scores are computed and saved as global variables. If random numbers are used to generate the score, or if you make changes to the score or to the program that generated it, you may not be able to regenerate the score at a later date. It is a good idea to save any score that you may want later.

Example 5.1.2: Using the Nyquist workspace functions

```
SAL> ; add my-first-score to the "workspace"
     exec add-to-workspace(quote(my-first-score))

SAL> ; write the workspace variables and
     ; values to workspace.lsp
     exec save-workspace()

SAL> ; to test, first destroy my-first-score
     set my-first-score = nil

SAL> ; now see if we can restore my-first-score
     load "workspace" ; loads workspace.lsp
     ; loading "workspace.lsp"
     workspace loaded

SAL> ; score-print is implemented in Lisp and
     ; uses Lisp conventions (parentheses) for
     ; lists
     exec score-print(my-first-score)
((0 0 (SCORE-BEGIN-END 0 NIL))
(0 0.7 (NOTE vel: 100 pitch: 60))
(0.7 1.4 (NOTE vel: 100 pitch: 60))
)

SAL> ; my-first-score was restored!
```

Example 5.1.2 illustrates how to save and restore my-first-score, which was computed in Example 5.1.1. The idea is that a list of global variables constitutes a "workspace" that can be saved to a file, workspace.lsp, and restored from that file. (The .lsp extension indicates that the workspace file is written in Lisp.) The add-to-workspace function adds a global variable to the workspace. You can have as many variables in the workspace as you like. Notice that the input parameter is normally quoted: You are adding the variable *name* to the workspace, and without the quote you will get the variable *value*. The save-workspace function writes all variables and their values to the file workspace.lsp. Later, if you load this file, the values of all the workspace variables will be restored. (This will also replace any current values that exist, so be careful not to overwrite values you want to keep.)

In addition to saving the program that generated the score, or saving the score itself in the workspace, you may wish to save a score to a MIDI file (.mid). Saving a Nyquist score as a standard MIDI file means you can readily combine the power of Nyquist with the functionality of a MIDI sequencer. Use the score-write-smf function to write a MIDI file as shown in Example 5.1.3. The file my-first-score.mid will be saved in the current directory, which you can discover by evaluating print setdir(".").

Example 5.1.3: Calling score-write-smf

```
SAL> exec score-write-smf(my-first-score,
                          "my-first-score.mid")
```

Table 5.1.1 gives an overview of the file formats discussed in Section 5.1.

Table 5.1.1 File formats

File Type	File Suffix	Description	Command(s) Associated with File Creation
Nyquist/SAL source	.sal	File contains Nyquist (SAL syntax) program code	Use the jnyqide program to edit and save programs
Nyquist/XLISP source	.lsp	File contains Nyquist (XLISP syntax) program code	Use the jnyqide program to edit and save programs
Nyquist workspace file	.lsp	File contains XLISP code to restore variable values	add-to-workspace save-workspace
MIDI file	.mid	File contains MIDI data generated from a score	score-write-smf

5.2　Pitch and Rhythm Notation

Nyquist provides pre-defined variables so that programmers can use symbolic names for common pitches and rhythmic durations. Pitch names have the form *<pitch-letter><flat-or-sharp><octave>*, where the pitch letter is a through g. This is followed by an optional f or s to denote flat or sharp, and the last character is an octave number from 0 to 7. These pitch names are initialized to floating point numbers using the MIDI numbers for pitch (c4 = 60).

Rythmic durations are denoted by w, h, q, i, and s for whole, half, quarter, eighth, and sixteenth, followed by an optional d for dotted, or t for triplet. Again, these are ordinary variables initialized with floating point values. The values represent duration in quarter notes. It is often convenient to express durations in terms of these variables, then scale durations or stretch scores by some factor representing tempo, expressed in seconds per quarter note.

Example 5.2.1: Pitch and rhythm variables

```
SAL> print c0, bf4, b4, c5, cs5, b7
12 70 71 72 73 107

SAL> print w, h, q, i, s, hd, qt, st
4 2 1 0.5 0.25 3 0.666667 0.166667
```

5.3　Pattern Objects and Item Streams

In order to do something musically interesting, we certainly need to produce scores that have more than one pitch! The easiest way to create scores that have more than one pitch is to use *item streams*. Item streams are sequences of values generated by *pattern objects*. Pattern objects are created by functions to be described below. Once created, the next function causes a pattern object to generate the next item in an infinite sequence.

Example 5.3.1: pitch-cycle.sal

```
set pitch-cycle = make-cycle(list(c4, d4, e4, f4))
set pitch-cycle-score =
    score-gen(score-len: 8,
              pitch: next(pitch-cycle),
              dur: 0.4)
```

In Example 5.3.1, we use make-cycle to make a cycle pattern. The cycle pattern circularly selects items from the list, reading left to right for as many items are required. The cycle is assigned to the global variable pitch-cycle using set. score-gen is then used to build a score. Notice the value for pitch: is an expression to retrieve the next item of pitch-cycle. This expression is evaluated once for each note in sequence, so each note will have a new pitch value. Try printing and playing the result. Manipulating patterns using item streams is a simple yet very powerful approach to algorithmic composition.

Let's consider another example.

Example 5.3.2: item-streams.sal

```
set pitch-cycle = make-cycle(list(c4, c6, nil))
set   vel-cycle = make-cycle({75 100 125})
set   dur-cycle = make-cycle({0.3 0.5 0.7})
exec score-gen(save: quote(item-streams),
               score-len: 10,
               pitch: next(pitch-cycle),
               vel:   next(vel-cycle),
               ioi:   next(dur-cycle))
```

This example introduces the save: keyword, which means set the following variable (which is quoted because we want the variable *name*, not its value) to the computed score. This is equivalent to using set as in the previous example. After evaluating these expressions, the value of item-streams is the following:

Example 5.3.3: Output from item-streams.sal

```
SAL> exec score-print(item-streams)
((0  0 (SCORE-BEGIN-END 0 NIL))
 (0 0.3 (NOTE vel: 75 pitch: 60))
 (0.3 0.5 (NOTE vel: 100 pitch: 84))
 (0.8 0.7 (NOTE vel: 125 pitch: NIL))
 (1.5 0.3 (NOTE vel: 75 pitch: 60))
 (1.8 0.5 (NOTE vel: 100 pitch: 84))
 (2.3 0.7 (NOTE vel: 125 pitch: NIL))
 (3 0.3 (NOTE vel: 75 pitch: 60))
 (3.3 0.5 (NOTE vel: 100 pitch: 84))
 (3.8 0.7 (NOTE vel: 125 pitch: NIL))
 (4.5 0.3 (NOTE vel: 75 pitch: 60))
)
```

Notice that the pitch: keyword parameter is an expression that gets the next item from pitch-cycle. The expression is evaluated for every note and the cyclic pattern continues for the ten events specified by the score-len: slot. When the pitch: is nil, no note is performed, so in musical terms, this is a rest. Even when the pitch: is nil, the other parameters, vel: and dur:, are computed from their cycles. The rest gets a duration of .7 seconds from the dur-cycle pattern. Since time: is not specified explicitly, it defaults to the end time of the previous note.

Table 5.3.1 and Table 5.3.2 describe the different pattern classes. In each case, you make a pattern object with a function make-*patternclass* and store the pattern object in a variable with set. Then, you access successive items from the pattern with the expression next(*patternobject*). The pattern classes in Table 5.2.1 all take a list of items as a parameter and deliver the items according to different rules.

Other pattern objects operate on the stream of items retrieved from another pattern. Pattern objects of this type are created by a function of the form make-*patternclass*, which takes another pattern object as input.

Often, these pattern objects operate on groups of items. Items retrieved from pattern objects are grouped into *periods*. For example, each repetition of a cycle pattern is one period. In a heap pattern, one period is some permutation of all the items of the input list. The period length can also be specified by the for: keyword parameter, which we will see in later examples.

Table 5.3.1 : Pattern objects that take item lists as input

Pattern Class	Description	Example in Accompanying Media	Notes
cycle	Circles through the data items provided in a list parameter.	cycle.sal	
heap	Plays through the data items in random order but will not repeat an item until all items have been played.	heap.sal	
palindrome	Plays through the data item list forwards and backwards.	palindrome. sal	The keyword parameter elide: may have a value of first:, last:, #t, or #f and determines if events are repeated when the pattern changes direction.
random	Each successive item is selected randomly from the input list.	random.sal	Items may be paired with weights for a weighted random selection.
line	Iterates through a list and repeats the last element until no more events are required.	line.sal	
markov	Generate items from a Markov model.	markov-graph.sal	The markov pattern is covered in a later chapter.
accumulation	For each item in the input list, output all the items up to and including the item	accumulation. sal	Example: (a b c) generates a a b a b c, and then repeats.

Table 5.3.2: Pattern objects that take pattern objects as input

Pattern Class	Description	Example in Accompanying Media	Notes
accumulate	Each output item is the sum of the previous *output* item and the next item of an *input* stream.	accumulate. sal	Items from the input stream must be numbers.
copier	Copies periods of the input stream to the output stream.	copier.sal	The repeat: parameter tells how many copies to make. The merge: parameter tells whether repeated periods should be output as one period (#t) or separate periods (#f).
length	Regroups items from the input stream into periods of a specified length.	length.sal	The first parameter is the input pattern, the second is the period length.
window	Outputs items in a sliding window over input items.	window.sal	Parameters are input pattern, window size and window skip.
eval	Re-evaluates expression for each item.	pwl-pat-fm.sal	Parameter is a Lisp expression.

5.4 A Complete Example

Example 5.4.1 uses score-merge to combine 6 scores. The merge is preceded by 6 generators producing scores 1, 2, 3a, 3b, 3c, and 3d. The merge is based on the *octatonic scale*, initially presented in series. The octatonic scale is a series of eight pitches that alternate whole and half steps for one octave. Permutations of the octatonic scale form the pitch material of the remaining generators as a means of creating pitch homogeneity.

Example 5.4.1: my-first-merge.sal

```
; Compute and merge 6 different scores:
;    1, 2, 3a, 3b, 3c and 3d.

; Score-1 is the "melody", derived from an octatonic
; scale emitted by a palindrome pattern.
set pitch-1 = make-palindrome(
            list(ef3, e3, fs3, g3, a3, bf3, c4, cs4))
set rhythm-1 = make-accumulation(
                {.22 .23 .25 .26 .28 .29 .31})

define function score-1-helper(count)
  set vel-1 = interpolate(count, 0, 40, 47, 125),
      ioi-1 = next(rhythm-1)

exec score-gen(save: quote(score-1), score-len: 48,
            pre: score-1-helper(sg:count),
            pitch: next(pitch-1),
            ioi: ioi-1,
            vel: vel-1,
            dur: vel-1 * 0.01 * ioi-1)

; Score-2: chords that punctuate the melodic material

set pitch-2 = make-random(
            list(list(list(c2, d3, ef4, f5)),
                 list(nil),
                 list(list(cs1, ds2, e3, fs4)),
                 list(gs5)))
set rhythm-2 = make-random(
        list(i, id, list(s, keyword(weight), .5), sd))
set vel-2 = make-heap({80 90 100})

define function score-2-helper()
  set vel-2-item = next(vel-2)

exec score-gen(save: quote(score-2), begin: 7,
            score-dur: 4.5,
            pre: score-2-helper(),
            pitch: next(pitch-2),
            ioi: next(rhythm-2),
            vel: vel-2-item,
            dur: vel-2-item * 0.005)
```

```
; Scores 3a-3d: an accompaniment to pitch material

set pitch-3a = make-cycle(list(c4, d5, ef6, f6))
set rhythm-3a = make-heap({0.01 0.035 0.048})
exec score-gen(save: quote(score-3a), begin: 2.8,
               score-len: 4,
               pitch: next(pitch-3a),
               vel: interpolate(sg:count, 0, 60, 3, 80),
               ioi: next(rhythm-3a),
               dur: 0.1)

set pitch-3b = make-cycle(list(cs3, ds4, e5, fs6, gs7))
set rhythm-3b = make-heap({0.01 0.035 0.048})
exec score-gen(save: quote(score-3b), begin: 3.75,
               score-len: 5,
               pitch: next(pitch-3b),
               vel: interpolate(sg:count, 0, 60, 4, 80),
               ioi: next(rhythm-3b),
               dur: 0.1)

set pitch-3c = make-cycle(list(c4, d5, ef6, f6))
set rhythm-3c = make-heap({0.01 0.035 0.048})
exec score-gen(save: quote(score-3c), begin: 4.1,
               score-len: 4,
               pitch: next(pitch-3c),
               vel: interpolate(sg:count, 0, 60, 3, 80),
               ioi: next(rhythm-3c),
               dur: 0.1)

; 3d generates chords
set pitch-3d = make-cycle(list(list(cs2, ds3, e4),
                               nil,
                               list(ds3, e4, fs5),
                               list(e4, fs5, g6),
                               list(fs5, g6, gs7),
                               list(g6, a7, as7)))
set rhythm-3d =
          make-heap({0.12 0.124 0.126 0.128 0.132})
exec score-gen(save: quote(score-3d), begin: 4.1,
               score-len: 6,
               pitch: next(pitch-3d),
               vel: interpolate(sg:count, 0, 40, 5, 70),
               ioi: next(rhythm-3d),
               dur: 0.1)

;; now merge the scores
set the-score = score-merge(score-1, score-2, score-3a,
                            score-3b, score-3c, score-3d)
```

Notice how each score is generated: first, various pattern objects are created and assigned to global variables. Variable names are chosen to avoid duplication. Trying to use the same variable for two different purposes is called "name collision," and is one of the hazards of using global variables. There are more sophisticated programming techniques to avoid this problem, but for now, we will take a simple approach and just be careful with name choices.

After creating the pattern objects to be used, score-gen is used to create a score. Again, global variables retain the scores (the save: keyword provides the variable name). At the very end, score-merge is used to combine all the score parts into one score.

Most note parameters such as pitch: are generated independently with the expression next(*pattern-object*), which just takes the next item from the pattern. In this example, ioi: and dur: in score-1 depend on the value of next(*rhythm-1*), but if we simply evaluated this expression twice (once for ioi: and once for dur:) we would get two different items from the rhythm-1 pattern. Instead, we evaluate next(rhythm-1) just once per generated note and use set to store the value in the variable ioi-1. Then, we use ioi-1 in two different expressions to specify the ioi: and dur: parameters. Similarly, dur: depends on vel:, so we introduce the variable vel-1 and use it in two places.

To compute ioi-1 and vel-1 once for every note, we use the pre: keyword. The expression following pre: is evaluated *once before* each note. (There is also an optional post: keyword to evaluate an expression *after* each note.) Notice that pre: (and all keywords) must be followed by an expression, but set is a command, so we cannot say something like pre: set ioi-1 = next(rhythm-1). However, we *can* call a function, so we define score-1-helper to do the assignments. Again, there are more sophisticated ways to do this, but we opt for the approach that uses concepts we have already seen.

Now that we understand how the score-1 generator is structured, let us look more closely at what it computes. The rhythm-1 pattern is the accumulate pattern applied to a list of durations. It returns the sequence .22, .22, .23, .22, .23, .25, .22, .23, .25, .26, etc. score-1 will have a length of 48 notes, as indicated by the :score-len parameter.

The variable vel-1 is computed by

    set vel-1 = interpolate(sg:count, 0, 40, 47, 125)

The interpolate function has parameters x, *x1, y1, x2, y2*. It computes the *y* value at *x* on the line from point (*x1, y1*) to (*x2, y2*). In this case, sg:count is an index that starts at 0 and increments after each note is generated. Thus, sg:count takes on the values 0 through 47 for the 48 notes of score-1. The remaining parameters say that when sg:count is 0, the output (*y*) should be 40, and when sg:count is 47, the output should be 125. The output is interpolated (or extrapolated) for other values of sg:count. Thus, the result values will increase smoothly from 40 to 125 over the 48 notes in score-1. The variable ioi-1 is simply the next item from the rhythm-1 pattern.

The ioi: and vel: parameters are specified by very simple expressions: just an unquoted symbol. Recall that a symbol evaluates to the value of the indicated variable. The dur: expression scales the duration by the velocity so that louder notes are also longer. Since velocity values range (normally) from 1 to 127, an extra scale factor of 0.01 is used so that the scale factor is between 0.01 and 1.27.

score-2 uses chords. Notice how the pattern object for pitch (stored in the variable pitch-2) is created. make-random chooses between items in a list, and in this case, the items themselves are lists: (c2, d3, ef4, f5), nil, (cs1, ds2, e3, fs4), and gs5. You might think the input to make-random should therefore be something like {{c2 d3 ef4 f5} {} {cs1 ds2 e3 fs4} gs5}; however, when make-random sees a list as an item, it expects to find an item followed by keywords weight:, min:, or max:. To tell make-random that the items themselves are lists, an additional level of nesting must be used, so the input is actually {{{c2 d3 ef4 f5}} {{}} {{cs1 ds2 e3 fs4}} gs5}. Instead of braces {}, the program uses list to construct lists so that the pitch names, which are global variables, will be evaluated to produce numbers. (Note that {c4} is a list containing the *symbol* c4, whereas list(c4) is equivalent to {60}.)

To finish this discussion on lists of pitches, remember that when a score is played, if the pitch: keyword contains a list, the note expression is expanded into one note for each element of the list. Thus, the generated "notes" will be chords. The empty list "expands" into no notes, so it is effectively a rest.

Previously, it was stated that the parameter expressions are evaluated once for each note. To be more precise, we should say the expressions are evaluated once for each score event, which may be a note, a chord, or a rest. Similarly, the score-len: parameter is the number of score events, so chords and rests count the same as a single note.

To listen to the-score, use jnyqide to open "my-first-merge.sal" and push the load button. To see the score, type exec score-print(the-score), or to hear the score, type exec score-play(the-score).

5.5   Suggested Listening

"U" (The Cormorant) for violin, computer, and quadraphonic sound composed by Mari Kimura is motivated by the blight of the oil-covered cormorants in the Persian Gulf. The formal structure of the composition is quasi-palindromic, imitating the shape of the letter "U" (Kimura, 1992).

Phasing by John Woodruff is included in the electronic materials in its original version for Common Lisp (phasing-woodruff.lsp), translated to SAL (phasing-woodruff.sal), and as a sound file (phasing.wav).

Chapter 6   Printing, Reading, and Debugging

This chapter introduces you to writing output, reading data from the computer keyboard, and debugging programs. Displaying information on your monitor is very helpful in locating problems in your programs.

6.1   print Command

We have already seen the print command, which causes expressions to be evaluated and printed. The print template is

print *expression₁, expression₂, ...*

print will print a constant, symbol, string, or the value of a variable or expression. A newline is printed first; then each value is printed followed by a space.

Example 6.1.1: The print command

```
SAL> print 45
45

SAL> print quote(a-symbol)
A-SYMBOL

SAL> print "hello world!"
hello world!

SAL> print *default-sound-srate*
44100

SAL> print 2 + 3 + 4
9
```

6.2   format Command

The function format allows you greater control of the formatting of your output. The format template is

format(#t, *format-control-string, things-to-print*)

format is followed by true (#t) to indicate that we want to print to the monitor. (Later we will see how to direct output to a file.) A string is used as the *format-control-string*. Since format is a function, we use an `exec` command to call it. `format` is not a command like `print`.

Example 6.2.1: format

```
SAL> exec format(#t, "I love Nyquist!")
I love Nyquist!
```

The *format-control-string* is always enclosed in double quotes. The *format-control-string* may include `format` directives – special characters in the *format-control-string* that cause output to appear in certain ways. `format` directives always begin with the tilde (~). Table 6.2.1 gives an overview of the most useful `format` directives.

Table 6.2.1: format directives

format Directive	Result
~%	Move to a new line
~A	Print the value of a variable or expression
~S	Print the value of a variable or expression using quotes around strings
~~	Print the tilde character

Example 6.2.2: The ~% format directive

```
SAL> exec format(#t,
"~%this is the first line ~%and this is the second")
this is the first line
and this is the second
```

Example 6.2.3: The ~A format directive

```
SAL> set count = 43
SAL> exec format(#t, "The count is ~A~%", count)
The count is 43
```

Notice that in Example 6.2.3 the characters "~A" in the format string are replaced by the value of `count` which appears as an input to `format`.

In Example 6.2.4, "~A" appears twice in the `format` string, so there are a total of four input parameters. Also, note that `error-msg` is inserted into the formatted output without quotation marks.

Example 6.2.5 is identical to 7.2.4 except that "~S" is used in the format string. Notice the output is similar, but the printed version of `error-msg` includes quotation marks.

Example 6.2.4: format multiple items

```
SAL> set error-msg =
             "you entered a negative number"
SAL> set error-value = -7
SAL> exec format(#t, "Error: ~A, ~A",
                 error-msg, error-value)
Error: you entered a negative number, -7
```

Example 6.2.5: ~S format directive

```
SAL> set error-msg =
             "you entered a negative number"
SAL> set error-value = -7
SAL> exec format(#t, "Error: ~S, ~A",
                 error-msg, error-value)
Error: "you entered a negative number", -7
```

6.3 display Command

"Debugging" is the process of finding errors (bugs) in your programs. When debugging, it often helps to print out values of variables and expressions to confirm that the program is operating as expected. Printing makes the computation process more observable. Although format is a perfectly usable function for debugging, a special command, display, can be even easier. The first input to display is a string that is simply printed. After that, any expression is printed along with its value.

Example 6.3.1: display

```
SAL> display "display example",
             *default-sound-srate*, count
Display example : *DEFAULT-SAMPLE-RATE* = 44100 COUNT = -7
SAL> exec format(#t,
"Format example : *default-sound-srate* = ~A count = ~A~%",
                 *default-sound-srate*, count)
Format  example:: *default-sample-rate* = 44100 count = -7
```

In Example 6.3.1, equivalent output is generated using display and format. Notice the display version is more compact.

6.4 Debugging with #display and #print

Sometimes, it may be useful to monitor the values of one or more expressions. SAL has a function, #print, that accepts one input, prints it, and returns the same value as the input. Thus, you can convert any expression *x* into #print(*x*) without changing the behavior of your program except for the fact that the value of *x* will be printed each time expression *x* is evaluated.

The "#" part of #print has a special meaning in SAL. Recall that SAL programs are evaluated by first translating them into Lisp. Ordinarily, any function name or variable name in SAL is translated to the same name in Lisp, making it easy to call Lisp functions from SAL and vice-versa. However, in this case, the desired Lisp function is named print, which is in conflict with the print *command* in SAL. In SAL, if you try to call print as a function (rather than a command), SAL merely reports a syntax error. To work around problems like this, SAL translates symbols prefixed with "#" into the Lisp symbol without the prefix. Thus, #print in SAL means print in Lisp, and this avoids the naming conflict with SAL's print command.

Another use of the "#" prefix is to access the Lisp display function. The Lisp display function is essentially identical to the SAL display command, but it can be used where expressions are required. See Example 7.3.1 for an example.

There are a few exceptions to the "#" prefix rule: In particular, we have already seen that #t and #f are special values in SAL. The variable t does happen to be the Lisp name for "true," but the variable f does not normally have any value at all.

To illustrate the use of #print, let's say you'd like to learn more about the Nyquist functions score-gen and exponential-dist. We will use #print to print a number to the display whenever exponential-dist is evaluated within a score-gen expression. exponential-dist is used to compute note durations.

From the printout, we can see the printed duration values that are computed by exponential-dist and we can confirm that these values are used for durations in the score. Also, since these numbers appear before the score, we can surmise that the score is completely evaluated immediately resulting in a list. This may seem obvious to some, but it is conceivable that duration computation could be deferred until the score is accessed or even until the duration of each note is read. You might also wonder whether durations are *recomputed* each time the score is played, but since the same random numbers printed when the score is computed appear in the score, it should be clear that the numbers are computed just once.

Example 6.4.1: print.sal

```
SAL> load "distributions" ; defines exponential-dist
SAL> exec score-print(
              score-gen(save: quote(score-exp-dist),
                        score-dur: 10,
                        dur:
                        #print(exponential-dist(0.5)),
                        pitch: 72, vel: 100))
1.53382
0.121667
5.98811
0.544893
0.522198
0.377926
4.15305
8.28694
0.74661
0.282558
((0 0 (SCORE-BEGIN-END 0 9.28256))
 (0 1.53382 (NOTE :VEL 100 :PITCH 72))
 (1 0.121667 (NOTE :VEL 100 :PITCH 72))
 (2 5.98811 (NOTE :VEL 100 :PITCH 72))
 (3 0.544893 (NOTE :VEL 100 :PITCH 72))
 (4 0.522198 (NOTE :VEL 100 :PITCH 72))
 (5 0.377926 (NOTE :VEL 100 :PITCH 72))
 (6 4.15305 (NOTE :VEL 100 :PITCH 72))
 (7 8.28694 (NOTE :VEL 100 :PITCH 72))
 (8 0.74661 (NOTE :VEL 100 :PITCH 72))
 (9 0.282558 (NOTE :VEL 100 :PITCH 72))
 )
SAL>
```

6.5   Tracing Pattern Evaluation

Patterns are a very powerful way to generate data, but pattern behavior can be confusing, especially with complex, nested pattern expressions. To help debug programs with patterns, patterns have a built-in facility for monitoring their evaluation. The following example uses the window pattern:

Example 6.5.1: Pattern evaluation

```
SAL> set winpat = make-window(
                  make-cycle({a b c d}), 6, 1)
SAL> print next(winpat, t)
(A B C D A B)
```

```
SAL> print next(winpat, t)
(B C D A B C)
```

With these nested patterns, make-cycle produces the sequence A
B C D A B C D A B C D ..., and make-window regroups these into
periods of length 6 with a sliding window that is advanced by one
item each period. To illustrate the step-by-step computation in both
cycles, use trace: and name: keyword parameters as shown in the
next example:

Example 6.5.2: Tracing evaluation

```
SAL> set winpat =
        make-window(
          make-cycle({a b c d}, trace: t,
                                name: "cycle"),
        6, 1, trace: t, name: "window")
SAL> print next(winpat, t)
pattern cycle advanced to A
pattern cycle advanced to B
pattern cycle advanced to C
pattern cycle advanced to D
pattern cycle advanced to +EOP+
pattern cycle advanced to A
pattern cycle advanced to B
pattern window advanced to A
pattern window advanced to B
pattern window advanced to C
pattern window advanced to D
pattern window advanced to A
pattern window advanced to B
pattern window advanced to +EOP+
(A B C D A B)

SAL> print next(winpat t)
pattern cycle advanced to C
pattern window advanced to B
pattern window advanced to C
pattern window advanced to D
pattern window advanced to A
pattern window advanced to B
pattern window advanced to C
pattern window advanced to +EOP+
(B C D A B C)
```

The trace shows the order of evaluation of the patterns. Notice that patterns generate an explicit marker +EOP+ that indicates the end of a period. This marker is not returned by next, but it is printed by the trace facility. You can see that periods are obtained by repeatedly generating the next item until +EOP+ is returned. To generate the first period of the window pattern, cycle is called to fill the 6-item window. Then, window can return the six items to next. For the next period, the window slides forward one item by dropping the first item (A) and calling cycle for a new item (C). It then returns a new period of 6 items.

Later, we will see more advanced uses of patterns where patterns are used to control other patterns. Along with expressive power comes the potential for great confusion. The pattern trace facility is one way to get detailed information that can help you understand pattern evaluation.

6.6   Reading Data from the Computer Keyboard

The function read accepts input from the computer keyboard. Generally, read is used to assign a variable. The read template is
> read()

We can allow the user to enter data from the computer keyboard during the evaluation of an algorithm or generator. Because of the looping behavior of algorithms and generators, Nyquist evaluates the read function as many times as the generator or algorithm loops. Consider the following example that assigns the pitch atribute using read.

This score-gen creates 5 notes. The vel:, dur:, ioi:, and name: properties are simple values. The pitch: property is given by a function that prints a prompt and reads a value. When evaluated, the user is prompted for each of 5 pitch numbers, which are incorporated into the score.

When using the Nyquist IDE, be sure to type all input into the text entry box at the upper left. The input will appear automatically in the Output window. (You cannot type directly into the Output window where the prompt appears.)

Example 6.6.1: Read pitches from user

```
SAL> define function enter-note-number()
        begin
           exec format(#t, "Enter a note number: ")
           return read()
        end

SAL> set my-score =
              score-gen(name: quote(note),
                        score-len: 5, vel: 100,
                        dur: 0.25, ioi: 0.5,
                        pitch: enter-note-number())
Enter a note number: 60
Enter a note number: 62
Enter a note number: 64
Enter a note number: 66
Enter a note number: 68

SAL> exec score-print(my-score)
((0 0 (SCORE-BEGIN-END 0 2.25))
(0 0.25 (NOTE :PITCH 60 :VEL 100))
(0.5 0.25 (NOTE :PITCH 62 :VEL 100))
(1 0.25 (NOTE :PITCH 64 :VEL 100))
(1.5 0.25 (NOTE :PITCH 66 :VEL 100))
(2 0.25 (NOTE :PITCH 68 :VEL 100))
)
```

Chapter 7 Variable Assignment and Scoping

This chapter introduces you to how to assign and reference variables in SAL (and Nyquist). Variables save values for reuse, avoiding the need to recompute them. Variables also offer a way to name values, making programs easier to understand. You will become familiar with several more SAL functions and the concept of the *scope* of a variable.

7.1   set Command

In Chapter 4, we used the set command to assign a list (a Nyquist score) to the variable my-score. The association between a variable and its value is called a *binding*. In addition to the *assignment* operation denoted by set, bindings are created by parameter passing, with, and other commands. We say the *scope* of the variable my-score is *global* because the variable and its value are valid everywhere in the program. The scope of a variable is the region in which a variable's value is known.

The general set command template is

set *variable₁* = *value₁*, *variable₂* = *value₂*, ...
    variableₙ = *valueₙ*

For example, set a = 1, b = 2, c = 3 will assign the variable a the value of 1, b the value of 2, and c the value of 3.

Example 7.1.1 shows the variable a4 evaluates to 69. We define a function transp that adds an interval to a pitch number. The body of the function returns the sum of the pitch and the interval. When we call the function with an input of a4 and 5, a4 is evaluated to obtain 69, which is passed to transp along with 5. The sum, which is 74, is returned. Printing the value of a4 indicates that the global variable has not been reassigned. Printing the value of pitch indicates that the variable pitch has no value. What does this mean?

This example demonstrates some of the differences between local and global variables. The parameter pitch in the function transp acts as a *local* variable. pitch is considered a local variable because its value is known only within the scope of its function. We demonstrate the scope of pitch by calling the function transp where pitch is bound to the value 69 and used to compute the result value 74. But pitch is local to the function transp, demonstrated by trying to evaluate it outside of the transp function.

Example 7.1.1: Local and global variables

```
SAL> print a4
69

SAL> define function transp(pitch, interval)
        begin
            return pitch + interval
        end

SAL> print transp(60, 3)
63

SAL> print transp(a4, 5)
74

SAL> print a4
69

SAL> print pitch
error: unbound variable - PITCH
Call traceback:
    SAL top-level command interpreter

SAL>
```

When we call the function transp with an input of a4, the function returns the transposed value of the global variable a4. A subsequent access of a4 indicates its value is unchanged. The global variable a4 is unchanged because it was not explicitly reassigned using set. It is the *value* of a4, not a4 itself, that is associated with the pitch parameter in transp. a4 is not affected by the function, and even pitch is unchanged from its initial value, because there is no set.

Example 7.1.2 uses set in the body of the function definition to reassign the value of a4. A function call followed by a print demonstrates that set reassigns the value of the global variable a4.

Example 7.1.2: Global variable

```
SAL> define function transp-a4-with-set(interval)
        begin
          set a4 = a4 + interval
          return a4
        end

SAL> print transp-a4-with-set(0.1)
69.1

SAL> print a4
69.1
```

Local and global variables of the same name can exist at the same time without interference. In Example 7.1.3, the variable v is used as both a global and a local. When both are active (inside the function), v refers to the local variable, but outside of the function body, v refers to the global.

Example 7.1.3: Local variable

```
SAL> define function my-fn(v)
        begin
          display "inside my-fn", v
        end

SAL> set v = "v is a global"
SAL> exec my-fn("v is a local")
inside my-fn : V = v is a local

SAL> display "outside my-fn", v
outside my-fn : V = v is a global

SAL>
```

7.2   begin, end, and with

Until now, we have mostly used begin-end to enclose the body of a function without any explanation. The more complete story is this: SAL expects a single command as the function body. Wherever SAL allows a command, you can instead write a begin-end block containing any number of commands. Function definitions do not actually require a begin-end block; but since they expect a single command, it is usually a good idea to use begin and end so that you can write any number of commands.

The same is true of the if-then-else command introduced in Section 4.5 and described more fully in Chapter 8. After then and else, SAL expects a single command, but a begin-end block can be used to contain several commands.

Besides its role in packaging multiple commands into a single command, another function of the begin-end block is to create local variables. So far, we have created local variables in the input list of a user-defined function. You can also create local variables in a begin-end block using with. with creates local variables and initializes them to the value of an expression (or nil by default). The template for a begin-end block with local variables is

```
begin
    with variable₁ = expression₁,
         variable₂ = expression₂, ...
    command₁
    command₂
    ...
end
```

The introduction of a local variable is called a *declaration*. The "= $expression_n$" part of each local variable declaration is optional; if it is missing, then the variable is initialized to nil (false).

In Example 7.2.1, the user-defined function average-of-three uses with to calculate the average (mean value) of three numbers passed as inputs to the function.

Example 7.2.1: average-of-three.sal

```
SAL> define function average-of-three(n1, n2, n3)
         begin
             with sum = (n1 + n2 + n3)
             return list(quote(the), quote(average),
                 quote(of),
                 n1, n2, n3, quote(is), sum / 3.0)
         end

SAL> print average-of-three(1, 2.5, 4)
{THE AVERAGE OF 1 2.5 4 IS 2.5}
```

We enter the body of the function with three inputs. A with is used to create the local variable sum and initialize it to the sum of the three inputs. list is used to construct a list by combining the quoted symbols the, average, of and is with the values of the input parameters and the value of the expression sum / 3.0.

When multiple variables are declared after with, they are created and initialized in order. Example 7.2.2 illustrates this point. The user-defined function more-averaging computes the average of three numbers in two steps. The first step computes sum as before, and the second step computes average as sum / 3.0.

Example 7.2.2: more-averaging.sal

```
SAL> define function more-averaging(n1, n2, n3)
       begin
         with sum = n1 + n2 + n3,
              average = sum / 3.0
         return list(quote(the),
                     quote(average), quote(is),
                     average)
       end

SAL> print more-averaging(1, 2.5, 4)
{THE AVERAGE IS 2.5}
```

7.3   score-gen and Local Variables

When computing scores with score-gen, local variables are created and updated automatically. Sometimes, it is useful to write expressions that depend on these variables. These variables are prefixed by "sg:". Note that the colon (:) *within* a variable name has no specific meaning; in SAL and Lisp; a colon can be used like any letter within a variable name. (SAL uses a colon suffix to indicate keywords, and Lisp uses a colon *prefix* to indicate keywords, so you should avoid variable names like :foo and bar: in any Nyquist program.)

sg:score-len is the maximum length of the score (in notes) specified by the score-len: keyword parameter, and sg:count is the number of notes generated so far.

sg:score-dur is the maximum length of the score (in seconds) specified by the score-dur: keyword parameter, and sg:start is the starting time of the current note.

sg:dur is the duration of the current note, and sg:ioi is the time from sg:start to the start of the *next* note.

Example 7.3.1 illustrates the use of sg:count and sg:start by printing these values as the score is computed. In Example 7.3.1, we call score-gen to create a score of 5 notes. Recall that in score-gen, expressions after keywords are evaluated for each note. Before each note, the pre: expression (not present in this example) is evaluated, and after each note, the post: expression is evaluated. In this example #display is used to print the values of sg:count and sg:start. Recall that #display is the functional form of the command display. SAL syntax rules say that an expression (not a command) must follow a keyword in an input list, so we must use #display rather than the command display. As you can see in the output, the printed values change for each note.

Example 7.3.1: monitoring-count-and-start.sal

```
SAL> define function monitoring-count-and-start()
        begin
          return score-gen(
            vel: 100, pitch: 60, ioi: 0.2,
            dur: 0.1, save: quote(myscore),
            score-len: 5,
            post:
            #display("show-count-and-start",
                      sg:count, sg:start))
        end

SAL> exec score-print(
            monitoring-count-and-start())
show-count-and-start : SG:COUNT = 0   SG:START = 0
show-count-and-start : SG:COUNT = 1   SG:START = 0.2
show-count-and-start : SG:COUNT = 2   SG:START = 0.4
show-count-and-start : SG:COUNT = 3   SG:START = 0.6
show-count-and-start : SG:COUNT = 4   SG:START = 0.8
((0 0 (SCORE-BEGIN-END 0 0.9))
(0 0.1 (NOTE :PITCH 60 :VEL 100))
(0.2 0.1 (NOTE :PITCH 60 :VEL 100))
(0.4 0.1 (NOTE :PITCH 60 :VEL 100))
(0.6 0.1 (NOTE :PITCH 60 :VEL 100))
(0.8 0.1 (NOTE :PITCH 60 :VEL 100))
)
```

7.4   Combining with and score-gen

Why are local variables important? In most cases, you can substitute global variables for locals, omit with expressions, and programs will compute exactly the same results. We saw, for example, the use of many globals in Chapter 5; we assigned pattern objects to global variables and used them in score-gen expressions. This is fine for small examples, but there can be problems when programs get larger. How can you be sure that you do not try to use the same global variable for two different purposes?

In general, if you only need a variable within a limited scope, you should use a local variable instead. The advantages of local variables are (1) programs are easier to read and understand – a global can be read or modified anywhere in the program, whereas a local is only visible within a limited range of program text, and (2) since local variables are invisible to code outside of their scope, future modifications to your program are unlikely to affect local variables – extensive use of global variables is asking for trouble and confusion.

Example 7.4.1 illustrates how to use with with score-gen so that pattern objects are held by local variables. This example is derived from Example 5.2.2, with globals converted to locals using with. Notice that the with cannot be embedded in score-gen. Among other problems, we want the with to compute and initialize the patterns one time only, whereas expressions within score-gen are re-evaluated for every note.

Example 7.4.1: with-example.sal

```
SAL> begin
        with pitch-cycle =
                make-cycle(list(c4, c6, nil)),
             vel-cycle =
                make-cycle({75 100 125}),
             dur-cycle =
                make-cycle({0.3 0.5 0.7})
        exec score-gen(
                save: quote(item-streams),
                score-len: 10,
                pitch: next(pitch-cycle),
                vel: next(vel-cycle),
                dur: next(dur-cycle))
        exec score-print(item-streams)
      end
((0 0 (SCORE-BEGIN-END 0 9.3))
(0 0.3 (NOTE :VEL 75 :PITCH 60))
(1 0.5 (NOTE :VEL 100 :PITCH 84))
(2 0.7 (NOTE :VEL 125 :PITCH NIL))
(3 0.3 (NOTE :VEL 75 :PITCH 60))
(4 0.5 (NOTE :VEL 100 :PITCH 84))
(5 0.7 (NOTE :VEL 125 :PITCH NIL))
(6 0.3 (NOTE :VEL 75 :PITCH 60))
(7 0.5 (NOTE :VEL 100 :PITCH 84))
(8 0.7 (NOTE :VEL 125 :PITCH NIL))
(9 0.3 (NOTE :VEL 75 :PITCH 60))
)
```

When local variables are used, it is safe to use generic-sounding names like pitch-cycle because local variables will not affect or interact with other parts of the program. If there is a global variable named pitch-cycle defined elsewhere in the program, it will be invisible inside the scope of the with expression, and assignments within this scope (from the declaration to the **end** token) will have no effect on the global with the same name.

Locals can also be useful for computing coordinated values using score-gen. Consider that score-gen ordinarily computes each note attribute independently. To coordinate the computation of parameters, compute a value for a local variable, and then compute note attributes from the local variable.

Example 7.4.2: with-example-2.sal

```
SAL> begin
        with pitch-pattern =
                make-random(
                    list(c4, d4, e4, f4, g4, a4, b4)),
                octave-pattern =
                make-random({0 12 24}),
                pitch
        exec score-gen(
                save: quote(let-example-2),
                score-len: 10,
                pre: setf(pitch, next(pitch-pattern) +
                                    next(octave-pattern)),
                pitch: pitch,
                vel: pitch + 20,
                dur: step-to-hz(c3) /
                    step-to-hz(pitch))
        exec score-print(let-example-2)
    end

((0 0 (SCORE-BEGIN-END 0 9.44545))
(0 0.0834275 (NOTE :VEL 111 :PITCH 91))
(1 0.0743254 (NOTE :VEL 113 :PITCH 93))
(2 0.264866 (NOTE :VEL 91 :PITCH 71))
(3 0.198425 (NOTE :VEL 96 :PITCH 76))
(4 0.187288 (NOTE :VEL 97 :PITCH 77))
(5 0.148651 (NOTE :VEL 101 :PITCH 81))
(6 0.297302 (NOTE :VEL 89 :PITCH 69))
(7 0.198425 (NOTE :VEL 96 :PITCH 76))
(8 0.374577 (NOTE :VEL 85 :PITCH 65))
(9 0.445449 (NOTE :VEL 82 :PITCH 62))
)
```

Example 7.4.2 demonstrates this approach. pitch, a local variable, is computed from a pattern generator in the pre: expression. As in Example 6.4.1 and Example 7.3.1, here we have another case where we would like to use a command, "set pitch = next(pitch-pattern) + next(octave-pattern)," in a list of (keyword) parameters for score-gen, but this is syntactically not allowed. As before, the solution is to use a Lisp function that accomplishes the equivalent of a

SAL command. In this case, we use Lisp's setf function, which is actually a special form (not a true function) that sets the first input (usually a variable name) to a value.

This pre: expression that sets pitch is evaluated before any note attributes. Then, the pitch: and dur: and vel: attributes are computed from the value of pitch.

In Example 7.4.2, pitch is the sum of a pitch pattern and an octave pattern. The pitch pattern randomly chooses from a scale, and the octave pattern randomly chooses from an octave offset. Before each note is computed, the pre: expression sets pitch to a value based on the pitch and octave patterns. This computed value (a local variable created in the with command) is used directly for the note pitch (pitch:), and it is incremented by 20 to form the note velocity (vel:). The note duration (dur:) depends inversely on the fundamental frequency of the note, as determined by step-to-hz. The lowest pitch, C4, will have a duration of 0.5, and the duration will be cut in half for each additional octave. Try exec score-play(let-example-2) to hear the result.

7.5   Understanding Variable Scope in SAL

The *scope* of a variable is the region in which its value is known. We have seen variables that have both local and global scope.

There are two ways to create variables with global scope. So far, we have seen *implicit* creation – just mentioning a variable name creates a global variable, but it is an error to access the variable's value until it is set, normally by using a set command. The second way to create a global is *explicit* creation using define variable. Example 7.5.1 shows a problem with implicit creation and Example 7.5.2 shows how to create global variables explicitly.

Before going any further, why would anyone include operators such as "*" and "+" in variable names? Asterisks surrounding a global variable name are merely a programming *convention* in Lisp, where there are no infix operators. While this may not be the best convention for SAL programs, many global variables in Nyquist (meaning they are common to XLISP and SAL) use this convention.

Since SAL function and variable names can contain operator characters, "a*b" is a variable name, but "a * b" is an expression. Even experienced programmers can be very confused if they intend to multiply a times b but instead get an error that a*b is uninitialized. To help avoid this problem, SAL checks all variables for embedded operator symbols and generates a warning if the variable is unknown. The warning does not prevent the initialization of the global, but it can be annoying to see these warnings when the program is actually correct. In fact, these warnings would be so common with hyphenated names, that SAL does not give warnings for variables with embedded "-" characters. In Example 7.5.1, the attempt to initialize an implicitly declared global variable with set generates a warning message because of the asterisks in the name.

Example 7.5.1: Implicitly defined variable

```
SAL> set *my-global* = 50
>>> parse warning: Identifier contains operator
character(s).
          Perhaps you omitted spaces around an
operator.
>>> in <console>, line 1, col 5.

set *my-global* = 50
    ^

SAL> print *my-global*
50
```

To avoid warning messages, you can declare variables explicitly with the define variable command. The syntax for this command is similar to with, but the command should not be embedded in a begin-end block. Notice that the warning that appeared in Example 7.5.1 does not appear in Example 7.5.2. Also, notice that multiple variables can be declared and initialized with one statement. Initialization is optional, and nil (false) is the default initial value. *Unlike set, define variable does not change a variable that already has a value. Therefore, initialization only takes effect once, even if a file containing define variable is reloaded.*

Example 7.5.2: define variable

```
SAL> define variable *my-global* = 50,
                      motive = {60 61 72 71}
```

Declaring a variable using with creates a local variable. The with is always the first command of a begin-end pair, and the with must be followed by one or more non-with commands. The local variables introduced by with are only visible from the point of declaration up to the matching end. This region is called the scope or the lexical context of the variable.

Local variables including function parameters are independent of any global with the same name. In Example 7.5.3, with creates variable b. b is initialized to 2 and then set to a new value. Notice how the variable b is not known or visible outside the begin-end command where it was created.

Example 7.5.3: Limited scope of a local variable

```
SAL> begin with b = 2
        set b = b * 2
        print b
     end
4

SAL> print b
SAL> error: unbound variable - B
Call traceback:
     SAL top-level command interpreter
```

Example 7.5.4 demonstrates again how local variables are independent of any global variables that might share the same name. Within a begin-end command, we create a local variable a initialized to the value 3. The body of the begin-end contains a set that increments the value of the local variable a by one and a print command that prints the value of a. The result is "4" as expected. Now that the begin-end command has finished, the local variable a no longer exists. What has happened to the global variable named a? We query the value of a at the "SAL>" prompt and see that the global variable a has retained its value of 0. Example 7.5.4 demonstrates how two variables of the same name have different lexical contexts. When scopes overlap, the innermost scope takes precedence and "hides" any other variable definitions. *This is an important language feature because it can reduce interference between different sections of programs.*

Example 7.5.4: Locals and globals that share a name

```
SAL> set a = 0 ; initialize global variable a
SAL> begin with a = 3 ; create local a
        set a = a + 1
        print a
     end
4

SAL> print a
0
```

7.6   Increment, Decrement, and Other Operators

The assignment operators += and -= can be used to increment and decrement a variable by some value. In the case of Example 7.6.1, += and -= increment and decrement the global variable a.

Example 7.6.1: Shortcuts to increment and decrement variables

```
SAL> set a = 1
SAL> set a += 1
SAL> print a
2

SAL> set a -= 2
SAL> print a
0
```

Another useful assignment operator is @=, which uses cons to insert a new element at the beginning of a list. The command "set *var* @= *expression*" is equivalent to the command "set *var* = cons(*expression*, *var*)."

Example 7.6.2: Using set and @=

```
SAL> set the-list = {b c}
SAL> set the-list @= quote(a)
SAL> print the-list
{a b c}
```

In Example 7.6.3, a global variable c is assigned a value of 0. We define a function increase that increases the value of c by a user-specified amount signified by the input x.

Example 7.6.3: Changing globals in functions

```
SAL> set c = 0

SAL> define function increase(x)
        set c += x
```

In Example 7.6.4, the function call to increase increases the value of c by 3.

Example 7.6.4: Testing the increase function

```
SAL> exec increase(3)

SAL> print c
3
```

A function definition that modifies a global variable is usually considered to be in poor style. If functions change global variables, then the behavior of the program as a whole depends upon the internal details of every function. It is usually better if functions compute a value and return it without any "side effects" that change global variables. Changing a global variable in a function is also an indication that the programmer may not fully understand how programs can be written more clearly using local variables. Example 7.6.5 shows an improvement of the definition of the function increase.

Example 7.6.5: Eliminating a global variable

```
SAL> define function increase(c, x)
        return c + x
```

In Example 7.6.6, we call the function increase with inputs of c and 3. The value of the global variable c (currently 3) is used in the evaluation.

Example 7.6.6: Calling the new increase function

```
SAL> print increase(c, 3)
6
```

A query shows that the global variable c still has a value of 3. The global variable c has not been reassigned; we merely computed the sum of c and x.

Example 7.6.7: The global has not changed

```
SAL> print c
3
```

In order to reassign the global variable c, we need to assign it using set as seen in Example 8.6.11.

Example 7.6.8: Updating a global

```
SAL> set c = increase(c, 3)

SAL> print c
6
```

While this version is slightly longer than the code in Example 7.6.3 and Example 7.6.4, the advantage here is that you can see clearly that we are changing the value of c. You might be thinking: "But what if *this* code (Example 7.6.8) is contained within another function? Isn't

Chapter 7 · Variable Assignment and Scoping

this just another case of a function modifying a global variable?"
This is absolutely true. One solution would be to declare c as a local
variable to the function that calls increase. This would avoid using a
global entirely.

7.7 Assigning Local Variables Interactively

In Section 6.6, we learned how SAL accepts data from the computer
keyboard using the function read. We can use read in conjunction
with with to interactively assign local variables.

Example 7.7.1 is a SAL user-defined function, simple-add, that
accepts two numbers from the computer keyboard and assigns those
numbers to local variables using the with command. simple-add
returns the sum of the two numbers.

Example 7.7.1: Reading into variables in simple-add.sal

```
SAL> define function simple-add()
        begin
          exec format(#t,
                  "Please enter a number ")
          begin
            with x = read()
            exec format(#t,
              "Please enter another number ")
            begin
              with y = read()
              exec format(#t,
                  "~A plus ~A equals ~A~%",
                  x,        y,        x + y)
            end
          end
        end

SAL> exec simple-add()

Please enter a number 6

Please enter another number 8

6 plus 8 equals 14
```

Notice that there are begin commands nested to three levels deep.
Variables must be declared immediately after begin, but in this case,
we want to alternate the creation and initialization of local variables
with the printing of prompts. This is a good illustration of how

begin-end commands can be nested, but the program becomes rather cluttered, so a cleaner version using set to bind local variables is shown in Example 7.7.2. *Warning: Any* program that prompts the user for input should test for valid entries and give the user a chance to confirm, reenter, or cancel the operation. We leave this as an exercise for the reader.

Example 7.7.2: An alternative implementation, simple-add-2.sal

```
SAL> define function simple-add()
        begin with x, y
          exec format(#t,
                  "Please enter a number ")
          set x = read()
          exec format(#t,
              "Please enter another number ")
          set y = read()
          exec format(#t,
                  "~A plus ~A equals ~A~%",
                  x,      y,        x + y)
      end
```

Example 7.7.3 uses local variables and read in a score generator. We use with to create the local variables the-pitch and the-amplitude. We use a pre: expression to prompt for and assign the values of these local variables. The program must use something of the form

pre: *expression,* pitch: the-note, vel: the-amplitude

where *expression* reads the-note and the-amplitude.

A complication with this plan is that, first of all, SAL does not normally allow assignments as expressions, so we need a slight "trick" to bind the-pitch using an expression. We saw the solution to this problem in Example 7.4.2: call the function setf in place of the command set.

The second problem is that we want to assign *two* variables rather than one. Why not call a function to read and initialize the variables? Since these are local variables, they are not in the scope of another function, so they cannot be manipulated outside of their enclosing begin-end block. We could use global variables instead, but this practice is frowned upon as discussed earlier.

The simplest solution uses the fact that setf can take any number of inputs, alternating variables with the expressions to be evaluated to determine the variables' new values. We could write this expression:

Chapter 7 · Variable Assignment and Scoping

```
               setf(the-pitch, read(), the-amplitude, read())
```
to initialize both variables with one expression. This would work, but
what if we want to prompt the user for input?

A more general solution is required. The Lisp form, progn,
evaluates any number of expressions in sequence and returns the
value of the last one. Although not recommended for SAL programming in general, it can be a useful way to obtain sequential behavior
in an expression as opposed to using a sequence of commands sur-
rounded by begin-end. Within the progn expression, we can use the
format function to print prompts, and the setf function to set local
variables. Compare Example 7.7.3 to Example 6.6.1.

Example 7.7.3: interactive-assign.sal

```
SAL> begin with the-note, the-amplitude
        exec score-gen(
          save: quote(interactive-assign),
          score-len: 3, ioi: .5, dur: .35,
          pre: progn(format(#t,
              "Please enter a note number: "),
            setf(the-note, read()),
            format(#t,
              "Please enter an amplitude: "),
            setf(the-amplitude, read())),
          pitch: the-note,
          vel: the-amplitude)
      end
Please enter a note number: 60
Please enter an amplitude: 75
Please enter a note number: 48
Please enter an amplitude: 80
Please enter a note number: 36
Please enter an amplitude: 90

SAL> exec score-print(interactive-assign)
((0 0 (SCORE-BEGIN-END 0 1.35))
 (0 0.35 (NOTE :VEL 75 :PITCH 60))
 (0.5 0.35 (NOTE :VEL 80 :PITCH 48))
 (1 0.35 (NOTE :VEL 90 :PITCH 36))
)
```

7.8   Suggested Listening

Systems Management is a composition by tENTATIVELY, a
cONVENIENCE (2009). *Systems Management* was performed by
HiTEC (Histrionic Thought Experiment Cooperative) on several

occasions in Pittsburgh. In *Systems Management,* a giant "wheel of fortune" is spun to select a number, which corresponds to a *system.* A system is a set of directions or a musical thought experiment for the orchestra members, called *systems managers.* (An example can be viewed online: http://www.youtube.com/watch?v= tMpa9VMyWmU.) Each system is like a computer program for musicians to follow. In computational terms, you can think of spinning the wheel as assigning a random number to a variable called system-number. In the next chapter, we will see how computers can perform actions that depend upon the values of variables.

Chapter 8   Conditionals

Evaluating data and making decisions is an important part of describing music algorithmically. In this chapter, we will learn how to make decisions using SAL's if statement and the special function #? (no, we're not cursing, that's really the name of the function). Programming constructs that choose an action based on a value are called *conditionals*. For example, make notes shorter *if* they are above C5. Using conditionals, we can write programs that create music based on a condition or set of conditions.

8.1   if Command

The if command has a test expression that is evaluated to obtain a true or false value (anything other than nil – the same as #f – is considered to represent true). When the test-clause evaluates to true, the true-consequent command is evaluated. When the test-clause evaluates to false (#f), an optional false-consequent command is evaluated. If the false-consequent command is omitted, the program continues with the next command.

The templates for if are:
> if *test-expression* then *true-consequent*
> if *test-expression* then *true-consequent* else *false-consequent*

In Example 8.1.1, we use define variable at the "SAL>" prompt to create global variables *pitch* with a value of 60 and *vel*, initially nil. We would like to assign a global variable *vel* a value of 90 if *pitch* is less than 60. Otherwise, we will assign *vel* a value of 50. Example 8.1.1 illustrates the conditional assignment of the variable *vel*.

Example 8.1.1: Using if

```
SAL> define variable *pitch* = 60, *vel*

SAL> if *pitch* < 60 then set *vel* = 90
                     else set *vel* = 50

SAL> print *vel*
50
```

In Example 8.1.1, the test-clause *pitch* < 60 uses the relational operator < to see if the current value of *pitch* is less than 60. Because *pitch* was initialized with a value of 60, the test-expression evaluates to #f and the false-consequent, "set *vel* = 50," is performed. The effect can be seen by printing the new value of *vel*.

SAL if commands may be nested to make more complex decisions. The nesting of if is accomplished when another if takes the role of a true-consequent or false-consequent. Typically, programs are more readable if only the false-consequent is another if command.

The template for a nested if using the false-consequent command is

> if *test-expression₁* then *true-consequent₁*
> else
>   if *test-expression₂* then *true-consequent₂*
>   else *false-consequent*

In Example 8.1.2, we write a SAL function test-range that uses a nested if to determine if the variable a-note is within the range of the MIDI specification.

Example 8.1.2: nested-if.sal

```
define function test-range(a-note)
  begin
    if a-note < 0 then
      return quote(too-low)
    else
      if a-note > 127 then
        return quote(too-high)
      else
        return quote(in-range)
  end
```

Given an input of −5, the function test-range evaluates the test-expression "is −5 less than 0?" The test-expression evaluates to true and the symbol too-low is returned by the function. (Recall that too-low is quoted to indicate the symbol itself should be returned rather than being evaluated as a variable.)

Given a MIDI note input of 129, the function test-range evaluates the test-expression "is 129 less than 0?" The test-expression evaluates to #f and program control transfers to the next test clause "is 129 greater than 127?" This test-expression evaluates to true and the symbol too-high is returned by the function.

Given an input of 60, the function **test-range** evaluates the test-expression "is 60 less than 0?" The test-expression evaluates to #f and program control transfers to the next test "is 60 greater than 127?" This test-expression also evaluates to #f and the symbol in-range is returned by the function.

8.2 #? Special Form

While if is a command, #? can be used to create a conditional expression. Just as if takes a test and one or two consequent commands, the #? form takes a conditional expression and one or two consequent *expressions*.

We can use #? to rewrite Example 8.1.1 in a slightly more compact form. Example 8.2.1 uses #? to select which value (90 or 50) to assign to *vel*:

Example 8.2.1: Using #?

```
SAL> define variable *pitch* = 60, *vel*

SAL> set *vel* = #?(*pitch* < 60, 90, 50)

SAL> print *vel*
50
```

#? is a "special form" – an operation that is written in the form of a function but uses special rules to control the evaluation of its input parameters. The evaluation of a #? form is similar to the evaluation of an if command. Evaluation begins with the first input, the test-expression. Depending upon whether this is true or false, #? evaluates the first or the second expression (but not both). Note that if this were a true function, all inputs would be evaluated.

As with any form of expression, #? can be nested to form more complex conditionals. In Example 8.2.2, we rewrite the test-range function to use #? instead of if commands.

Example 8.2.2: Nested #? in nested-if-2.sal

```
define function test-range(pitch)
  begin
    return #?(pitch < 0, quote(too-low),
              #?(pitch > 127,
                 quote(too-high),
                 quote(in-range)))
  end
```

8.3 Using if with begin-end

In the examples presented so far, the consequent statements of if have been single commands, or in the case of the nested if, one consequent was another if command. In general, you may need to perform multiple actions based on a single test. This can be accomplished by calling a function containing many commands, or you can enclose the commands in a begin-end block, which is syntactically equivalent to a single command.

In Example 8.3.1, we use if to write a function make-valid-pitch that simply returns pitch numbers that fall within the range of 0 to 127, but otherwise prints "out of range" and returns 60.

Example 8.3.1: if-then-begin-end.sal

```
define function make-valid-pitch(pitch)
  begin
    if test-range(pitch) != quote(in-range)
    then
      begin
        print "out of range"
        set pitch = 60
      end
    return pitch
  end
```

First, make-valid-pitch calls test-range to obtain one of too-low, in-range, or too-high. This value is compared to in-range. If the two values are not equal (!=), the if performs the begin-end command that follows "then." This prints a message and changes pitch to 60. Regardless of the outcome of the conditional, pitch is returned. Consider an alternative implementation that replaces "set pitch = 60" with "return 60". Convince yourself that both produce the same result values and output.

8.4 Using Conditionals in Algorithmic Composition

Conditionals offer a powerful way to delineate form and sculpt musical events in the realization of a compositional algorithm. In Example 8.4.1, we create a musical gesture of 99 note events that change their pitch content during each third of the score. To achieve continuity, we maintain the same intervallic distances between the pitches in each set. We use a pitch set that follows the intervallic succession M2 m3 M2 M2. To achieve variety, we transpose the pitch set up a M2 for the second third of the container and down a M2 for the last third of the container.

Example 8.4.1: Conditional in composition

```
begin
  with notes = make-heap(
                  list(c4, d4, f4, g4, a4)),
       vels = make-heap({20 40 60}),
       durs = make-heap(list(s, sd, i))
  exec score-gen(
       save: quote(cond), score-len: 99,
       pitch: next(notes) + #?(sg:count < 33, 0,
                              #?(sg:count < 66, 2,
                                                -2)),
       vel: #?(sg:count < 49, next(vels),
                              next(vels) + 60),
       ioi: next(durs))
  end
```

The score cond has 99 notes. A #? is used to test the value of sg:count which increments from 0 to 98. The total number of events is divided into three cases. In the first case, if sg:count is less than 33, the pitch attribute will be assigned a value from the pitch set {c4, d4, f4, g4, a4} using the heap pattern type. In the second case, where sg:count is between 34 and 65 inclusive, the pitch attribute will be based on the same pitch set but transposed up a major second. The third case, where sg:count is greater than or equal to 66, calculates the pitch transposed down a major second from the original set.

A #? is also used to determine the set of amplitudes for any particular note. The value of the variable sg:count is tested and if we are in the first half of the score, an amplitude from the set {20, 40, 60} is picked. If we are in the second half of the score (sg:count is 50 or more), an amplitude is selected from the same set and incremented by 60. This algorithm allows the musical material to grow in amplitude as the number of note events increases. You can play it using the command "exec score-play(cond)". How would you make the average amplitude grow steadily instead of making one change at the midpoint of the score?

Notice that in this example, both pitch: and vel: are computed as the sum of an item from a pattern and some offset. For pitch:, we "factored out" the call to next(notes) and use the nested conditional to compute the offset (0, 2, or −2). For vel:, we wrote the entire computation in each consequence, so "next(vels)" appears twice. Either approach is "correct," but unless you are trying to demonstrate different possibilities, it would be better to be consistent.

In Example 8.4.2, we create a musical gesture for a duration of ten seconds that changes pitch content and amplitude during each second.

Example 8.4.2: Ascending melody in ascent.sal

```
begin
  with pitch-a = make-heap(list(c4, d4, e4)),
       pitch-b = make-heap(list(cs4, ds4, f4)),
       pitch-c = make-heap(list(d4, e4, fs4)),
       pitch-d = make-heap(list(ds4, f4, g4)),
       pitch-e = make-heap(list(e4, fs4, gs4)),
       pitch-f = make-heap(list(f4, g4, a4)),
       pitch-g = make-heap(list(fs4, gs4, as4)),
       pitch-h = make-heap(list(g4, a4, b4)),
       pitch-i = make-heap(list(gs4, as4, c5)),
       pitch-j = make-heap(list(a4, b4, cs5)),
       vel-a = make-cycle({20 40 60}),
       vel-b = make-cycle({40 75 80}),
       vel-c = make-cycle({60 80 100}),
       vel-d = make-cycle({80 100 120}),
       vel-e = make-cycle({100 120 127}),
       pitch, vel, s ;; s = note start time
  exec score-gen(
       save: quote(ascent), score-dur: 10,
       ioi: .2,
       pre: progn(setf(s, round(sg:start)),
                  #?(s < 2, setf(pitch, next(pitch-a),
                                 vel, next(vel-a))),
                  #?(s = 2, setf(pitch, next(pitch-b),
                                 vel, next(vel-b))),
                  #?(s = 3, setf(pitch, next(pitch-c),
                                 vel, next(vel-c))),
                  #?(s = 4, setf(pitch, next(pitch-d),
                                 vel, next(vel-c))),
                  #?(s = 5, setf(pitch, next(pitch-e),
                                 vel, next(vel-d))),
                  #?(s = 6, setf(pitch, next(pitch-f),
                                 vel, next(vel-d))),
                  #?(s = 7, setf(pitch, next(pitch-g),
                                 vel, next(vel-d))),
                  #?(s = 8, setf(pitch, next(pitch-h),
                                 vel, next(vel-e))),
                  #?(s = 9, setf(pitch, next(pitch-i),
                                 vel, next(vel-e))),
                  #?(s > 9, setf(pitch, next(pitch-j),
                                 vel, next(vel-e)))),
       pitch: pitch, vel: vel)
  end
```

This call to score-gen is nested within a begin-end command that creates stream objects for pitch and velocity. The long progn expression uses many #? expressions to determine which stream objects are used for each note. Recall that sg:start is the starting time of the note whose attributes are being computed. This start time is rounded to an integer s, and each different value of s selects a pair of patterns for pitch and velocity. In every case, variables pitch and vel are set, and these are then used as the values for keyword parameters pitch: and vel:. In this particular example, the resultant music creates a gradually rising chromatic figure that increases in pitch and loudness as time progresses. Play it with "exec score-play(ascent)".

In this example, a series of conditionals is used to select changing patterns as time passes. Often, a long list of nearly identical program statements like these is an indication that the program could be expressed more cleanly some other way. In this case, the variable s acts as a selector among many choices. The primitive nth uses an integer to select an element from a list. How would you rewrite Example 8.4.2 to use nth? In this program, it happens that there are exactly 5 notes per second, so with one small exception, each pattern is accessed 5 times. Earlier, we saw how patterns can be composed. How would you rewrite this example to draw pitches and velocities from nested patterns to yield the same result without the long series of conditionals?

8.5 Conditionals vs. Formulas

Example 8.4.2 uses a rather elaborate scheme to spell out the computation in great detail. The previous paragraph hinted at some possible simplifications. We can also observe that the general trend is a chromatically rising pitch center and increasing loudness. In the next example, we replace the conditionals with a more numerical approach, using formulas to calculate the change in pitch and velocity. We will use the same "trick" of rounding the note time to obtain an integer, but rather than select an expression with the integer, we will use the integer directly to compute pitch and velocity.

This example is not exactly equivalent to Example 8.4.2, but it does generate similar output, and it is certainly much more compact. It is worth considering the advantages and disadvantages of these two approaches. The first approach is more amenable to fine tuning. It would be simple to change just one or two pitch patterns to include a half step or a large interval, whereas the formula example only has one fixed pitch pattern. It would also be simple to vary the amplitude patterns in Example 8.4.2, for example to make a very quiet section just before a loud ending. On the other hand, the #? expressions are awkward to extend to greater durations. Each additional second requires another expression. In contrast, the formula approach can run for any duration with only slight changes necessary to limit velocity and pitch values. It is also possible to vary the overall shape of the pitch or velocity contour in Example 8.5.1 by editing a single expression rather than editing every pitch or velocity pattern. For example, the pitch pattern will go down if you just subtract the rounded start time rather than add it.

Example 8.5.1: formula.sal

```
begin
  with pitch-stream =
          make-heap(list(c4, d4, e4)),
       vel-stream =
          make-cycle(list(20, 40, 60))
  exec score-gen(save: quote(formula),
                 score-dur: 10, ioi: .2,
                 pitch: next(pitch-stream) +
                        round(sg:start),
                 vel: next(vel-stream) +
                      round(sg:start) * 10)
end
```

At a deeper level, this discussion is really about *abstraction*, one of the central concepts of algorithmic composition. We use algorithms to make music in order to shift the focus (and labor!) from the detailed specification of each note to more general, more abstract notions such as contour, texture, duration, and temporal evolution. An important task for the composer is to design algorithms that afford the "right" kind of control, depending on individual musical goals and expressive needs.

The last two examples illustrate two very different algorithms that yield similar music. The question is not which one is faster, better, simpler, or smaller. The important question is: Which approach best lends itself to the musical goals of the composer? Programs rarely if ever produce masterpieces or even good material without a significant amount of experimentation and refinement. Part of the process of algorithmic composition is designing programs that represent musical decisions in a way that supports musical exploration.

8.6 Suggested Listening

Matices Coincidentes (converging colors) composed by Pablo Furman was inspired by the use of perspective in art and architectural design. Pablo Furman explores the convergence and blending of tone colors using electronics (Furman, 1998).

British group Halal Kebab Hut uses various algorithmic techniques to generate music from everyday "junk." The piece *Variazioni con Shish No.4* uses inputs (in the form of surrounding sounds) in a set of rules for the performer to follow (http://www. halalkebab.co.uk/download/MP3s/Kebabish/ 02%20Variazioni%20con%20Shish.mp3).

Chapter 9   Sets and Tables

A *set* is a collection of objects. In SAL, we can represent finite sets as lists. Each object in a set is called an *element* or a *member*. In algorithmic composition, sets may be manipulated to achieve a compositional result.

9.1   Introduction to Set Theory

The analysis of atonal music using mathematical set theory was codified by Allen Forte in his landmark book, *The Structure of Atonal Music* (1973). His theory of atonal music develops a comprehensive framework for the organization of collections of pitches referred to as *pitch class sets*. We will introduce the concept of *pitch class*, and then describe Forte's concept of *pitch class set*.

Since SAL uses braces {} to denote lists and mathematicians use braces to denote sets, we need to be careful with notation. Here, braces with comma-separated items, all in this font (Times New Roman), are used to denote sets. Lists are denoted by parentheses () and comma-separated items, also in this font. If we use SAL's notation for lists, it will always be with the Lucinda Sans font and without commas:

> {this, is, a, set, of, words}
> (this, is, a, list, of, words)
> {this is a list of words too}

A *pitch class* is a set of pitches, one from each octave, that have the same note names. Informally, we are just saying that the pitch classes are all the A's, the B-flat's, the B's, etc. There are 12 pitch classes. Mathematicians are not happy with informal definitions, so "all the A's" is represented more precisely by a set. For example, $\{A_0, A_1, A_2, ...\}$ is a pitch class (here, A_4 denotes the A above middle C, A_3 is an octave lower, etc.), and $\{B_0, B_1, B_2, ...\}$ is another. In mathematics, these pitch classes are examples of *equivalence classes*. Members of the classes are equivalent in the sense that they have the same note names. There are other equivalence relations that induce other equivalence classes; for example, the "white keys" and "black keys" are equivalence classes. We say that equivalence classes form a *partition* over the set of all pitches, dividing the pitches into subsets.

Pitch classes could be named "A," "B-flat," "B," etc., but Forte names them with integers in the range 0 to 11. Pitch class assignment in twelve-tone equal temperament is as follows: C (or its enharmonic equivalent) is 0, C-sharp (or its enharmonic equivalent) is 1, D (or its enharmonic equivalent) is 2, and so on. Notice that in terms of MIDI pitches (key numbers), the pitch class is just the remainder of dividing the key number by 12. An aside: the *integers* are also a set, and the equivalence relation "has the same remainder after division by 12" forms equivalence classes over the integers that correspond to musical pitch classes. We represent pitches as integers rather than symbols to facilitate this kind of pitch manipulation and computation.

A *pitch class set*, or *pc set*, is a collection of pitch classes. Thus, a pc set is really a set of sets, but it is less confusing to think of a pc set as all the note names that occur in a collection of pitches. Intuitively, this amounts to removing all the octave names and octave doublings from a collection of pitches. What's left is a set of pitch classes. How many pitch class sets are there? Consider that there are 12 pitch classes, and each pitch class offers two choices: it can be in the set or not in the set. Thus, there are $2 \times 2 \times 2 \times 2 \times 2 \times 2 \times 2 \times 2 \times 2 \times 2 \times 2 \times 2$, or 2^{12}, or 4096 possible sets (including the empty set). In keeping with Forte's naming scheme, we represent pitch class sets as sets of the integers from 0 to 11.

Forte names each pc set based on its *prime form*. To understand the prime form, think of the pitch classes 0-11 organized around a circle. The pitch class structure is circular because a minor second above 11 (B) is 0 (C). To generate the *prime form* from a pc set, we list the pitch classes in clockwise order, starting at any pitch class. For example, the D-minor triad {D, F, A} or {2, 5, 9} in clockwise order generates the lists (2, 5, 9), (5, 9, 2), and (9, 2, 5). Next, we transpose the lists to begin at zero. Remember that these numbers represent pitch classes without octaves, so 1 (D-flat) transposed down by 3 (a minor third) is 10 (B-flat), not −2 (also B-flat, but not in the range 0-11). After transposition, our lists are (0, 3, 7), (0, 4, 9), and (0, 5, 8). Next, we also generate the *inversions* of these lists by subtracting each pitch class from 12. The effect is to exchange descending intervals for ascending ones. The results in our example are (0, 9, 5), (0, 8, 3), (0, 7, 4), and these are sorted into increasing order to get (0, 5, 9), (0, 3, 8), (0, 4, 7). Finally, the prime form is the list from among the original and inverted lists that is "most compact," meaning that the last element is smallest. In this case, there is a tie between (0, 3, 7) and (0, 4, 7), so we break the tie by taking the list with the smallest next-to-last element, (0, 3, 7).

Notice that two pc sets may have the same form. For example, all transpositions of minor triads have the prime form (0, 3, 7), and because inversions are considered equivalent, all *major* triads have the same prime form as all minor triads. Thus, prime forms are *equivalence classes* of pitch class sets: two pitch class sets are considered equivalent if they have the same prime form. Forte names prime forms with two numbers. The first number is the length of the prime form, which is also the number of elements in the corresponding pc sets. (The number of elements in a set is called the *cardinality* of the set.) The second part is derived by listing all prime forms from most to least compact. For example, set 4-1 is comprised of pitch classes (0 1 2 3). The 4 in the pc set name represents the cardinality of the set. The 1 is the unique integer identifier associated with that set. Only pc-sets with a succession of three minor seconds will have the Forte number 4-1.

The prime form is only one of many equivalence relations that can partition the 4096 pitch class sets. For example, if Forte had not considered inversions to be equivalent, then major and minor triads would not have the same prime form, and a different kind of equivalence relation would be obtained. Another interesting equivalence relation is obtained from the *interval vector*, which is a tally of all pair-wise intervals in a pitch class set. For example, the pitch class set {G, B, D, F} or {7, 11, 2, 5} has the following pairs: (7, 11), (7, 2), (7, 5), (11, 2), (11, 5), (2, 5). The corresponding intervals are 4, 5, 2, 3, 6, 3. Note that "interval" is defined as the smallest number of half steps from one pitch class to the other without regard for direction. For example, the interval from 7 to 2 is 5 (not −5), and the interval from 11 to 2 (B to D) is 3 because D lies 3 half steps above B. The *interval vector* is an ordered list of the number of intervals of size 1, size 2, size 3, and so on up to size 6, the largest interval. This example contains one interval of size 2, two intervals of size 3, and one each of sizes 4, 5, and 6, so the interval vector is 012111. This is the interval vector of all dominant seventh and half diminished chords, corresponding exactly to the prime form 4-27.

Not all prime forms have a unique interval vector. For example, the prime form (0, 1, 3, 5, 6), number 5-12, and prime form (0, 1, 2, 4, 7), number 5-36, have the same interval vector: 222121. Forte calls prime forms with the same interval vector "Z-related sets," or "Z correspondents," and he adds the letter Z to the designation, so these prime forms are actually named 5-Z12 and 5-Z36. You will see the letter Z in the names of some of the prime forms used in examples below.

9.2   List and Set Operations

Nyquist provides a number of functions that perform operations on lists or sets. These primitives are helpful in analyzing or composing music that is based on sets.

append, which was first discussed in Chapter 3, is very helpful in manipulating sets. append may take two or more lists as input and return a list of all of the elements of the first list followed by all of the elements of the second. When appending lists, the template for append is

append(list-1, list-2)

In the following example, we assign pitch class sets to two global variables s6-1 and s5-2. We use append to create a list of the two pc sets in succession.

Example 9.2.1: append with pitch class sets (as lists)

```
SAL> set s6-1 = {0 1 2 3 4 5}

SAL> set s5-2 = {0 1 2 3 5}

SAL> print append(s6-1, s5-2)
(0 1 2 3 4 5 0 1 2 3 5)
```

Example 9.2.2: append.sal

```
begin
  with c-major = list(c4, e4, g4),
       f-major = list(f4, a4, c5),
       g-major = list(g4, b4, d5),
       pitch-pattern = make-cycle(
                   append(c-major, f-major,
                          g-major, list(c5))),
       ioi-pattern = make-heap({0.2 0.3 0.45}),
       rhythm

  exec score-gen(score-len: 10,
                 save: quote(append-example),
                 pre: setf(rhythm,
                         next(ioi-pattern)),
                 pitch: next(pitch-pattern),
                 ioi: rhythm,
                 dur: rhythm * 2,
                 amp: interpolate(sg:count,
                         0, 10, 9, 120))
  end
```

In Example 9.2.2, we use major triads on C, F and G as sets. Local variables are created and initialized to lists that represent these triads. The variables that represent the lists are appended and converted into a cyclic item stream using make-cycle.

The functions reverse and nth were introduced in Chapter 3. Example 9.2.3 uses reverse in a score generator.

Example 9.2.3: reverse.sal

```
begin
  with c-major = list(c4, e4, g4),
       f-major = list(f4, a4, c5),
       g-major = list(g4, b4, d5),
       pitch-pattern = make-cycle(
         append(g-major,
               reverse(f-major), c-major)),
       rhythm-pattern = make-heap(
                         {0.2 0.3 0.35}),
       rhythm
  exec score-gen(
          save: quote(reverse-example),
          score-len: 9,
          pitch: next(pitch-pattern),
          pre: setf(rhythm,
                    next(rhythm-pattern)),
          ioi: rhythm,
          dur: rhythm * 2,
          amp: interpolate(sg:count,
                          0, 10, 8, 120))
end
```

In Example 9.2.4, we use nth to randomly access elements in a set. with is used to assign the local variables s6-z36 and amp-pattern and to create index, pitch, and octave. These variables are used in score-gen. This example could also be written using make-random to select random elements rather than using nth and random.

Example 9.2.4: nth.sal

```
begin
  with s6-Z36 = {0 1 2 3 4 7},
  ;;; 0 1 2 3 4 7 is set 6-Z36 according to
  ;;; Allen Forte's "Structure of Atonal Music"
       amp-pattern = make-heap(
                           {20 30 40 50 100}),
       index, pitch, octave
  exec score-gen(
    save: quote(nth-example),
    score-len: 25,
    pre: setf(index, random(6),
              pitch, nth(index, s6-Z36),
              octave, nth(random(2), {36 48})),
    pitch: octave + pitch,
    amp: next(amp-pattern),
    ioi: 0.2, dur: 0.3)
end
```

The predicate **member** checks to see if an element is included in a list. If the element is not found in the list, **member** returns nil. If the element is found, **member** returns the remainder of the list beginning with the found member.

Example 9.2.5: Using member

```
SAL> print member(6, {0 1 2 3 5})
#f

SAL> print member(3, {0 1 2 3 5})
{3 5}
```

Why is **member** considered a predicate if it returns a list? Recall that in SAL, any non-nil value is considered to mean "true."

Example 9.2.6 creates a melody, accompaniment, and final-chord using three calls to **score-gen**. In the melody, certain pitch classes (2, 4, 5, and 7) are emphasized by giving them a high amplitude. **member** is used to test whether the pitch class is in the list (2, 4, 5, 7). If so, the #? test expression is true, so an amplitude value between 100 and 119 is computed. Otherwise, an amplitude value between 10 and 39 is computed.

Example 9.2.6: member.sal

```
;; melody is drawn from pitches in 6-Z3, 6-Z36,
;; 5-Z38 and 7-Z38 (first two pitches, 0 and 1,
;; in these sets are omitted
begin
  with notes-1 = make-heap({2 3 4 7}),    ;; 6-Z3
       notes-2 = make-heap({2 3 5 6}),    ;; 6-Z36
       notes-3 = make-heap({2 5 8}),      ;; 5-Z38
       notes-4 = make-heap({2 4 5 7 8}),  ;; 7-Z38
       amp-pattern = make-cycle(
           {10 20 30 40 50 60 70 80 90
            10 20 30 40 50 60 70 80 90
            10 20 30 40 50 10 20 30 40 50
            10 20 30 40 50 10 20 30 40 50
            10 20 30 40 50 60 70}),
       rhythm-pattern =
           make-heap(list(q, qd, h, hd)),
       pitch

  ;; The first score is member-melody: select a
  ;; pattern and shift by 2 to 5 octaves depending on
  ;; the starting time
  exec score-gen(save: quote(member-melody),
          score-dur: 20,
          pre: setf(pitch,
                    #?(sg:start < 5,
                       24 + next(notes-1),
                       #?(sg:start < 10,
                          36 + next(notes-2),
                          #?(sg:start < 15,
                             48 + next(notes-3),
                             60 + next(notes-4)))))),
          pitch: pitch,
          ;; emphasize certain pitch classes with high
          ;; amplitude; pitch class is remainder of
          ;; pitch divided by 12. "%" is the remainder
          ;; operator.
          ;; Use member to test if pitch class is one
          ;; of 2, 4, 5, or 7:
          vel: #?(member(pitch % 12, {2 4 5 7}),
                  100 + random(20), ;; pick 100 to 119
                  10 + random(30)), ;; pick 10 to 39
          ioi: 0.1)
```

```
;; a second score is computed called member-accomp.
;; When the pitch: parameter is a list, a chord is
;; generated, so this creates 5- to 7-note chords.
exec score-gen(save: quote(member-accomp),
        score-dur: 20,
        pre: setf(pitch,
                #?(sg:start < 5,
                    {50 51 52 53 54 57},
                    #?(sg:start < 10,
                        {60 61 62 63 65 66},
                        #?(sg:start < 15,
                            {70 71 72 75 78},
                            {80 81 82 84 85 87 88})))),
        pitch: pitch,
        vel: next(amp-pattern),
        ioi: next(rhythm-pattern),
        dur: 0.15)

;; the third score is a final chord
exec score-gen(save: quote(member-final),
        score-len: 1,
        pitch: {24 25 38 51 64 77 90 103 104},
        ;; chord is based on union of all four sets:
        ;; (0 1 2 3 4 5 6 7 8) or set 9-1. Each
        ;; pitch class is transposed up a successive
        ;; octave. (the lowest and highest pitches
        ;; are adjusted up to fall into the range of
        ;; the piano)
        vel: 120, dur: 2)

;; combine all the scores
set member-example =
    score-merge(member-melody, member-accomp,
            score-shift(member-final, 20))
end
```

Further explanation of the program is included in the program as comments. The program sets global variables to scores representing each part (member-melody, member-accomp, member-final) as well as their combination in member-example. It would be good programming practice to at least make member-melody, member-accomp, and member-final local variables by declaring them in the with command, but they are left as globals here so that they can still be printed and played after the begin-end command exits. You can play any of the scores with score-play.

The function intersection takes two lists as input and returns a list of the elements that are common to both lists, corresponding to set intersection.

In Example 9.2.7, we take the intersection of pc sets 6-Z3 and 6-Z36. Note that in sets, the order of the elements does not matter.

Example 9.2.7: Using intersection

```
SAL> print intersection({0 1 2 3 5 6},
                        {0 1 2 3 4 7})
{3 2 1 0}
```

The function union takes two lists as input and returns a list of the elements that are found in either set.

Example 9.2.8: Using union

```
SAL> print union({0 1 2 3 5 6}, {0 1 2 3 4 7})
{7 4 6 5 3 2 1 0}
```

Example 9.2.9 demonstrates how the set operations intersection and union may be used in algorithmic composition. We use with to define some pc sets and then take the intersection and union of set combinations. The resulting sets are converted to item streams which are then used in score-gen to compute various note attributes.

Example 9.2.9: sets.sal

```
begin
  with s6-Z36 = {0 1 2 3 4 7},
       s6-Z3 = {0 1 2 3 5 6},
       s5-Z38 = {0 1 2 5 8},
       s7-Z38 = {0 1 2 4 5 7 8},
       common-set1 = make-heap(
           intersection(s6-Z36, s6-Z3)),
       common-set2 = make-heap(
           intersection(s5-Z38, s7-Z38)),
       inclusive-set1 = make-cycle(
           union(s6-Z36, s6-Z3)),
       inclusive-set2 = make-cycle(
           union(s5-Z38, s7-Z38))
  exec score-gen(save: quote(sets-example),
    score-len: 15,
    pitch: next(common-set1) + 60,
    vel: 10 + next(inclusive-set1) * 10,
    ioi: max(next(common-set2) * 0.5, 0.05),
    dur: max(next(inclusive-set2) * 0.5, 0.05))
end
```

The function set-difference performs set subtraction. set-difference takes two lists as input and returns a list consisting of all the elements in the first list that are not also in the second list. set-difference returns a new list and does not change either of the two input lists. Notice that the empty list prints as #f.

Example 9.2.10: Using set-difference

```
SAL> print set-difference({0 1 2 3 5 6},
                          {0 1 2 3 4 7})
{5 6}

SAL> print set-difference({0 1 2 3 4 7},
                          {0 1 2 3 5 6})
{4 7}

SAL> print set-difference({0 1 2 3}, {4 5 6 7})
{0 1 2 3}

SAL> print set-difference({0 1 2 3}, {0 1 2 3})
#f
```

The predicate subsetp accepts two lists as input and returns true if the first list is a subset of the second and false if not.

Example 9.2.11: Using subsetp

```
SAL> print subsetp({0 1 2 3 4 7},
                   {0 1 2 3 4 5 6 7 8})
#t

SAL> print subsetp({0 1 2 3 4 7}, {0 1 2 5 8})
#f
```

9.3   Tables

Tables can be built in SAL by making lists of lists. In fact, a table can be thought of as a nested indexed list. In SAL or Lisp, sometimes tables are referred to as association lists or simply a-lists. Consider the table in Table 9.3.1 that makes a correspondence between pitch class name and number.

Table 9.3.1: A simple table

Name	Number
C	0
C-sharp	1
D	2
D-sharp	3
E	4

In Table 9.3.1, we refer to the pitch class name as the key to the table and the note number as its value. For example, key C-sharp has a value of 1.

We represent tables or a-lists in SAL or Lisp as nested lists. Example 9.3.1 converts the table representation of Table 9.3.1 to a nested list and uses it to initialize the global variable *simple-table*.

Example 9.3.1: Creating a table

```
SAL> define variable *simple-table* =
        {{C 0}
         {C-sharp 1}
         {D 2}
         {D-sharp 3}
         {E 4}}
```

Now that we have a table stored in memory, we can look up things in the table. SAL performs table lookup using the function assoc. When assoc is given a key in a table, it returns a list comprised of the key and its corresponding value(s). It may be helpful to think of assoc as returning a specified row in a table as a list.

Example 9.3.2: Using assoc

```
SAL> print assoc(quote(D), *simple-table*)
{D 2}
```

If we want to find the value associated with a particular key, we simply use list functions to point to the element of interest.

Example 9.3.3: Accessing a table value

```
SAL> print second(assoc(quote(D),
                        *simple-table*))
2
```

Performing table lookup is such a common occurrence, we define a function table-lookup in Example 9.3.4 to simplify the procedure.

Example 9.3.4: table-lookup function

```
define function table-lookup(key, table)
   return second(assoc(key, table))
```

In the next example, we demonstrate calling this function to perform a lookup in *simple-table*.

Example 9.3.5: Using table-lookup

```
SAL> print table-lookup(quote(D),
                            *simple-table*)
2
```

Example 9.3.6 demonstrates how you can use tables in Nyquist. This example generates music from text by mapping letters to pitches. The length of the score is the length of the text string. Each letter of the string is mapped to a pitch number using a table lookup. The function char-to-symbol is defined to take a string and an index as inputs. It returns a symbol corresponding to the character at the given position in the string. The first step here is to take the substring from index to index + 1 using the subseq function. The resulting single-letter string is converted to upper case using the string-upcase function. This upper-cased string is converted to a symbol using the intern function. (Note that *strings are not symbols,* so intern is necessary.) The reason for the upper case conversion is that SAL automatically converts program text to upper case, so symbol names in the table will use upper case, but the intern function will not automatically convert to upper case. We must convert the case or else table lookups will not work.

Instead of converting each character to a symbol to match the symbol keys in the table, we could have used strings as keys in the table and called table-lookup with strings. Unfortunately, the assoc function does not ordinarily work with strings as keys. We could fix this by adding the keyword parameter "test: quote(equal)" to tell assoc to use a slightly more expensive key-comparison function. It is normal that there are several ways to solve programming problems.

Not all characters are letters. Characters that are not letters will not be found in the table, so in table-lookup, assoc returns nil, and second(nil) returns nil. Conveniently, a pitch value of nil is interpreted as a rest, so the spaces and any non-alphabetic characters in the text are converted to rests. We will revisit the idea of text to music in Section 16.3.

Example 9.3.6: table.sal

```
;; table to map letters to pitches
;; in this mapping, consonants are chromatic
;; from 40 to 60
;; vowels are pitches 35, 67, 78, 89, and 100
define variable *letter-to-pitch* =
 {{a 35} {b 40}
  {c 41} {d 42} {e 67} {f 43} {g 44} {h 45}
  {i 78} {j 46} {k 47} {l 48} {m 49} {n 50}
  {o 89} {p 51} {q 52} {r 53} {s 54} {t 55}
  {u 100} {v 56} {w 57} {x 58} {y 59} {z 60}}

define function table-lookup(key, table)
  return second(assoc(key, table))

define function char-to-symbol(text, index)
  return intern(string-upcase(
              subseq(text, index, index + 1)))

begin
  with text = "This text is the source data for
music generation",
        pitch
  exec score-gen(save: quote(table-example),
    score-len: length(text),
    pitch: table-lookup(char-to-symbol(
                            text, sg:count),
                      *letter-to-pitch*),
    dur: 0.3, ioi: 0.2)
end
```

Example 9.3.7 integrates many of the concepts we have learned in this chapter and applies them using SAL. This example uses four techniques to select random values:

1. A table of pitch-class sets maps random integers to values.
2. nth maps random integers to pitch classes stored in a list.
3. #? translates ranges of values of sg:count into different expressions to compute pitch:. (Admittedly, sg:count is not random, but the same technique could be used with random values.)
4. ioi-pattern and amp-pattern are used to select random values from lists (in this case, make-heap does not reuse a selection until all values have been selected).

Example 9.3.7: table-with-sets.sal

```
define function table-lookup(key, table)
  return second(assoc(key, table))

; Generator table-with-sets defines a table of the
; first four pitch-class sets of cardinality 6. A
; random number selects one of four keys in the range
; 0-3 that corresponds to sets 6-1, 6-2, 6-Z3 and
; 6-Z4.  Use the table-lookup to return the pitch
; classes associated with the key. Assign a pitch
; to the note slot by picking a random element of the
; selected list, accessed using nth.

begin
  with table-cardinal6 = {{0 {0 1 2 3 4 5} s6-1}
                          {1 {0 1 2 3 4 6} s6-2}
                          {2 {0 1 2 3 5 6} s6-Z3}
                          {3 {0 1 2 4 5 6} s6-Z4}},
       key1 = random(4),
       key2 = random(4),
       key3 = random(4),
       key4 = random(4),
       set1 = table-lookup(key1, table-cardinal6),
       set2 = table-lookup(key2, table-cardinal6),
       set3 = table-lookup(key3, table-cardinal6),
       set4 = table-lookup(key4, table-cardinal6),
       ioi-pattern = make-heap({.2 .4 .5}),
       amp-pattern = make-heap({20 30 40 100}),
       index
  exec score-gen(save: quote(table-with-sets-score),
                 score-len: 60,
                 pre: setf(index, random(6)),
                 pitch: #?(sg:count < 15,
                           nth(index, set1) + 40,
                       #?(sg:count < 30,
                           nth(index, set2) + 50,
                       #?(sg:count < 45,
                           nth(index, set3) + 60,
                           nth(index, set4) + 70))),
                 ioi: next(ioi-pattern),
                 dur: 0.1,
                 amp: next(amp-pattern))
end
```

Since algorithmic composing often uses constrained random selection, you should check your understanding of each of these four techniques by reviewing Example 9.3.7.

In Example 9.3.8, we rewrite Example 9.3.7 using patterns for all random selection. The result is more compact, but at least for many readers, it will be harder to understand because the behavior of nested patterns can be rather subtle. The "correct" way to make random selections is really a matter of taste and programming expertise.

Example 9.3.8: all-patterns.sal

```
begin
  with period = 15,
       pitch-pattern = make-heap(
       list(make-random({0 1 2 3 4 5}, for: period),
            make-random({0 1 2 3 4 6}, for: period),
            make-random({0 1 2 3 5 6}, for: period),
            make-random({0 1 2 4 5 6}, for: period)
            )),
       offset-pattern =
       make-copier(make-line({40 50 60 70}, for: 1),
                   repeat: period, trace: t),
       ioi-pattern = make-heap({.2 .4 .5}),
       amp-pattern = make-heap({20 30 40 100})
  exec score-gen(save: quote(all-patterns-example),
                 score-len: period * 4,
                 pitch: next(pitch-pattern) +
                        next(offset-pattern),
                 ioi: next(ioi-pattern),
                 dur: 0.1,
                 amp: next(amp-pattern))
end
```

In this example, the pitch-pattern is a heap that selects from four pitch class sets. In Example 9.3.7, the selection is random and a given pitch class set might be selected more than once. To get this behavior, use make-random rather than make-heap. With make-heap, each of the four pitch class sets will be used one time. In Example 9.3.7, the nested #? expression determines that 15 pitches are selected from each pitch class set. Here, we make a variable period and initialize it to 15, and we represent each pitch class set by a make-random pattern that randomly selects an element from the pitch class set. These patterns have a period length of period, so 15 pitches will be generated in sequence before the next pitch class set pattern is selected.

Example 9.3.7 also offsets each group of 15 pitch class set values by a different value. These values are generated here by offset-pattern, which uses make-copier to make 15 copies each of the offset values 40, 50, 60, and 70. Notice that make-copier copies whole pattern *periods* rather than individual items, so the period length of make-line must be set to 1 using the for: keyword parameter.

Finally, notice how many patterns in this implementation and the score length (`score-len:`) all depend on the variable period, representing one quarter of the length of the score. To make the score longer, all you need to do is replace 15 with a different value. In contrast, to get the same effect in Example 9.3.7, you would need to study the program to find and replace the numbers 60, 15, 30, and 45 with appropriate new values. In general, numerical constants like 15 are frowned upon by good programmers, especially when the same number is used two or more times in different places. Programs are usually more readable if the numerical constant is used only once to initialize a variable that is used throughout the program. In the future, if the "constant" value changes, it is easier to change the variable initialization than to track down and change all the occurrences of the number. On the other hand, compositions are full of numbers, and part of the art of algorithmic composition is judiciously deciding what values are truly fixed and what values might be adjusted. To paraphrase Alan J. Perlis, "One composer's constant is another composer's variable."

9.4   Arrays

Both SAL and Lisp implement a data structure called an *array*. An array is a container that holds other values. Each value is stored at a location within the array, and locations are indexed by an integer starting at zero. Arrays, as one-dimensional sequences of values, are similar to lists, and both SAL and Lisp emphasize lists, so we will not work with arrays in this book. In some cases, arrays can allow more compact representations and faster processing, so advanced programmers should certainly learn about them. Arrays are generally used to implement tables that are accessed via an integer index.

9.5   Suggested Listening

Late August by Paul Lansky is one in a series of his pieces that explores the conversations of everyday life. In this composition, Paul Lansky recorded a conversation between two Chinese students sometime in late August, 1989. Their processed speech, in conjunction with pitch material motivated by set theory, became the foundation for this composition (Lansky, 1990; Simoni, 1999).

Norman Megill developed an algorithm to convert mathematical proofs to music. The algorithm converts the proof by the depth of its proof tree into a series of values. These values are then scaled to a range of notes and a MIDI file is created with the corresponding output (http://us.metamath.org/mpegif/mmmusic.html#algorithm).

Chapter 10 Functional Programming

Functional programming is a programming style that emphasizes the combination of functions to produce *values* as opposed to the sequential evaluation of commands and the modification of *variables*. One advantage of functional programming is that functional programs are often easier to reason about than non-functional alternatives. This chapter introduces some functional programming concepts and illustrates their use in computing scores.

10.1 Introduction to Functional Programming

Lisp was one of the first languages to support functional programming, and by encouraging functional programming, Lisp has had a tremendous impact on many modern languages such as Java, Python, and ML. The main attraction of functional programming is that behaviors of functional expressions do not depend upon the changeable and hidden values of variables or the sequential order of assignment statements. Often, functional programs enjoy the good qualities of mathematical equations, which are designed for communication and expressiveness.

Proponents of other styles of programming, particularly *Object-Oriented Programming*, argue that variables and assignment statements are actually features that allow programs to more naturally model real-world objects that do in fact change over time. In our experience, *functional programming, object-oriented programming,* and other programming paradigms all have advantages and disadvantages. The best approach often depends on the problem at hand.

SAL is a bit of a compromise. It is built above a Lisp implementation and therefore has access to the functional programming features of Lisp. However, SAL has a much greater emphasis on sequential execution and assignment to variables, so it does not strongly encourage functional programming. The occasional need to access special Lisp forms such as progn and setf could be seen as a weakness of SAL.

10.2 Mapping a Function over a List

One powerful concept of functional programming is the use of functions as parameters. In other words, we can have functions of functions, also called higher-order functions. The primitive mapcar al-

lows you to apply a function to each element of a list. The applied
function may be another primitive or a user-defined function.
mapcar is thus a higher-order function. In SAL, when you pass a
function to a function, the passed function is normally a quoted
symbol. The template for mapcar is

mapcar(quote(*function*), *list*)

Recall that the primitive sqrt returns the square root of its input.

Example 10.2.1: sqrt function

```
SAL> print sqrt(25.0)
5
```

Since mapcar allows you to map a function onto a list, we can
take the square root of each element of a list by passing sqrt to
mapcar.

Example 10.2.2: mapcar and sqrt

```
SAL> print mapcar(quote(sqrt),
                  {25.0 36.0 81.0})
{5 6 9}
```

Notice the syntax of mapcar. The function passed to mapcar
must be quoted. The inputs to the passed function are given as a list.

Recall in Example 8.2.2, we wrote a user-defined function that
used #? to determine if a MIDI note is within the range of the MIDI
specification.

Example 10.2.3: test-range (as presented in Chapter 8)

```
define function test-range(pitch)
  begin
    return #?(pitch < 0, quote(too-low),
             #?(pitch > 127, quote(too-high),
                quote(in-range)))
  end
```

Using mapcar, we can determine if an entire list of MIDI notes is
in range.

Example 10.2.4: mapcar and test-range

```
SAL> print mapcar(quote(test-range),
                  {0 -5 129 127 54})
{IN-RANGE TOO-LOW TOO-HIGH IN-RANGE IN-RANGE}
```

Since returning a list that describes the range status of a list of MIDI notes may not be helpful in composing music, we alter our function in Example 10.2.4. Any MIDI note outside the range of the MIDI specification is recalculated to fall in range. The new function, called rangify, is defined in Example 10.2.5.

Example 10.2.5: rangify

```
define function rangify(note)
  begin
    return #?(note < 0, 0,
              #?(note > 127, 127, note))
  end
```

The function rangify uses an algorithm that returns 0 for all MIDI notes less than 0 and 127 for all MIDI notes greater than 127. rangify is one of many algorithms that may be used to correct for values that fall outside of the range of the MIDI specification.

In Example 10.2.6, we map the function rangify onto a list of values. Notice all values less than 0 return 0 and all values greater than 127 return 127.

Example 10.2.6: mapcar and rangify

```
SAL> print mapcar(quote(rangify),
                  {0 -5 129 127 54})
{0 0 127 127 54}
```

So far, the functions that we've passed to mapcar only have one input. It is possible to pass mapcar functions that have more than one input. Consider the function definition and function call in Example 10.2.7.

Example 10.2.7: my-transpose

```
SAL> define function my-transpose(
                              note, interval)
        return note + interval

SAL> print my-transpose(60, -12)
48

SAL> print my-transpose(72, 6)
78
```

The function my-transpose requires two inputs: a note and an interval. my-transpose transposes the note by the specified interval.

In Example 10.2.8, we use `mapcar` to transpose a list of notes by a list of specified intervals. `mapcar` returns a list of the transposed notes.

Example 10.2.8: `mapcar` over two lists

```
SAL> print mapcar(quote(my-transpose),
                  {20 30 40 50}, {-5 5 -10 10})
{15 35 30 60}
```

10.3 Using the `score-apply` Function

Now that you have a taste of passing functions as parameters to modify the behavior of another function (in this case, `mapcar`), let's look at a higher-order function for editing and transforming scores. `score-apply`, introduced in Chapter 4, applies a function to each note in a score. Since the function to be applied is provided by the caller, you can tailor `score-apply` to solve many tasks. The template for `score-apply` is

```
score-apply(score, quote(function),
            from-index: index1, to-index: index2,
            from-time: time1, to-time: time2)
```

As with other "score-" functions, all the keyword parameters, starting with `from-index`, are optional, so to apply a function to every note in a score, you would write something like

```
score-apply(score, quote(function))
```

The *function* input is a symbol – the name of a function that must accept three parameters: the start time of the note, the duration of the note, and the note expression. So if the score is

```
{{0 0 {score-begin-end 0 3}}
 {0 2 {flute pitch: 74 vel: 100}}
 {2 1 {flute pitch: 75 vel: 90 }}}
```

then the function will be called once with the parameters

```
0, 2, {flute pitch: 74 vel: 100}
```

and once with the parameters

```
2, 1, {flute pitch: 75 vel: 90}
```

Example 10.3.1 demonstrates the use of `score-apply` to transform a score. In this example, notes that have pitch classes 1, 3, 6, 8, and 10 are transposed up an octave and played using the function `violin`. Other notes are unchanged.

Essentially all of the work in this example is in the definition of `transform-accidentals`. As described earlier, this function takes three parameters: the start time, duration, and sound expression. There are two cases, handled by the if-then-else construct. The first case applies when the pitch class is in the set {1, 3, 6, 8, 10}, so the first problem is to extract the pitch from the note expression. The function expr-get-attr (described in Example 4.5.9) is used to find the value for any given keyword. Once we have the pitch, we use member to test for membership in the set, represented by a list. If that condition is true, we need to transform the current note into one with violin as the instrument and pitch raised one octave. The technique is to construct a new note in terms of the old note. The form of a note is

{start-time *duration expression*}

so we can use list to construct a list of these three elements. We use the same start time and duration as the original note, and these are just the parameters start and dur, so the note expression begins with list(start, dur, ...). Now we just need to construct the note expression. Take a moment to think about what is going on here. We are going to write a SAL expression that, when evaluated, returns a Lisp expression that will eventually be evaluated again to compute a note. This idea that Lisp programs can be both data and programs is very powerful and one of the big attractions of Lisp.

Example 10.3.1: score-apply.sal

```
    define function transform-accidentals(
                                      start, dur, expr)
      begin
        if member(expr-get-attr(expr,
                            keyword(pitch)) % 12,
                {1 3 6 8 10}) then
            return list(start, dur,
                    cons(quote(violin),
                        params-transpose(rest(expr),
                            keyword(pitch), 12)))
        else
            return list(start, dur, expr)
      end

    set new-score = score-apply(my-score,
                        quote(transform-accidentals))
```

Getting back to our problem, the note expression is a list starting with violin and followed by a list of alternating keywords and values. To just replace the first item in a list, we can write

cons(quote(violin), rest(*expr*))

where *expr* is the original note expression. rest is used to get the "rest" of the expression (a list) after the first item, and cons is used to insert a new item at the head of the list. Effectively, this replaces the head of the list with violin.

However, we need to do more than this. We also want to transpose the pitch: attribute by 12. For this, we use another convenient function, params-transpose, that can be used to add a numerical offset to the value of any keyword parameter:

params-transpose(*parameter-list*, keyword(*attribute*), *offset*)

The *parameter-list* is just a list of alternating attribute symbols (keywords) and values. This should not be a complete note expression with an initial function symbol. That's why we pass in rest(expr) in Example 10.3.1. For the attribute, we pass in keyword(pitch) because that is what we want to transpose, and the *offset* is 12 (semitones) to get one octave.

Putting all this together, the expression to compute a new note with the function changed to violin and the pitch transposed up one octave is

```
list(start, dur,
    cons(quote(violin),
        params-transpose(
            rest(expr), keyword(pitch), 12)))
```

The rest of Example 10.3.1 handles the second case where the pitch is not in the set {1, 3, 6, 8, 10}. This case merely reconstructs the original note using list:

```
list(start, dur, expr)
```

and returns this value from the if command. This completes the definition of transform-accidentals.

Finally, we pass transform-accidentals to score-apply to apply the function to each note and return a new score. Notice how quote is used so that transform-accidentals is not treated as a variable.

There is no set or other data-altering expression in Example 10.3.1. This is typical in functional programming: there is input data, often consisting of a complex structure such as a score, there is a function that "walks" through the data, either extracting useful information or rebuilding a transformed version of the data, and finally a completely new data structure is returned. In this case, the value of my-score (the input data) is unaltered, so unless we do something with the result of score-apply, this whole program has no real effect. In practice, you might want to play the outcome:

```
exec score-play(score-apply(my-score,
                quote(transform-accidentals)))
```

Or, while functional purists might object to the use of set, you might want to save the final result as a variable:

```
set my-new-score = score-apply(my-score,
                quote(transform-accidentals)))
```

You have now seen a rather detailed example of functional programming used to perform a customized operation on score data. In this example, notes that met a certain condition were transformed in a couple of ways. While there are many built-in functions for manipulating scores, it is important for a composer to have the power to create whatever comes from the imagination. You should not be limited to a fixed palette of editing operations. The transformations you apply can include various uses of random numbers to select notes and control how they are changed. The possibilities are endless!

Chapter 11   Recursion

Recursion is an important concept in computer science. In this chapter, we will explore what it means for a function to call itself and why that might be a good idea.

11.1   Introduction to Recursion

Recursion occurs when something refers to itself. For example, a recursive definition uses the term being defined within the definition. A *recursive function* is a function that calls itself. A classic example of a recursive process is generating the Fibonacci series. In the Fibonacci series, the first two terms are defined as 0 and 1. Thereafter, the next term is calculated as the sum of the previous two terms. The mathematical relationship between terms may be stated as

$$next\text{-}term = current\text{-}term + previous\text{-}term$$

For example, the six terms followed by the initial two terms of 0 and 1 are

$$0\ 1\ 1\ 2\ 3\ 5\ 8\ 13 \ldots$$

Another example of a recursive process is decrementing a given starting value by 1 until it is equal to 0. We calculate the value of the next term as

$$next\text{-}term = current\text{-}term - 1$$

Given a starting value of 4, the resultant series is

$$4\ 3\ 2\ 1$$

Notice in both cases, recursion reduces the current problem to a simpler one that can be solved by the same function (with different inputs). Typically, the process eventually terminates in a special case. (The second example terminates at zero.)

Perhaps the easiest way to begin writing recursive functions is to study recursive functions. After studying several examples, patterns emerge for different kinds of recursive conditions. This chapter introduces templates for recursion and gives examples of their use.

11.2   Single-Test Tail Recursion

Single-test tail recursion is a method of recursion when a condition terminates processing and the recursive function call occurs as the default case of an if-then-else statement (e.g. the "tail end" of an if-then-else). Example 11.2.1 shows the template for single-test tail recursion.

Example 11.2.1: Template for single-test tail recursion

```
define function function-name(input)
  begin
    if end-test then
      return end-value
    else
      return function-name(reduced-input)
  end
```

In addition to referencing a template when writing a recursive function, it is important to understand how a recursive process works. Here are some guidelines for writing a recursive function:

1. What is the test that terminates the recursion? (e.g. end-test)
2. What do you want the function to return? (e.g. end-value)
3. How do you take one step? (e.g. reduced-input)

Consider the example of decrementing a given number by 1 until it is equal to 0. Let's say that our starting number is 4. Our recursive function should output the values 4, 3, 2, 1, and done as seen in Example 11.2.2.

Example 11.2.2: Recursive function output

```
4
3
2
1
DONE
```

Consider the guidelines for writing a recursive function in relation to this output. We stop the recursion when the number is equal to 0 so the *end-test* is $x = 0$. Our recursive function returns done when it is completed so the *end-value* is quote(done). Each step in the process subtracts one from the previous term so the *reduced-input* is $x - 1$.

Now that we've sketched some guidelines, we're ready to apply the template and write the function.

Example 11.2.3: recursive-dotimes.sal

```
define function recursive-dotimes(x)
  begin
    if x = 0 then
      return quote(done)
    else
      begin
        print x
        return recursive-dotimes(x - 1)
      end
  end
```

Example 11.2.4: Output from recursive-dotimes

SAL> **load "recursive-dotimes.sal"**

SAL> **exec recursive-dotimes(4)**
4
3
2
1
DONE

11.3 List-Cons'ing Recursion

List-cons'ing recursion is a recursive process that creates lists by cons'ing a new element onto a list. Example 11.3.1 shows a template for list-cons'ing recursion.

Example 11.3.1: Template for list-cons'ing recursion

```
define function function-name(inputs)
  begin
    if end-test then
      return nil ; return the empty list
    else
      return cons(new-element,
                  function-name(reduced-inputs))
  end
```

Consider the example of creating a list that starts at a particular value and ends after a certain number of elements have been generated. For example, we want to write a function that starts at MIDI note 60 and generates a list of 6 pitch numbers that ascend chromatically. Our recursive function should return

{60 61 62 63 64 65}

The recursive way to think about this problem is to note that the solution is just 60 followed by a list of 5 notes starting at 61. This is in turn just 61 followed by a list of 4 notes starting at 62, and so on. Once you can think of the problem in these terms, the programming task is almost a direct translation of the problem statement.

The function requires two inputs: a starting MIDI note value and the number of notes to generate. Let's call these start and number-of-notes. From the template, notice that the if returns nil if the end test is met. Under what condition should the function return nil? nil represents an empty list, i.e. there are zero notes, so the condition is number-of-notes = 0. If there are more than zero notes, the second else command uses cons to add *new-element* to the front of the list returned by a recursive call. The *new-element* becomes the first element of the list, so it must be start. The *reduced-inputs* for the recursive call will be the next start value, which is start + 1, and the remaining number of notes, which is number-of-notes - 1. Now we can more-or-less just plug these expressions into the template to produce a solution, shown in Example 11.3.2. Example 11.3.3 shows an example application of the function.

Example 11.3.2: recursive-make-chromatic-lick.sal

```
define function
  recursive-make-a-chromatic-lick(start,
                                      number-of-notes)
    begin
      if number-of-notes = 0 then
        return nil
      else
        return cons(start,
          recursive-make-a-chromatic-lick(start + 1,
                                      number-of-notes - 1))
    end
```

Example 11.3.3: Output from recursive-make-a-chromatic-lick

```
SAL> load "recursive-make-chromatic-lick.sal"

SAL> print recursive-make-a-chromatic-lick(60, 6)
{60 61 62 63 64 65}
```

Sometimes, adding a display command to a recursive process helps clarify what is going on. Example 11.3.4 is the same function as Example 11.3.2 with a display command prior to the recursive call.

Example 11.3.4: recursive-make-chromatic-lick-display.sal

```
define function
  recursive-make-a-chromatic-lick(start,
                                    number-of-notes)
    begin
      if number-of-notes = 0 then
        return nil
      else
        begin
          display "recursion", start, number-of-notes
          return cons(start,
            recursive-make-a-chromatic-lick(start + 1,
                                    number-of-notes - 1))
        end
    end
```

Example 11.3.5: Output from recursive-make-chromatic-lick

```
SAL> print recursive-make-a-chromatic-lick(60, 6)
recursion: START = 60, NUMBER-OF-NOTES = 6
recursion: START = 61, NUMBER-OF-NOTES = 5
recursion: START = 62, NUMBER-OF-NOTES = 4
recursion: START = 63, NUMBER-OF-NOTES = 3
recursion: START = 64, NUMBER-OF-NOTES = 2
recursion: START = 65, NUMBER-OF-NOTES = 1
{60 61 62 63 64 65}
```

11.4 Conditional Augmenting Tail Recursion

Conditional augmenting tail recursion is used to examine the elements of a list and perform some operation when list elements satisfy some condition. A simple example is counting the number of things that meet a certain test. Example 11.4.1 shows the template for conditional augmenting tail recursion.

Consider the example of counting the number of MIDI notes that exceed the range of the MIDI specification. Given the list of MIDI notes {87 67 129 776 43}, the function should return 2.

Let's think about this in recursive terms. If the list is empty, the count is zero. If the first value is out of range, the count is one plus the number of out-of-range elements in the rest of the list. If the first value is in range, the count is just the number of out-of-range elements in the rest of the list.

The function requires two inputs: a list of MIDI notes and a variable to count the number of MIDI notes outside of the range. We will use the-list and result for the parameter names. The recursion stops when we receive an empty list, so the *end-test* is null(the-list). If the list is not empty, there are two more cases, depending on whether the first element is out-of-range or in-range. The *augment-condition* is this test, and the *augment-command* should increment result, e.g. set result += 1. The *reduced-inputs* are rest(the-list) and result. A solution is found in Example 11.4.2, and Example 11.4.3 is an example application of the function.

Example 11.4.1: Template for conditional augmenting tail recursion

```
define function function-name(inputs)
  begin
    if end-test then
      return end-value
    else
      if augment-condition then
        begin
          augment-command
          return function-name(reduced-inputs)
        end
      else
        return function-name(reduced-inputs)
```

Example 11.4.2: recursive-count-outliers.sal

```
define function recursive-count-outliers(
                          the-list, result)
  begin
    if null(the-list) then
      return result
    else
      if (first(the-list) < 0) |
         (first(the-list) > 127)
      then
        begin
          set result += 1
          return recursive-count-outliers(
                  rest(the-list), result)
        end
      else
        return recursive-count-outliers(
                  rest(the-list), result)
  end
```

Example 11.4.3: Output from recursive-count-outliers

```
SAL> print recursive-count-outliers(
              {87 67 129 776 43}, 0)
   2
```

Sometimes, it is helpful to insert display commands prior to the recursive calls to track the changing values of the variables as seen in Example 11.4.4. You should test your understanding of this example by predicting the printed output and then compare your predictions to the output shown in Example 11.4.5.

Example 11.4.4: recursive-count-outliers-2.sal (with print)

```
define function recursive-count-outliers(
                            the-list, result)
    begin
      if null(the-list) then
        return result
      else
        if (first(the-list) < 0) |
           (first(the-list) > 127)
        then
          begin
            set result += 1
            display "outlier", result, the-list
            return recursive-count-outliers(
                    rest(the-list), result)
          end
        else
          begin
            display "no outlier", result, the-list
            return recursive-count-outliers(
                    rest(the-list), result)
          end
    end
```

Example 11.4.5: Output from Example 11.4.4

```
SAL> exec recursive-count-outliers(
              {87 67 129 776 43}, 0)
no outlier: RESULT = 0, THE-LIST = (87 67 129 776 43)
no outlier: RESULT = 0, THE-LIST = (67 129 776 43)
outlier: RESULT = 1, THE-LIST = (129 776 43)
outlier: RESULT = 2, THE-LIST = (776 43)
no outlier: RESULT = 2, THE-LIST = (43)
   2
```

11.5 Double-Test Tail Recursion

Double-test tail recursion terminates based on one of two conditions. Example 11.5.1 shows the template for double-test tail recursion.

Example 11.5.1: Template for double-test tail recursion

```
define function function-name(input)
  begin
    if end-test₁ then
      return end-value₁
    else if end-test₂ then
      return end-value₂
    else
      return function-name(reduced-input)
```

Let's modify recursive-count-outliers in Example 11.4.2 so that the function returns the first occurrence of a MIDI note number outside of the range of the MIDI specification. Given the list of MIDI notes {87 67 129 776 43}, the function should return 129. If no MIDI notes are outside the range of the MIDI specification, the function returns nil.

The function requires a list of MIDI notes as input. We stop recursion when we reach the end of the list. Recursive processing can also stop if we find a MIDI note outside of the range of the MIDI specification. Since there are two ways that processing terminates, we have two end tests. The first is null(midi-note-list) with an end value of nil. The second test is first(midi-note-list) < 0 | first(midi-note-list) > 127 with an end value of first(midi-note-list). That is why this technique is called double-test tail recursion.

As in the previous examples, we look at this problem from a recursive point of view. If the input list is nil, the result is nil. Otherwise, if the first note is out of range, we return the first note. If neither test is true, we recursively apply the function to the sub-problem consisting of the rest of the list. An implementation of this function is found in Example 11.5.2, and Example 11.5.3 gives an example application of the function.

Example 11.5.2: recursive-find-first-outlier.sal

```
define function recursive-find-first-outlier(
                                  midi-note-list)
  begin
    if null(midi-note-list) then
      return nil
    else
      begin
        if first(midi-note-list) < 0 |
           first(midi-note-list) > 127 then
          return first(midi-note-list)
        else
          return recursive-find-first-outlier(
                      rest(midi-note-list))
      end
  end
```

Example 11.5.3: Output from Example 11.5.2

```
SAL> print recursive-find-first-outlier(
                      {87 67 129 776 43})
129
```

Example 11.5.4: recursive-find-first-outlier-2.sal (with print)

```
define function recursive-find-first-outlier(
                                  midi-note-list)
  begin
    if null(midi-note-list) then
      return nil
    else
      begin
        if first(midi-note-list) < 0 |
           first(midi-note-list) > 127 then
          return first(midi-note-list)
        else
          begin
            display "recursive", midi-note-list
            return recursive-find-first-outlier(
                          rest(midi-note-list))
          end
      end
  end
```

As we saw before, it is helpful to insert a display command prior to the recursive call. The modified function appears in Example 11.5.4.

Again, predict what will be printed when this function is run on the data in Example 11.5.3 above; then compare your answer to Example 11.5.5.

Example 11.5.5: Output from Example 11.5.4

```
SAL> exec recursive-find-first-outlier(
                          {87 67 129 776 43})
recursive: MIDI-NOTE-LIST = (87 67 129 776 43)
recursive: MIDI-NOTE-LIST = (67 129 776 43)
129
```

11.6 Multiple Recursion

A function uses multiple recursion if it makes more than one recursive call at each pass of the function. Generating the Fibonacci series requires multiple recursion because the next term is derived by the sum of the previous two terms:

$$fib(n) = fib(n - 2) + fib(n - 1)$$

Example 11.6.1 shows the template for multiple recursion.

Example 11.6.1: Template for multiple recursion

```
define function function-name(input)
   begin
      if end-test₁ then
         return end-value₁
      else
         begin
            if end-test₂ then
               return end-value₂
            else
               return combiner(
                          function-name(first-reduced-input,
                          function-name(second-reduced-input))
         end
   end
```

The Fibonacci function requires a number as input that corresponds to the number of the desired term. Two conditions terminate the recursion: when the input number is 0 and when it is equal to 1. These conditions allow us to return the first two terms. The final else establishes the relationship between terms by multiple recursion: fibonacci(x - 1) + fibonacci(x - 2). The function returns the nth element of the Fibonacci sequence beyond the initial term of 0. An implementation with a display command for execution tracing is found in Example 11.6.2.

Example 11.6.2: fibonacci.sal

```
define function fibonacci(n)
  begin
    display "Fibonacci", n
    if n = 0 then
      return 0
    else
      if n = 1 then
        return 1
      else
        return fibonacci(n - 1) +
                fibonacci(n - 2)
  end
```

Example 11.6.3: Output from Example 11.6.2

```
sal> print fibonacci(5)
fibonacci: N = 5
fibonacci: N = 4
fibonacci: N = 3
fibonacci: N = 2
fibonacci: N = 1
fibonacci: N = 0
fibonacci: N = 1
fibonacci: N = 2
fibonacci: N = 1
fibonacci: N = 0
fibonacci: N = 3
fibonacci: N = 2
fibonacci: N = 1
fibonacci: N = 0
fibonacci: N = 1
5
```

The output from multiple recursion can at first glance appear baffling. Figure 11.6.1 helps make sense of what SAL is doing when it is given the function call fibonacci(5). The solid arrows indicate recursive calls, and the dashed arrows with numbers indicate the return value. The circled numbers indicate the order in which the value of the input is printed. At the deepest levels of recursion (at the bottom of the figure), "Fibonacci" is abbreviated as "Fib" to make the figure layout more compact. Incidentally, the output sequence shown in Example 11.6.3 has some interesting compositional possibilities.

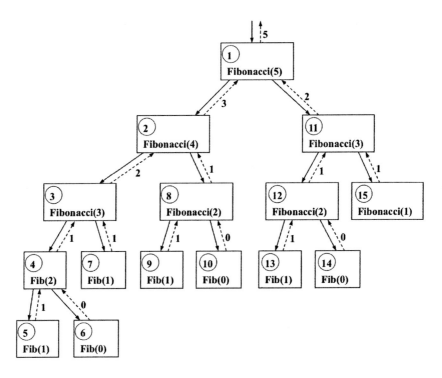

Figure 11.6.1: Graphic representation of fibonacci(5), the order of evaluation indicated by numbers in circles

11.7 Tracing Function Evaluation

In Example 11.6.2, we used display to follow the recursive evaluation of fibonacci. XLISP has a built-in facility for this called trace that we can use on SAL functions. When a function is *traced*, the function and its inputs are printed when the function is entered, and the return value is printed when the function exits. Nested functions are indented to help keep track of recursive calls, and you can trace as many different functions as you wish.

To trace a function, call trace with the function you want to trace. Call untrace with the function name to stop tracing. trace and untrace are special functions that automatically quote their inputs, so you should not use "quote." trace and untrace return a list of functions currently being traced. Example 11.7.1 shows how to use trace to trace the evaluation of fibonacci(5). The display statement is *not* included in this definition of fibonacci as in Example 11.6.2, so only output from trace is printed here.

Example 11.7.1: The use of trace on fibonacci from Example 11.6.2, indentation produced by trace output exaggerated here for greater readability

```
SAL> print trace(fibonacci)
{FIBONACCI}

SAL> print fibonacci(5)
Entering: FIBONACCI, Argument list: (5)
   Entering: FIBONACCI, Argument list: (4)
      Entering: FIBONACCI, Argument list: (3)
         Entering: FIBONACCI, Argument list: (2)
            Entering: FIBONACCI, Argument list: (1)
            Exiting: FIBONACCI, Value: 1
            Entering: FIBONACCI, Argument list: (0)
            Exiting: FIBONACCI, Value: 0
         Exiting: FIBONACCI, Value: 1
         Entering: FIBONACCI, Argument list: (1)
         Exiting: FIBONACCI, Value: 1
      Exiting: FIBONACCI, Value: 2
      Entering: FIBONACCI, Argument list: (2)
         Entering: FIBONACCI, Argument list: (1)
         Exiting: FIBONACCI, Value: 1
         Entering: FIBONACCI, Argument list: (0)
         Exiting: FIBONACCI, Value: 0
      Exiting: FIBONACCI, Value: 1
   Exiting: FIBONACCI, Value: 3
   Entering: FIBONACCI, Argument list: (3)
      Entering: FIBONACCI, Argument list: (2)
         Entering: FIBONACCI, Argument list: (1)
         Exiting: FIBONACCI, Value: 1
         Entering: FIBONACCI, Argument list: (0)
         Exiting: FIBONACCI, Value: 0
      Exiting: FIBONACCI, Value: 1
      Entering: FIBONACCI, Argument list: (1)
      Exiting: FIBONACCI, Value: 1
   Exiting: FIBONACCI, Value: 2
Exiting: FIBONACCI, Value: 5
5
```

11.8   SAL Is Recursive

Recursion is fundamental to SAL (and to most other programming languages). While we have not described the meaning of a SAL program in any formal sense, programming languages are often defined recursively. To evaluate a normal SAL expression (we will discuss special forms separately), we first evaluate each input expression in order. This is where recursion comes into play: the evaluator for each input expression is the same as the evaluator for the whole expression. In other words, the evaluator is recursive. Special forms, such as quote, trace, and setf, are handled by passing the inputs to the functions as expressions or atoms *without* evaluating them. In most cases, the special form *does* eventually evaluate at least some of the inputs by calling the built-in evaluator function. Since the call to the special form is already within an instance of the evaluator function, the evaluation of input expressions by a special form also uses recursive calls to the evaluator.

To keep track of recursive calls, a *stack* is used. The stack is a mostly hidden structure used internally by Lisp to store functions, input values, and local variables for the duration of a function evaluation. The stack supports two operations: a new item can be *pushed* on top of the stack, causing the stack to grow, and an item can be *popped* from the stack, causing the stack to shrink. Items are only added or removed from the top of the stack. The stack traces described in Section 3.10 are representations of the stack.

When a function is called, the function name and its input values are pushed onto the stack where they remain until the function returns. While the function is being evaluated, it may make calls to other functions or even recursively to itself. When that happens, the new function and its input values are pushed onto the stack, and this may happen many more times before the evaluation eventually gets back to the original function call. Thus, the stack is an inherently recursive structure: a stack is a top-most item sitting on top of a stack!

Local variables are created on the stack and popped from the stack when the program leaves the scope of the variables. Just as the stack helps to manage multiple invocations of recursive functions, it also helps manage multiple instances of local variables.

Full coverage of Lisp evaluation and semantics could easily fill a book (Allen 1978), and it is a fascinating subject. For composers using Lisp or SAL, the most important thing is to understand that recursive functions are really just an interesting case of nested function calls that are pervasive in programs.

11.9 Using Recursive Forms in Nyquist

Example 11.9.1 integrates many of the recursive techniques described in this chapter. The function rec-make-chrom-lick uses list-cons'ing recursion to generate a specified number of chromatic notes. The function random-in-range uses tail recursion to generate a specified number of random numbers in a user-specified range. The function select-in-range uses double-test tail recursion to select the notes that fall within a user-specified range (lower and upper bound inclusive).

These SAL functions are used within a call to score-gen to generate the score recursion-etude. The function rec-make-chrom-lick is used to generate the pitches, which are then used to create a heap pattern. The function random-in-range is used to generate a list of 15 random numbers in the range 0.25 to 0.98. The list is assigned to the variable ioi-list that is used to create a cyclic pattern called ioi-pattern. The variable ioi-list is also used as input to the function select-in-range as we look for values between 0.5 and 0.8 inclusive. The result is used to form a cycle pattern for the note velocities. What happens if there are no values between 0.5 and 0.8? (Hint: this is a bug!) How would you fix the program to avoid this problem?

Example 11.9.1: recursion-etude.sal

```
;; Make a chromatic lick for note events
;;
define function rec-make-chrom-lick(
                              start, number-of-notes)
  if number-of-notes = 0 then return nil
  else return cons(start,
              rec-make-chrom-lick(start + 1,
                          number-of-notes - 1))

;; Define a recursive function that generates a
;; prescribed number of random values in a user-
;; specified range
;;
define function random-in-range(
                        lowest, highest, how-many)
  if how-many = 0 then return nil
  else return cons(real-random(lowest, highest),
                  random-in-range(lowest,
                        highest, how-many - 1))

;; Define a recursive function that returns a list of
;; elements inside a user-specified range
;;
define function select-in-range(
                        the-list, lowest, highest)
  if null(the-list) then return nil
  else
    if first(the-list) >= lowest &
       first(the-list) <= highest then
      return cons(first(the-list),
              select-in-range(rest(the-list),
                          lowest, highest))
    else
      return select-in-range(rest(the-list),
                        lowest, highest)
```

```
;; Create a score that uses the three recursive
;; functions: rec-make-chrom-lick, random-in-range,
;; and select-in-range. These three functions
;; highlight three recursive processes: list-cons'ing
;; recursion, single-test tail recursion, and double-
;; test tail recursion.
;;
begin
  with pitch-pattern =
         make-heap(rec-make-chrom-lick(60, 12)),
       ioi-list = random-in-range(0.25, 0.98, 15),
       ioi-pattern = make-cycle(ioi-list),
       vel-pattern = make-cycle(
         select-in-range(ioi-list, 0.5, 0.8))
  exec score-gen(save: quote(recursion-etude),
                 score-len: 15,
                 pitch: next(pitch-pattern),
                 ioi:   next(ioi-pattern),
                 vel:   next(vel-pattern) * 100)
  exec score-play(recursion-etude)
end
```

11.10 Suggested Listening

On Growth and Form by Bruno Degazio for mixed ensemble and electronic sounds explores the recursive structure of fractals. As the composer states, "Drawing on the chaotic energy of fractal processes, *On Growth and Form* is a sort of ritual dance of life, the by-product of a recursive explosion of musical events" (Degazio, 1992).

Profile for tape by Charles Dodge is a three-voice composition in which the choice of pitch, timing, and amplitude is determined by application of a 1/f algorithm. The structure of the work is like a fractal in that recursive processes are used to determine multiple levels of scale and self-similarity (Dodge, 1988).

Chapter 12 Iteration

Iteration in programming means repeated evaluation. In SAL, iteration is accomplished through loops. Loops evaluate a set of expressions over and over again. A loop should terminate after a specified number of repetitions or when a condition is met. SAL has several iterative forms, including a loop command with many variations. This chapter will show how to solve many of the same problems presented in Chapter 11, only using iteration instead of recursion, so the reader can easily compare recursive and iterative forms.

12.1   The loop Command with a for-below Clause

The most general iterative form in SAL is the loop command, which like a begin-end block organizes a set of commands, but unlike begin-end, the commands are repeated. Loop commands can include clauses that create, initialize, and update local variables for each repetition. Loop commands can also include clauses that stop the repetition when certain conditions are met. For now, we will start with a simple form of loop, using a for clause to control the number of iterations.

The template for this simple form of loop is

```
loop
    for counter below count-expression
    commands
end
```

This loop is evaluated as follows: First, *counter* (a variable) is initialized to zero, and *count-expression* is evaluated to obtain a number we will call *limit*. If *counter* is less than *limit*, *commands* (any number of commands) are evaluated. Then *counter* is incremented by 1, and the loop repeats by again comparing *counter* to *limit* and evaluating *commands* again. When *counter* reaches or exceeds *limit*, the loop ends.

In Example 12.1.1, we use a loop to increment the counter count. As we enter the loop, the variable count starts counting at 0. We enter the body of the loop and print the value of count. count is then incremented (to 1). Because the new value of count is less than the count expression (4), the body of the loop is executed again. The iterative process stops when count equals 4. The number of iterations

148

is given by the limit (4), and the values of the count range from 0 to *limit* − 1.

Example 12.1.1: A simple loop

```
SAL> loop
        for count below 4
        display "loop", count
        end
loop : COUNT = 0
loop : COUNT = 1
loop : COUNT = 2
loop : COUNT = 3
```

In Example 12.1.2, we define a function make-a-chromatic-lick using iteration rather than recursion. The purpose of the function is to create a list that generates a specified number of half steps from a starting key number. The begin statement first initializes the variable the-list (to nil). The notes we generate will be collected into the-list. The body of the begin contains a loop. The loop counter is index, and the *count-expression* is the number-of-notes we need to create. When the list ends, we return the-list of notes. In the body of the loop, we use set with @= to cons the sum of starting-note and the index onto the-list. The list cons'ing process continues until the variable index is equal to the number-of-notes. The list is returned. To help understand the iterative process, a display statement has been inserted into the loop body.

Example 12.1.2: make-a-chromatic-lick.sal

```
define function make-a-chromatic-lick(
                starting-note, number-of-notes)
  begin
    with the-list
    loop
      for index below number-of-notes
      set the-list @= starting-note + index
      display "make-a-lick", index, the-list
    end
    return the-list
  end
```

When we call the function, we get the following results:

Example 12.1.3: output from make-a-chromatic-lick

```
SAL> print make-a-chromatic-lick(60, 6)
make-a-lick : INDEX = 0   THE-LIST = (60)
make-a-lick : INDEX = 1   THE-LIST = (61 60)
make-a-lick : INDEX = 2   THE-LIST = (62 61 60)
make-a-lick : INDEX = 3   THE-LIST = (63 62 61 60)
make-a-lick : INDEX = 4   THE-LIST = (64 63 62 61 60)
make-a-lick : INDEX = 5   the-list = (65 64 63 62 61
60)
{65 64 63 62 61 60}
```

Why does the list go from largest to smallest? Because we cons'ed the newly created element onto the front of the list (using @=). If we want a list in ascending order, we could use the reverse function on the-list. Alternatively, we could use the &= operator to put the newly created elements at the *end* of the list. Note that extending lists at the end takes longer than cons'ing to the front because the computer must first find the end of the list. Because it is more efficient, cons'ing followed by a list reversal is a common coding pattern. (Unless lists are very long, you are unlikely to notice any difference in evaluation time.)

Example 12.1.4: make-a-chromatic-lick-2.sal, a revision

```
SAL> define function make-a-chromatic-lick(
                      starting-note, number-of-notes)
     begin
       loop
         with the-list
         for index below number-of-notes
         set the-list @= starting-note + index
         display "make-a-lick", index, the-list
         finally return reverse(the-list)
       end
     end

SAL> print make-a-chromatic-lick(60, 6)
make-a-lick : index = 0   the-list = (60)
make-a-lick : index = 1   the-list = (61 60)
make-a-lick : index = 2   the-list = (62 61 60)
make-a-lick : index = 3   the-list = (63 62 61 60)
make-a-lick : index = 4   the-list = (64 63 62 61 60)
make-a-lick : index = 5   the-list = (65 64 63 62 61
60)
{60 61 62 63 64 65}
```

In Example 12.1.2, we created the-list in a begin-end block so that it would still be in scope after the loop terminated, allowing us to return the final value from the function. It turns out that the with clause is also allowed in the loop statement, which seems like a better place to create a variable that is mainly associated with the loop. However, variables declared inside the loop are local to the loop, so how can we access one to return from the function? Another loop clause is finally followed by a command to be performed when the loop exits. The finally command is within the scope of all loop variables, so we can write finally return the-list. Putting this all together in Example 12.1.4, compare this iterative approach to the recursive solution found in Example 11.3.2.

12.2   The Full Story of for-below

The for-below clause has many variations. The full template is

for *counter* from *from-expr term to-expr* by *step-expr*

The from part specifies the initial value of *counter*. If this part is omitted as in our examples above, the initial value is zero. The next word, *term*, tells when the loop will end. While the examples above use below to specify the number of iterations, any one of the words below, to, above, or downto may be used for *term*. below means that the loop ends when *counter*, after it is incremented, is equal or greater than the value of *to-expr*. The word to means stop when *counter* is greater than *to-expr*. above means stop when *counter* is less than or equal to *to-expr*, and downto means stop when *counter* is less than *to-expr*. Finally, the *step-expr* is evaluated once to obtain the value that is added to *counter* at the end of each iteration. The default value for *step-expr* is 1 when the count is increasing (implied by below and to) and −1 when the count is decreasing (implied by above and downto). With all these options, it is easy to generate a variety of sequences. For example, rather than looping from 0 to number-of-notes − 1, as in Example 12.1.4, one could start the count at starting-note by writing

```
for index from starting-note
        below starting-note + number-of-notes
```

Or, one could generate a whole-tone scale rather than a chromatic one by writing something like

```
for index from starting-note to ending-note by 2
```

12.3   Iterating over the Elements of a List

In Section 10.2, we used mapcar to iterate over elements of a list, apply a function to each element, and construct a list of result values.

Iterating over lists is a frequent task, and loop supports this operation with a variant of the for clause.

The template for iterating over a list using loop is

```
loop
    for element in list
    commands
end
```

Example 12.3.1 shows a simple application of this template.

Example 12.3.1: Printing elements of a list

```
SAL> loop
        for item in {60 61 62 63}
        print item
     end
60
61
62
63
```

Example 12.3.2: count-outliers.sal

```
define function count-outliers(midi-note-list)
    begin
      loop
        with result = 0, lower-bound = 0,
             upper-bound = 127
        for element in midi-note-list
        if element < lower-bound |
           element > upper-bound then
           set result += 1
        display "count-outliers", element, result
        finally return result
      end
    end
```

Example 12.3.2 defines a function count-outliers that counts the number of notes in a list that are outside of the range of the MIDI specification. We enter a loop and initialize the variable result to 0. result is incremented when a note exceeds the range of the MIDI specification. We initialize the lower and upper bounds of the MIDI specification to 0 and 127, respectively. The loop is controlled by a for-in clause that binds the variable element to each member of a list. We use if to compare the value of each element of the list to the upper and lower bounds. If the element exceeds either the lower bound or the upper bound, we increment the variable result. When the loop completes processing, it returns the value of the variable result from the function. A display statement is added to the body of the loop to track the values of the variables element and result. Compare Example 12.3.2 with the recursive solution found in Example 11.4.4.

When we call the function, we get the following results:

Example 12.3.3: Output from count-outliers

```
sal> print count-outliers({189 -5 129 78 64})
count-outliers : ELEMENT = 189  RESULT = 1
count-outliers : ELEMENT = -5  RESULT = 2
count-outliers : ELEMENT = 129  RESULT = 3
count-outliers : ELEMENT = 78  RESULT = 3
count-outliers : ELEMENT = 64  RESULT = 3
3
```

12.4 Using return in a loop

Sometimes, it is necessary to exit an iterative process before a loop has repeated a prescribed number of times. The way to force an early exit from a loop is through the return statement. In previous examples, we used return in a finally clause to return a function value after the last iteration of the loop. return can also be used in the ordinary loop body. When return is encountered, the loop computation ends immediately and the value is returned from the function to the caller.

return is generally preceded by a condition that forces an early exit from the loop. If a return-value is not specified, the loop returns nil.

Example 12.4.1: return-first-outlier.sal

```
define function return-first-outlier(
                              midi-note-list)
  begin
    loop
      with lower-bound = 0,
           upper-bound = 127
      for element in midi-note-list
      if element < lower-bound |
         element > upper-bound then
        return element
      finally return quote(none-found)
    end
  end
```

Example 12.4.1 is a modification of Example 12.3.2. Instead of counting the notes that fall outside of the MIDI specification, the function returns the first occurrence of a note outside of the range. If no notes in the list exceed the range of the MIDI specification, the symbol none-found is returned.

When we call the function, we get the following results:

Example 12.4.2: Output from return-first-outlier

```
SAL> print return-first-outlier({0 98 -5 129})
-5
```

12.5   The for-then Clause

So far we have seen three ways to introduce variables into a loop: The with clause creates and initializes variables before iteration starts, the for-below creates a counter that increments on each iteration of the loop, and for-in iterates over a list. A more general for clause initializes a variable to the value of an expression and then re-evaluates an expression to obtain a new value for each iteration. The for-then clause looks like this:

for *variable* = *expression₁* then *expression₂*

The first time the loop is evaluated, *expression₁* is evaluated and the value is assigned to *variable*. At the beginning of each new iteration, *expression₂* is evaluated and the value is assigned to *variable*. The then *expression₂* part is optional; if omitted, the *expression₁* is evaluated before each iteration.

Example 12.5.1: for-then.sal, using for-then in a loop

```
define function make-a-chromatic-lick-for-then(
                starting-note, number-of-notes)
  begin
    loop
      with the-list
      for index below number-of-notes
      for pitch = starting-note then pitch + 1
      set the-list @= pitch
      finally return the-list
    end
  end
```

In Example 12.5.1, we modify the function in Example 12.1.2, make-a-chromatic-lick, to use a for-then clause. Then, in Example 12.5.2, we call the function make-a-chromatic-lick-for-then with inputs of 60 and 6. The function returns a list of six pitch numbers starting on 65 and descending by half steps. Modify the code to put the list in order using three different methods: (1) use the reverse function, (2) change the set command, and (3) change the for-then command.

Example 12.5.2: Calling make-a-chromatic-lick-for-then

```
SAL> print make-a-chromatic-lick-for-then(60, 6)
{65 64 63 62 61 60}
```

You might think that it would be a good idea to use a for-then clause to update the-list in Example 12.5.1, e.g. "for the-list = cons(pitch, the-list)" could be used instead of the set command. This almost works, but for clauses are evaluated *before* determining if it is time for the loop to terminate. Thus, for clauses run once before each iteration *and* once after the last iteration when it is determined that the loop should exit. If the-list is updated in a for-then clause, it will have number-of-notes + 1 elements, which is one too many. It is worth the effort to try this for yourself and to experiment with different loop configurations. The loop command is very powerful, but it is easy to fall into the trap of expecting a loop to "do the right thing" without careful design and testing.

12.6   Loops with while and until

Sometimes, we need a loop to repeat until some condition is met. Example 12.4.1 used return to exit a loop "early" and return from a function. Alternatively, loops can use while and until clauses to exit the loop (but not return from a function) when a condition is met. In Example 12.6.1, we once again make a chromatic lick as we did in Example 12.1.2 and Example 12.5.2. This time, we use until.

Example 12.6.1: make-a-chromatic-lick-until.sal

```
define function make-a-chromatic-lick-until(
                starting-note, number-of-notes)
   begin
     with the-list
     loop
       with index = 0
       until index = number-of-notes
       set the-list @= index + starting-note
       set index += 1
     end
     return reverse(the-list)
   end
```

We create the-list, initially nil, in the begin block. In the loop, we initialize the variable index to 0. The loop immediately evaluates a condition where the value of index is compared to the variable number-of-notes. If the condition is true, the loop exits and the-list is returned. Otherwise, the remainder of the loop body is evaluated and we cons a note onto the-list using set. The index variable is incremented using another set. The iterative process continues until the index equals the number-of-notes.

When thinking about loops, it is sometimes helpful to think about *loop invariants*, predicates that are true each time through the loop. In this case, a loop invariant at the beginning of the until clause is

the number of notes in the-list *is equal to* index.

Since the loop body grows the-list by one and increments index by one, then if the invariant is true on one iteration, it is true on the next. You can see that this is initially true (index is 0 and the-list is nil), so it must always be true. The loop exits when the until expression is true, so at the end of the loop, we know the invariant is true: *the number of notes in* the-list *is equal to* index, and we know index = number-of-notes. Putting these together, we know *the number of notes in* the-list *is equal to* number-of-notes. Think about what invariant would help you to prove that the final list is a sequence of consecutive integers.

Next, we call the function to demonstrate that it works as expected:

Example 12.6.2: Calling make-a-chromatic-lick-until

```
SAL> print make-a-chromatic-lick-until(60, 6)
{60 61 62 63 64 65}
```

In Example 12.6.3, once again we search for MIDI note numbers that are outside the range of the MIDI specification as we did in Example 11.4.2 and Example 12.3.2. This time, we use loop with a while clause.

In the body of the function, we use with to create the variables element and result. The latter is initialized to 0 and used to count outliers. A loop is used to examine the elements of midi-note-list. On each iteration, the first element of midi-note-list is tested to see if it is an outlier. If the note is too high or too low, the variable result is incremented. Then the first element is removed from the list to prepare for the next iteration. The condition that terminates iterative processing uses while. The loop continues "while" there are list elements to examine, but when the list is empty, it is nil, which means "false," and the loop exits. The value of the variable result is returned.

Example 12.6.3: count-outliers-loop.sal

```
define function count-outliers-loop(
                                midi-note-list)
  begin
    with element, result = 0
    loop
      while midi-note-list
      set element = first(midi-note-list)
      if element < 0 | element > 127 then
        set result += 1
      set midi-note-list = rest(midi-note-list)
    end
    return result
  end
```

We call the function:

Example 12.6.4: Calling count-outliers-loop

```
SAL> print count-outliers-loop({189 -5 129 78 64})
3
```

12.7 Reading and Writing Records Using Iteration

In Chapter 6, we learned how to input data into a program from the computer keyboard using the primitive read. SAL also allows you to read data from a file. To read data from a file, you must
- Open the file, creating a file-stream;
- Save the file-stream in a variable;
- Read from the file-stream;
- Close the file-stream.

These steps are illustrated in the next example. Assume that the contents of the ASCII (plain text) file midi.dat look like this:

```
60 98 0
34 87 1
98 78 2
```

In Example 12.7.1, we define a function get-midi-data that opens the file midi.dat, reads data from the file, and outputs what it has read using format.

We use with to create and assign the variables my-data, the-note, the-velocity, and the-channel. my-data is initialized with the file-stream returned by open. The input passed to open is a path to the file. This string can be a path relative to the current directory or a full, absolute path. The exact specification of the path depends on your operating system. open returns nil if the file cannot be opened (or does not exist), and it is a good idea to test the return value to see if the open was successful. The test is omitted here to keep the example small.

Example 12.7.1: get-midi-data.sal

```
define function get-midi-data()
  begin
    with my-data =
          open("/Users/rbd/Desktop/midi.dat"),
         the-note = read(my-data),
         the-velocity = read(my-data),
         the-channel = read(my-data)
    exec format(#t,
                "The midi note ~a has velocity ~a ",
                the-note, the-velocity)
    exec format(#t, "on channel ~a~%", the-channel)
    exec close(my-data)
  end
```

After opening midi.dat, data is read from the file. Each call to read reads one token from the file, skipping over white space and newlines. The body of the begin uses a format to print the data read from the file. Finally, the file-stream is closed by calling close. The input to close must be an open file-stream.

In Example 12.7.2, we call the function get-midi-data.

Example 12.7.2: Calling get-midi-data

```
SAL> exec get-midi-data()
The midi note 60 has velocity 98 on channel 0
```

As you can see, the function get-midi-data only retrieved the first line of data from the file. We can use an iterative process to retrieve more than one line of data. Example 12.7.3 defines a function read-multiple-records. The function uses a loop to repeatedly process data from the file. The loop assigns the variables midi-note, velocity, and channel using a for-then clause (without the optional then part). read returns nil when it encounters the end of the file. The loop uses "while midi-note" so that when read returns nil, the loop will exit. Each time through the loop after data are read from the file, a format function prints the data.

Note that the file-stream assigned to my-data is opened before the loop and checked to make sure it is valid. If the file cannot be found or opened, my-data will be nil, the then part of the if statement will be evaluated, a message will be printed and the function will return. Also, notice that the file-stream is closed after the loop exits.

Example 12.7.3: read-multiple-records.sal

```
define function read-multiple-records()
  begin
    with filename = "/Users/rbd/Desktop/midi.dat",
         my-data = open(filename)
    if ! my-data then
      begin
        exec format(t,
            "read-mulitple-records: cannot open ~A~%",
            filename)
        return #t
      end
    loop
      for midi-note = read(my-data)
      for velocity = read(my-data)
      for channel = read(my-data)
      while midi-note
      exec format(t, "The midi note ~A has ",
                      midi-note)
      exec format(t, "velocity ~A on channel ~A~%",
                      velocity,      channel)
    end
    exec close(my-data)
  end
```

In Example 12.7.4, we call the function read-multiple-records. Note that this function depends upon having a file to read. The file data is formatted and printed.

Example 12.7.5 opens two files: one for input (midi.dat) and one for output (midi-out.dat). To open a file for output, pass the keyword direction: with value keyword(output) to open. (You can also pass the value keyword(input), but that is the default, so it is unnecessary when reading a file.) We use a loop to iteratively read from the input file. We use format in the body of the loop to write to the output file. Notice that format does not use #t to write to the terminal, but instead uses the variable out-data to direct printing to the output file.

Example 12.7.4: Calling read-multiple-records

```
SAL> exec read-multiple-records()
The midi note 60 has velocity 98 on channel 0
The midi note 34 has velocity 87 on channel 1
The midi note 98 has velocity 78 on channel 2
```

Example 12.7.5: write-multiple-records.sal

```
define function write-multiple-records()
  begin
    with in-data = open(
                  "/Users/rbd/Desktop/midi.dat"),
         out-data = open(
                  "/Users/rbd/Desktop/midi-out.dat",
                  direction: keyword(output))
    if ! in-data | ! out-data then
      begin
        display "error", in-data, out-data
        if in-data  then exec close(in-data)
        if out-data then exec close(out-data)
        return #t
      end
    loop
      for midi-note = read(in-data)
      for velocity = read(in-data)
      for channel = read(in-data)
      while midi-note
      exec format(out-data, "midi-note = ~a ",
                            midi-note)
      exec format(out-data,
                  "velocity = ~a channel ~a~%",
                  velocity,   channel)
    end
    exec close(in-data)
    exec close(out-data)
  end
```

If open fails to open either file, then in-data or out-data will be nil. This is caught and reported by an if statement. Notice that even if one file fails to open, the other file might be open and should be closed. We cannot just call close with an input of nil (this would raise an exception), so we use two more if statements to close each file-stream *if* the file-stream exists (is not nil). If no open error occurs, the files are closed after the loop near the end of the function. No tests are necessary here because we know that both files were opened successfully and need to be closed.

In Example 12.7.6, we call the function write-multiple-records. Since the format expression sends output to the out-data file-stream, nothing is printed to the standard output.

Example 12.7.6: Calling write-multiple-records

```
SAL> exec write-multiple-records()
```

All of the output from the function has been directed to the file midi-out.dat. When we view the contents of midi-out.dat (for example, you can use the File:Open command in the Nyquist IDE or open the file with any text editor) we see

```
midi-note = 60 velocity = 98 channel 0
midi-note = 34 velocity = 87 channel 1
midi-note = 98 velocity = 78 channel 2
```

12.8 score-gen as Iteration

We have already seen and used the score-gen function, and it should now be clear that some sort of iteration is involved in the implementation of score-gen. In score-gen, the body is iterated to compute notes in a score. One of the keyword parameters score-len: or score-dur: is used to determine when the iteration terminates. One thing that is different about score-gen is that it can only be used to compute a score. score-gen automatically accumulates notes (one note per iteration) into a list. This is similar to the expression in Example 12.1.4 that accumulates pitches into a list to make a chromatic scale:

```
set the-list @= starting-note + index
```

In score-gen, however, this accumulation step is performed automatically, and rather than just forming a list of pitches, score-gen creates a list of events, each with a start time, a duration, and a sound expression.

As a final exercise on iteration, we will construct a version of the "chromatic-lick" functions that returns a playable score. We will start with a score-gen version, and then write a version that is based directly on loop for comparison. The score-gen version is quite simple, as shown in Example 12.8.1.

Example 12.8.1: chromatic-lick-score-gen.sal

```
define function chromatic-lick-score-gen(
                starting-note, number-of-notes)
    begin
      return score-gen(
             score-len: number-of-notes,
             pitch: starting-note + sg:count,
             ioi: 0.5, vel: 100)
    end
```

While it would be possible to generate pitches from a pattern, it seems easier to use sg:count, which starts at zero and automatically increments by one after each note is computed.

Example 12.8.2 generates a score using loop. Notice that in this version, there is an explicit variable, score, to accumulate the list of notes, and an explicit loop that performs one iteration for each note. Each note is explicitly constructed using nested calls to list, and each note is cons'ed onto the front of score. Since this constructs a score in reverse time order, the last line reverses the score. It also sets the begin time and end time of the score so that it will be in the proper form.

Example 12.8.2: chromatic-lick-loop.sal

```
define function chromatic-lick-loop(
               starting-note, number-of-notes)
  begin
    loop
      with score, dur = 0.5
      for i below number-of-notes
      for start = 0 then start + dur
      set score @=
          list(start, dur,
             list(quote(note),
             keyword(pitch), starting-note + i,
             keyword(vel), 100))
      finally
        return
          score-set-end(
            score-set-begin(reverse(score), 0),
            start)
    end
```

Use score-print to print the scores returned by these two functions. Do you see any difference? Use score-play to play the scores. Do you hear any difference?

12.9 Suggested Listening

Functions to read files are introduced in this chapter, allowing programs to read data from various sources and use the data in compositions. *Atlas Eclipticalis*, by John Cage is based on an atlas of stars. Cage superimposed musical staves over the star chart, translating brightness into amplitudes. This piece also inspired the cover of this book.

Jem Finer's *Longplayer* is a 1000-year-long composition (Finer, *et al.* 2003). The work is based on cycles or iterations of musical sequences of different lengths that, like planets, come into alignment only rarely. In the case of *Longplayer,* the system will not repeat for 1000 years. *Longplayer* is currently streaming over the Internet from a synthesized source, but portions and variations of it have also been performed by live musicians. Details, sounds, and the ongoing piece itself are available at: http://longplayer.org.

Chapter 13   Algorithmic Composition Using Probabilistic Methods

Chapter 5 introduced the random item stream pattern type. Using the random item stream pattern type, we were able to select randomly among sets of values. In music, we often want some choices to be more likely than others, or a choice might depend upon the previous choice. In this chapter, we will explore probability theory and ways to make biased (and hopefully more musical) choices.

13.1   Introduction to Probability

Probability is a branch of mathematics that studies the chance or likelihood that an event will occur. A probability is expressed as a ratio – the number of times a given event is expected to occur divided by the total number of outcomes. If all outcomes are equally likely, the probability of some event is simply the number of outcomes in which the event is present divided by the total number of outcomes. For example, consider a six-sided die where each side is uniquely identified 1, 2, 3, 4, 5, and 6. The probability that a 1 will be rolled is 1:6. The ratio 1:6 may also be expressed as a real number between 0 and 1. Considering the example of the six-sided die, the sum of all possible outcomes is 6/6 or 1.0 (100%).

13.2   The random Pattern

A random pattern is created by calling make-random. The first input is a list of items to choose among. In the simplest case, a call to make-random might look like

```
make-random({2, 3, 5, 7, 11, 13, 17})
```

which generates a stream of small prime numbers chosen randomly from the list. In this case, the probability of choosing any particular number is 1/7.

To make some elements more likely than others, we can specify a *weight*. To associate a weight with an item, the item is replaced by a list containing the item, the keyword weight:, and the weight, a numerical value that defaults to 1. Example 13.2.1 illustrates a random pattern where the first element is assigned a weight.

Example 13.2.1: Random pattern with weights

```
set note = make-random({{c4 weight: 0.5} d4 e4})
```

Notice that while `weight:` has the appearance of a keyword in a parameter list, here it is just a symbol in a list, and since the list is constructed with braces, there are no commas separating any of the list elements. Because the weight for `c4` is 0.5, `c4` is 1/2 as likely to be selected as `d4` or `e4`, which have default weights of 1. Given that there are 3 notes and the sum of their probabilities must equal 1 (or 100%), and `c4` is 1/2 as likely to be selected as `d4` or `e4`, Table 13.2.1 shows the probabilities of the note events.

Table 13.2.1: Note probabilities for Example 13.2.1

Note Name	C4	D4	E4
Weight	0.2	0.4	0.4

To compute these probabilities, divide the weight of an element (e.g. 0.5 for `c4`) by the sum of all weights (e.g. 0.5 + 1 + 1, or 2.5). Thus the weight for `c4` is 0.5/2.5 = 0.2, and the weight for `d4` is 1/2.5 = 0.4.

If no weights are specified, the probabilities of all events are equal. The term "white" is often used informally to describe equal probability. This terminology comes from natural white light, which is light in which all visible frequencies (or colors) are present in equal strength. By analogy, we can describe audio as "white noise" when all audible frequencies are equally intense. It turns out that each individual audio sample value of digitized white noise is equally likely and unrelated to other samples, as if sample values were chosen by rolling a die. (Admittedly, it would be hard to find a die with 65,536 sides to represent all the different sample values in 16-bit digital audio!) Thus, a sequence of random outcomes from a die or any other random process with equally probable outcomes can be called "white noise." In Example 13.2.2, the range of events is the rhythms for a quarter, sixteenth, and eighth note.

Example 13.2.2: Random rhythm pattern

```
set rhythm-pattern = make-random(list(q, s, i))
```

Table 13.2.2 shows the selection of rhythms based on equal probability.

Table 13.2.2: Rhythm probability table

Rhythm	Quarter	Sixteenth	eIghth
Weight	.333	.333	.333

With random events such as flipping coins, rolling dice, or getting the next item from rhythm-pattern, the next outcome is completely independent of all previous outcomes. This can be counterintuitive: most people feel that after a coin toss yields "heads" four times in a row, the next toss is more likely to be "tails." This is known as the *gambler's fallacy*. The probability of the next toss coming up heads is always 0.5, regardless of what happened in the past.

Perhaps because we feel that an uninterrupted run of heads or tails is particularly unlikely, these runs stand out. Similarly, a melody may not sound "random" if pitches are repeated, and these repetitions may sound wrong or out-of-place. The random pattern is normally like a coin toss. To generate each item, the next function selects an item at random according to the weights. This may result in runs where the same item is chosen several times in a row.

To avoid this behavior, the option max: sets a maximum value an element may be repeated before a different element must be selected. Alternatively, the min: keyword forces a number of direct repetitions before a different element is selected. If min: or max: is used with make-random, it is possible that the generated sequence of items will not be in proportion to the specified weights. You can think of starting with a random sequence that is constructed according to the weights and then removing items that violate the max: constraints and inserting items to satisfy the min: constraints.

Example 13.2.3 indicates that 0.1 and 0.2 can repeat at most one time before a new (and different) event must be selected. 0.3 and 0.4 must repeat at least 2 times before a different event is selected.

Example 13.2.3: Using max: and min: in random pattern

```
set amplitude-pattern =
     make-random({{0.1 max: 1} {0.2 max: 1}
                  {0.3 min: 2} {0.4 min: 2}})
```

Example 13.2.4 illustrates a simple score with random pitch, duration, and velocity. The patterns are constructed first and bound to variables in the with expression. The body of the begin-end is a call to score-gen, which uses these patterns to construct successive notes. Patterns are constructed with make-random, which takes a list of items.

score-print is used to print the result. In this case there are 1 C4 (60), 5 D4s (62), and 6 E4s (64). There are 5 quarter notes (1), 6 eighth notes (0.5), and 1 sixteenth note (0.25). The vel: parameter does not have successive values of 70 or 80 (where max: is 1), and values of 90 and 100 (where min: is 2) always occur at least twice in succession.

Example 13.2.4: random.sal

```
SAL> begin
        with pitch-pattern =
          make-random(list(list(c4, weight: 0.5),
                           d4, e4)),
          rhythm-pattern =
            make-random(list(q, s, i)),
          velocity-pattern =
            make-random({{70 max: 1} {80  max: 1}
                         {90 min: 2} {100 min: 2}})
        exec score-gen(save: quote(random-score),
                       score-len: 12,
                       pitch: next(pitch-pattern),
                       ioi:   next(rhythm-pattern),
                       vel:   next(velocity-pattern))
      end
```

```
SAL> exec score-print(random-score)
((0  0  (SCORE-BEGIN-END 0 8.25))
(0      0.25 (NOTE vel: 70 pitch: 62))
(0.25 0.5  (NOTE vel: 90 pitch: 64))
(0.75 0.5  (NOTE vel: 90 pitch: 62))
(1.25 1    (NOTE vel: 90 pitch: 62))
(2.25 0.5  (NOTE vel: 100 pitch: 64))
(2.75 1    (NOTE vel: 100 pitch: 60))
(3.75 0.5  (NOTE vel: 80 pitch: 64))
(4.25 0.5  (NOTE vel: 100 pitch: 62))
(4.75 1    (NOTE vel: 100 pitch: 64))
(5.75 0.5  (NOTE vel: 100 pitch: 64))
(6.25 1    (NOTE vel: 90 pitch: 64))
(7.25 1    (NOTE vel: 90 pitch: 62))
)
```

In Example 13.2.4, notice that pitch-pattern and rhythm-pattern are specified using calls to list, but velocity-pattern is specified using braces {}. Most of the previous examples use braces because the syntax is simpler and easier to read. However, braces implicitly quote all of the list elements. This is fine when elements are numbers and/or symbols, but not good when we want to use the values of variables.

In Example 13.2.5, similar lists are formed using list and braces. Notice in the first two cases, using list, that the variable c4 is evaluated to obtain 60, but in the third case, c4 in braces is an unevaluated symbol, and the printout shows that the list contains the symbol c4. Use list to form lists when you want the values of variables such as symbolic pitches (c4) or durations (q).

This example also illustrates two ways to introduce a keyword into a list. The first uses keyword(*name*) to construct a symbol. The second uses weight: without a subsequent comma. This only works when the keyword is followed by another expression. (This notation is also used in Example 13.2.4).

Example 13.2.5: Comparing the list function to brace notation

```
SAL> print list(c4, keyword(weight), 0.5),
           list(c4, weight: 0.5),
           {c4 weight: 0.5}
{60 :WEIGHT 0.5} {60 :WEIGHT 0.5} {C4 :WEIGHT 0.5}
```

13.3   Graphs and Patterns

Graphs are often used to describe behaviors including music. In mathematics and computer science, a *graph* is a set of *nodes* and a set of *edges*. We will consider *directed graphs*, which are graphs with directed edges.

The graph in Figure 13.3.1 has three nodes – C4, E4, and DS4. Each node represents a symbolic note name. The arrows connecting the nodes specify the direction in which the graph may be traversed. For example, from node E4, we can go to C4 or DS4. From node C4, we can only go to E4.

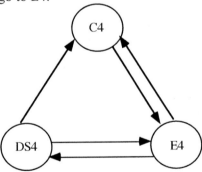

Figure 13.3.1: A directed graph

One way to model this graph is to represent each node with a pattern that selects the next node. Consider the program in Example

13.3.1. The variables c4-pattern, ds4-pattern, and e4-pattern represent nodes and contain pattern generators that generate the next node to visit. For example, the ds4-pattern will alternately generate c4-pattern and e4-pattern, corresponding to the edges from ds4 to c4 and e4. The variable current-node keeps track of the current location on the graph, and the function get-next-node traverses an edge as follows: (1) the value of current-node is a symbol. The eval function is applied to get the value of the symbol. (2) next is applied to the pattern to get the next item. (3) The item is stored in current-node. Finally, a table is used to translate the value of current-node (a symbol) into a pitch number.

The use of eval deserves further comment. We represent nodes with patterns that choose the next node. Thus, each pattern should return another pattern. However, when a pattern is an item of another pattern, the next function treats these as nested patterns, and it tries to generate a period of items from the nested pattern. (See Chapter 6 for examples and further explanation.) To avoid this in Example 13.3.1, patterns return *symbols*. Each symbol is the name of a global variable containing the associated pattern. eval is used to look up the variable's value. For example, current-node is initialized to the symbol c4-pattern. In line 8 (counting the blank line), eval is applied to the *value* of current-node, which is c4-pattern. The value of c4-pattern in turn is the cycle pattern created and assigned in the first line. This pattern object is assigned to the variable pattern and used to select the next value of current-node. Another way to implement this graph traversal is described in Section 13.4.

Example 13.3.1: get-next-node.sal

```
set c4-pattern = make-cycle({e4-pattern})
set ds4-pattern = make-cycle({c4-pattern e4-pattern})
set e4-pattern = make-cycle({c4-pattern ds4-pattern})
set current-node = quote(c4-pattern)

define function get-next-node()
  begin ;; note: current-node is a symbol
    with pattern = eval(current-node)
    set current-node = next(pattern)
    return second(assoc(current-node,
                      {{c4-pattern 60}
                       {ds4-pattern 63}
                       {e4-pattern 64}}))
  end
```

Example 13.3.2 calls get-next-node in a loop and prints a sequence of pitches that are generated. Note that the transitions from

E4 (64) alternate going to C4 (60) and DS4 (63), and DS4 (63) goes alternately to C4 (60) and E4 (64).

Example 13.3.3 incorporates get-next-node from Example 13.3.1 into a score generator. Listen to the output of this program. It is difficult to follow all the workings of the program, but you can easily hear, for example that the low note (C4) always makes a transition to the high note (E4), as shown in the graph of Figure 15.3.1.

Example 13.3.2 : Calling get-next-node

```
SAL> loop
        repeat 10
        exec format(#t, "~A ", get-next-node())
     end
64 60 64 63 60 64 60 64 63 64
```

Example 13.3.3: graph.sal

```
begin
  with dur-pattern = make-random({0.2 0.4 0.6}),
       vel-pattern = make-cycle({60 75 90 105})
  exec score-gen(save: quote(graph-score),
                 score-len: 30,
                 pitch: get-next-node(),
                 ioi: next(dur-pattern),
                 vel: next(vel-pattern))
end
```

13.4   The markov Pattern Generator

A *Markov process* is a probability system where the likelihood that an event will be selected is based on one or more past events. A *first-order* Markov process is one where the next state depends only on the current state. Note how a first-order Markov process can be represented as a directed graph. A node in the graph represents an event, and the probability of making a transition to another node (event) is represented by edges labeled with probabilities. Typically, only edges with non-zero probabilities are included in the graph.

An alternative to this graphical representation is a transition table that shows the probability that a certain event will be selected based on one or more past events. A *first-order* transition table describes the probability that an event will be selected given *one* past event, and a *second-order* transition table describes the probability that an event will be selected given *two* past events. (Higher orders are also possible.) The succession from one event to the other is called a *Markov chain*.

Table 13.4.1: A first-order transition table

	C4	D4	E4
C4	0.10	0.75	0.15
D4	0.25	0.10	0.65
E4	0.50	0.30	0.20

Table 13.4.1 is an example of a first-order transition table. The current events are listed in the zero[th] column and the possible next events are listed in the zero[th] row. We interpret the first row of the transition table as "if the current event is a C4, there is a 10% chance that another C4 will be selected, a 75% chance that D4 will be selected, and a 15% chance that E4 will be selected." Figure 13.4.1 shows a graph that is equivalent to this table. Notice that some edges lead from a node back to the same node.

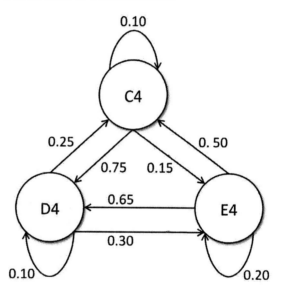

Figure 13.4.1: A first-order Markov process as a graph

Two frequent errors in constructing transition tables are loops and dead ends. The transition table in Table 13.4.2 will quickly fall into a loop that generates a chain of alternating D4s and E4s.

Table 13.4.2: A first-order transition table that loops

	C4	D4	E4
C4	—	.5	.5
D4	—	—	1.0
E4	—	1.0	—

A dead end occurs in a transition table when an event is specified and there is no way to select another event from that event. The transition table shown as Table 13.4.3 states that "if the current note is a C4, there is a 50% chance that D4 will be selected, a 25% chance that E4 will be selected, and a 25% chance that F4 is selected." If F4 is selected, it has no next event since there is no row in the transition table that considers F4 as a current event. The Markov chain reaches a dead end.

Table 13.4.3: A first-order transition table that dead-ends

	C4	D4	E4	F4
C4	—	.5	.25	.25
D4	—	—	1.0	—
E4	—	1.0	—	—

The function make-markov may be used to generate a pattern that constructs a Markov chain. To describe a Markov process using make-markov, each row of the transition table is specified by a list like this:

{current -> {next₁ weight₁} {next₂ weight₂} ... {nextₙ weightₙ}}

where states are symbols. *current* is the current state and *next₁* through *nextₙ* are the possible next states, which are listed with their associated transition weights. (Weights are relative and do not necessarily sum to 1.) The first input to make-markov is a list of transition rules.

Example 13.4.1 uses make-markov to produce a sequence of pitches using the first-order transition table described in Table 13.4.1. Notice that two keyword parameters are passed to make-markov in addition to the transition rules. The past: keyword gives the starting state. If this were a second-order Markov process, the list would contain two states: the previous one and the current one. The produces: keyword is used to convert the current state into a value. In this example, the value keyword(eval) says to evaluate the state name as a global variable to get the next value of the pattern generator. Since our state names are C4, D4, E4, and these happen to be Lisp variables that evaluate to 60, 62, and 64, keyword(eval) offers a convenient way to return pitch values rather than state names.

When markov.sal is evaluated, the note series shown in Figure 13.4.2 is generated. This series will be different each time the program is run.

Example 13.4.1: markov.sal

```
begin with markov-pattern = make-markov(
        {{c4 -> {c4 0.1}  {d4 0.75} {e4 0.15}}
         {d4 -> {c4 0.25} {d4 0.1}  {e4 0.65}}
         {e4 -> {c4 0.5}  {d4 0.3}  {e4 0.2}}},
        past: {c4}, produces: keyword(eval))
    exec score-gen(save: quote(markov1),
                   score-len: 12,
                   pitch: next(markov-pattern),
                   vel: 100, ioi: 0.5)
    end
```

Figure 13.4.2: Output from markov1.sal

An alternative version of this program illustrates another way to use the produces: parameter. In Example 13.4.2, each state is mapped explicitly to a value using a list, which has the form

$\{state_1\ value_1\ state_2\ value_2\ ...\ state_n\ value_n\}$

This example is identical to Example 13.4.1 except for the produces: keyword parameter.

Example 13.4.2: markov2.sal

```
begin
  with markov-pattern = make-markov(
      {{c4 -> {c4 0.1} {d4 0.75} {e4 0.15}}
       {d4 -> {c4 0.25} {d4 0.1} {e4 0.65}}
       {e4 -> {c4 0.5} {d4 0.3} {e4 0.2}}},
      past: {c4}, produces: {c4 60 d4 62 e4 64})
  exec score-gen(save: quote(markov2),
                 score-len: 12,
                 pitch: next(markov-pattern),
                 vel: 100, ioi: 0.5)
  end
```

13.5   Patterns Can Specify Next States and Weights

In the previous example, and in most models of Markov processes, the graph is static, meaning that the nodes and weights are fixed. However, the markov pattern allows you to specify next states and weights using patterns. When a pattern is used as a weight, the first item generated by the pattern is used as the "real" weight. Whenever the transition is taken, the weight on that transition is updated to the next item returned by the pattern. The next state can also be given by a pattern. If a pattern is used to specify a next state, then whenever that transition is taken, the next item generated by the pattern becomes the next state. It follows that the items generated by the pattern must be symbols that correspond to states.

Using patterns in rules, we can rewrite Example 13.3.1 using make-markov. Example 13.3.1 uses pattern generators to alternately choose one of the other two nodes as the next state for ds4 and e4. To incorporate these patterns into rules for make-markov, the variables ds4-pattern, e4-pattern, and markov-pattern are initialized in sequence. The rule for make-markov uses list to allow us to insert the *values* of ds4-pattern and e4-pattern into the rule expression. What would markov-pattern return if we used braces to form the list?

Example 13.5.1: markov-graph.sal

```
begin
  with ds4-pattern = make-cycle({c4 e4}),
       e4-pattern = make-cycle({c4 ds4}),
       markov-pattern = make-markov(
         list(
           list(quote(c4), quote(->), quote(e4)),
           list(quote(ds4), quote(->), ds4-pattern),
           list(quote(e4), quote(->), e4-pattern)),
         past: {c4}, produces: keyword(eval))
  exec score-gen(save: quote(markov-graph),
                 score-len: 12,
                 pitch: next(markov-pattern),
                 vel: 100, ioi: 0.5)
end
```

A true first-order Markov process chooses the next state based only on the current state, but Example 13.5.1 maintains some additional history in the pattern objects. The fact that this is not a true Markov process should not deter its use. The next example considers further extensions to the basic Markov model.

Weights can also be specified using patterns. Consider the simple Markov process shown in Figure 13.5.1. There are two states. If the transitions between states have high weights, then the music will tend to alternate states, but if the weights are small, the music will tend to "stick" at one state or the other. Example 13.5.2 uses a pattern to specify these weights. The pattern alternates between five high values and five low values. The same pattern is used for the weight from C4 to C5 and the weight from C5 to C4 so that transition weight changes will be synchronized.

The weight pattern is 0.1, 0.1, 0.1, 0.1, 0.1, 10, 10, 10, 10, 10, 0.1, 0.1, 0.1, 0.1, 0.1, ... This is created by first making a cycle pattern that returns 0.1, 10, 0.1, 10, ..., with a period of 1. Then make-copier is used to repeat each period five times.

The weight pattern, w-pattern, is used to initialize the second pattern, markov-pattern. Notice how we use list again to put the *value* of w-pattern into the transition rules.

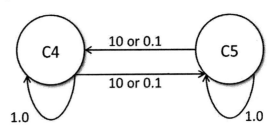

Figure 13.5.1: A Markov-like process with variable transition weights

Example 13.5.2: markov-weights.sal

```
begin
  with w-pattern =
        make-copier(make-cycle({10 0.1},
                    for: 1), repeat: 5),
       markov-pattern = make-markov(
        list(
          list(quote(c4), quote(->),
              quote(c4),
              list(quote(c5), w-pattern)),
          list(quote(c5), quote(->),
              quote(c5),
              list(quote(c4), w-pattern))),
          past: {c4}, produces: :eval)
  exec score-gen(save: quote(markov-weights),
              score-len: 50,
              pitch: next(markov-pattern),
              vel: 100, ioi: 0.2)
  end
```

Use score-play(markov-weights) to play the pattern created by Example 13.5.2. Can you follow the state transitions? Are they completely predictable? What happens if the weights are 100 and 0.01 instead of 10 and 0.1? What happens if the weights are both 1? See if you can predict what the music will sound like before you try changes.

13.6   Learning a Markov Process

Quite often, Markov processes are used to generate music based on a previous composition or set of compositions. It is not possible to determine the "true" transition probabilities from examples, but we can *estimate* the probabilities by counting the relative frequencies of actual transitions. Consider the folk melody "Aunt Rhody" as notated in Example 13.6.1.

Figure 13.6.1: "Aunt Rhody"

There is one occurrence of the note F5 and it always goes to E5. To describe this relationship in a first–order transition table, we would say given F5, there is 100% change that E5 will be selected.

{F5 -> E5}

There are two occurrences of the note G5. G5 may be followed by either another G5 or F5. To describe this relationship in a first-order transition table, we would say that given G5, there is a 50% chance that another G5 will be selected and a 50% chance that an F5 will be selected.

{G5 -> {G5 0.5} {F5 0.5}}

When a transition table is constructed, the sum of the weights for a row equals 1. make-markov can work with transition tables when the sum of a row does not equal 1. Under these circumstances, the Markov pattern generator scales the probabilities in relation to the other events in the row as was noted in the random pattern generator. For example,

{C4 -> {C4 .5} D4 E4)

means that C4 is 1/2 as likely to be selected as D4 and E4. Given a C4, the probability of selecting another C4 is 20%. The likelihood that D4 or E4 will be selected is 40% each.

The function markov-create-rules analyzes a list and returns a transition table that can be used as the first input to make-markov. markov-create-rules takes two or three inputs:

markov-create-rules(*sequence, order, generalize*)

where *sequence* is a list of states, *order* is the order of the Markov process (usually 1), and *generalize* is an optional input to be described below. Example 13.6.1 demonstrates the use of markov-create-rules using the note list from "Aunt Rhody." We request a first-order transition table. The rules are difficult to read as a flat list, so we call the built-in function pprint (short for "pretty print") to print the list in a nicer format.

Example 13.6.1: Using markov-create-rules

```
SAL> set rules = markov-create-rules(
            {e5 e5 d5 c5 c5 d5 d5 e5 d5 c5 g5 g5
            f5 e5 e5 d5 c5 d5 e5 c5}, 1)
SAL> print rules
{{E5 -> {E5 2} {D5 3} {C5 1}} {D5 -> {C5 3} {D5
1} {E5 2}} {C5 -> {C5 1} {D5 2} {G5 1}} {G5 ->
{G5 1} {F5 1}} {F5 -> {E5 1}}}
SAL> exec pprint(rules)
((E5 -> (E5 2) (D5 3) (C5 1))
 (D5 -> (C5 3) (D5 1) (E5 2))
 (C5 -> (C5 1) (D5 2) (G5 1))
 (G5 -> (G5 1) (F5 1))
 (F5 -> (E5 1)))
```

Next, we analyze the rhythm of "Aunt Rhody" using markov-create-rules. We specify a second-order transition table. Notice that this phrase of "Aunt Rhody" ends with a half note, but there is no next state after the half note. For now, we will extend the phrase with a quarter note so that there will be at least one transition out of the half-note state.

Example 13.6.2: Creating a second-order transition table

```
SAL> set iois = markov-create-rules(
            {q i i q q q q i i q q i i q q i i i
            i h q}, 2)
SAL> exec pprint(iois)
((Q I -> (I 4))
 (I I -> (Q 3) (I 2) (H 1))
 (I Q -> (Q 3))
 (Q Q -> (Q 2) (I 3))
 (I H -> (Q 1)))
```

The second-order transition table is more complex to read than a first order transition table. Consider the third row of the transition table in Example 13.6.2.

$$(I \ Q \ -> \ (Q \ 3))$$

The row is interpreted as "if the current rhythm is a Quarter note and it was preceded by an eIghth note, return a Quarter note" (there were three similar occurrences in the input sequence).

Given a first-order transition table for the selection of note events and a second-order transition table for the selection of rhythmic values, we can generate a melody that has note and rhythm transitions similar to those in "Aunt Rhody."

Example 13.6.3: markov-rhody.sal

```
begin
  with pitch-pat = make-markov(
          rules, past: {C5}, produces: :eval),
       rhythm-pat = make-markov(
          iois, past: {Q Q}, produces: :eval)
  exec score-gen(save: quote(markov-rhody),
                 score-len: 22,
                 pitch: next(pitch-pat),
                 ioi: 0.5 * next(rhythm-pat),
                 vel: 100)
end
```

Figure 13.6.2: Output from Example 13.6.3

All of the rules we have seen so far apply to specific states, but rules can also contain "*" which is a "wildcard" that matches any state. For example, the rule

$$\{* \ G5 \ -> \ \{G5 \ 1\} \ \{F5 \ 2\}\}$$

matches any pitch followed by G5, and

$$\{* \ * \ -> \ \{G5 \ 1\} \ \{F5 \ 2\}\}$$

matches any previous sequence of states. Rules are searched in order, so you can put a more general rule with wildcards after more specific rules. The rule with wildcards will then only be considered if none of the specific rules apply.

Sometimes, markov-create-rules generates transition tables that dead end. These dead ends generate the error message "Error, no matching rule found: ..." The error message can be avoided by reducing the order of the transition table or extending the transition table to include possible choices not returned by markov-create-rules. Another possibility is to specify #t (true) for the third (optional) parameter, *generalize*. *generalize* adds a rule that matches any state or sequence of previous states. The next state is chosen according to the estimated overall probability of states without considering the state history. Thus, there is always a transition to a next state, even though that transition did not appear in the data.

Example 13.6.4 uses the *generalize* option to compute transition rules from "Aunt Rhody." In this example, there is no added rhythm after the H(alf), thus no specific rule handles this case. Notice the last rule uses wildcard notation. This rule will be used in the event the Markov process reaches state H.

Example 13.6.4: Using the generalize option

```
SAL> set rules = markov-create-rules(
        {q i i q q q q i i q q i
         i q q i i i i h}, 2, #t)

SAL> print rules
((Q I -> (I 4)) (I I -> (Q 3) (I 2) (H 1)) (I Q
-> (Q 3)) (Q Q -> (Q 2) (I 3)) (* * -> (H 1) (Q
8) (I 9)))

SAL> exec pprint(rules)
((Q I -> (I 4))
 (I I -> (Q 3) (I 2) (H 1))
 (I Q -> (Q 3))
 (Q Q -> (Q 2) (I 3))
 (* * -> (H 1) (Q 8) (I 9)))
```

If you have a large MIDI file you'd like to analyze using markov-create-rules, it is easiest to read the MIDI file into SAL using score-read-smf. Example 13.6.5 assumes a MIDI file named teribus.mid resides in the current directory. (If you are using the Nyquist IDE, the current directory is automatically set to the directory of the last file you loaded with the "load" button or menu item.)

Example 13.6.5: Using score-read-smf

```
set teribus = score-read-smf("teribus.mid")
```

We use the newly created score that has been named teribus (i.e. the score is bound to the variable teribus) in Example 13.6.6. The score-apply function iterates through the score and extracts pitches into the variable pitches. It is important that the applied function return an event, so notice the extract-pitch function returns a list that simply reconstructs the event from the time, dur, and expr parameters. The *purpose* of calling score-apply is not to construct a score, but to accumulate pitches, accomplished using the @= operator. Since pitches are accumulated by pushing them onto the front of a list, the final value of the list has pitches in reverse order. Furthermore, MIDI program changes are encoded into scores with a pitch: attribute of nil, causing some occurrences of nil in pitches. The third expression in the example reverses pitches and removes nil's from the list. Finally, markov-create-rules is used to generate rules.

Example 13.6.6: markov-create-rules.sal, creating a Markov model from MIDI data

```
SAL> define variable pitches = nil
SAL> define function extract-pitch(
                                 time, dur, expr)
         begin
           set pitches @=
               expr-get-attr(expr, keyword(pitch))
           return list(time, dur, expr)
         end
SAL> exec score-apply(teribus,
                       quote(extract-pitch))
SAL> set pitches =
         remove(nil, reverse(pitches))
SAL> set rules = markov-create-rules(pitches,
                                      1, t)
SAL> exec pprint(rules)
((45 -> (33 1))
 (33 -> (57 1))
 (57 -> (55 10) (69 1))
 (55 -> (62 13) (69 3))
 (62 -> (61 18) (64 14) (67 18) (57 1) (55 3))
 (61 -> (62 18) (64 8))
 (64 -> (57 9) (67 9) (66 8) (62 8) (69 4))
 (67 -> (66 46) (64 8) (61 8) (62 4) (69 5))
 (66 -> (67 38) (69 8) (62 12) (64 8))
 (69 -> (66 12) (67 6) (55 3))
 (* -> (69 21) (66 66) (67 71) (64 38) (61 26)
       (62 55) (55 16) (57 11) (33 1)))
```

Notice that pitches are all numeric rather than symbolic. The file teribus.mid is intended to sound like bagpipes, and includes drones at A1 (= 33) and A2 (= 45). Since these are not part of the melody, it would make sense to remove these from pitches before computing rules, although in this case, there are no transitions to these states from any of the states from 55 to 69.

13.7 1/f² Noise or Brownian Motion

Brownian motion is the observed movement of small particles randomly bombarded by the molecules of the surrounding medium. The phenomenon was first observed by the biologist Robert Brown and was eventually explained by Albert Einstein. Brownian motion is also referred to as 1/f² noise.

Brownian motion in one dimension can be described by applying a random process to a succession of events in relation to a number line. Consider a seven-sided die that has values of $-3, -2, -1, 0, 1, 2,$ and 3. After tossing the die eight times, we derive a number series

$$-2, -3, +2, +2, +1, +2, -2, -2$$

That number series may be mapped to a number line to describe one-dimensional motion along the number line. Our number line is as follows:

If we assume a starting value of 60, the following number series is returned:

$$60, 58, 55, 57, 59, 60, 62, 60, 58$$
$$60 - 2 = 58$$
$$58 - 3 = 55$$
$$55 + 2 = 57$$
$$57 + 2 = 59$$
$$59 + 1 = 60$$
$$60 + 2 = 62$$
$$62 - 2 = 60$$
$$60 - 2 = 58$$

Example 13.7.1 implements this algorithm for one-dimensional Brownian motion. The SAL function brownian-motion accepts two inputs: the starting position and how many steps it should simulate. We enter a loop, initializing roll-die to a random pattern and the-list to nil. The repeat clause controls how many times the loop iterates, and each time, the for clause chooses a new value for note. The note values are cons'ed onto the head of the-list, and when the loop finishes, the-list is reverse'd and return'ed.

Since Example 13.7.1 is essentially just summing a sequence of numbers, we can use an accumulate pattern generator instead. In

Example 13.7.2, we use a line pattern generator to prefix a random number pattern with the value of start. (Recall that the line pattern returns each item of a list, repeating the last item as necessary.) A running total of these items is returned by the accumulate pattern.

Example 13.7.1: brownian-motion.sal

```
define function brownian-motion(start,
                                number-of-notes)
  loop
    with roll-die = make-random(
                      {-3 -2 -1 0 1 2 3}),
         the-list
    repeat number-of-notes
    for note = start then note + next(roll-die)
    set the-list @= note
    finally return reverse(the-list)
  end
```

Recall that patterns can return a stream of individual items, accessed one-at-a-time by calling next on the pattern object alone. Patterns can also return items grouped in lists called *periods*. The next period is obtained by calling next with a second, optional parameter equal to true (#t). Since we want a list of length number-of-notes, we use the for: keyword parameter to force the outermost pattern to return a period of length number-of-notes, and we access the period by calling next with a second parameter of #t. This programming "trick" eliminates the need to write a loop to accumulate a list of items from the pattern.

Example 13.7.2: brownian-motion-2.sal

```
define function brownian-motion(start,
                                number-of-notes)
  begin
    with pat =
      make-accumulate(
        make-line(list(start,
                       make-random(
                         {-3 -2 -1 0 1 2 3})))),
        for: number-of-notes)
    return next(pat, #t)
  end
```

We can combine this pattern approach with score-gen to create Brownian motion–based music, as illustrated by Example 13.7.3, which also shows the generated score.

Example 13.7.3: brownian-music.sal

```
SAL> begin
        with pitch-pat =
          make-accumulate(
            make-line(list(60,
                           make-random(
                           {-3 -2 -1 0 1 2 3})))))
        exec score-gen(
                  save: quote(brownian-music),
                  score-len: 10,
                  pitch: next(pitch-pat),
                  vel: 100, ioi: 0.2)
        end
SAL> exec score-print(brownian-music)
((0   0   (SCORE-BEGIN-END 0 2))
(0   0.2 (NOTE vel: 100 pitch: 60))
(0.2 0.2 (NOTE vel: 100 pitch: 63))
(0.4 0.2 (NOTE vel: 100 pitch: 61))
(0.6 0.2 (NOTE vel: 100 pitch: 61))
(0.8 0.2 (NOTE vel: 100 pitch: 59))
(1   0.2 (NOTE vel: 100 pitch: 58))
(1.2 0.2 (NOTE vel: 100 pitch: 59))
(1.4 0.2 (NOTE vel: 100 pitch: 61))
(1.6 0.2 (NOTE vel: 100 pitch: 64))
(1.8 0.2 (NOTE vel: 100 pitch: 61))
)
```

13.8 1/f Noise

A special class of noise called 1/f Noise has been discovered in many natural phenomena including rainfall patterns and sunspot activity. Oddly enough, the 1/f relationship has been found by analyzing recordings of non-random music in various styles (Voss, 1978). Number series generated using a 1/f formula correlate logarithmically with past values (Dodge, 1986). Because of this property, 1/f noise seems to have a memory for past values, conceptually similar to what we've seen with Markov processes. This property can be used to realize music that has highly-correlated attributes.

Richard F. Voss developed a simple algorithm to simulate 1/f noise (Gardner, 1986). His algorithm uses three six-sided dice: one red, one green, and one blue. The sum of the three dice ranges in value from 3 to 18 returning 16 possible values. These 16 values may be mapped to any 16 adjacent notes or any 16 musical parameters.

Voss uses a table similar to that found in Table 13.8.1 to create 1/f music. The numbers 0 through 7, base 10, are located in the leftmost column. The three-digit binary equivalent of the decimal value is found in the rightmost three columns. Each binary position is associated with a die color noted in the column heading.

The algorithm commences by rolling all three dice returning a value between 3 and 18. This initial action corresponds to Row 0 in the table. When comparing Row 0 to Row 1, we note that only the red value changes (from 0 to 1). Our corresponding action is to pick up the red die and throw it, calculating a new sum for the three dice. The new sum is used to select the next note of the composition. We are ready to generate a new note, so we compare Row 1 with Row 2 and find that both the green and red values change. Our corresponding action is to pick up the red and green dice and throw them. The dice are summed and the new sum corresponds to another new note. This process is repeated until the prescribed number of notes is generated. If the end of the table is reached, the process continues back at the first row.

Table 13.8.1: Voss-inspired table for 1/f noise

	Blue	Green	Red
$0_{10} =$	0	0	0
$1_{10} =$	0	0	1
$2_{10} =$	0	1	0
$3_{10} =$	0	1	1
$4_{10} =$	1	0	0
$5_{10} =$	1	0	1
$6_{10} =$	1	1	0
$7_{10} =$	1	1	1

Example 13.8.1 is a SAL implementation of a slightly modified version of the algorithm by Voss. The principal modification is that Example 13.8.1 simulates three five-sided dice. Each die returns the values 0, 1, 2, 3, or 4. The sum of the three dice ranges from 0 to 12 that easily maps to an octave.

The SAL function 1-over-f accepts as input a number representing the number of events it should generate. A loop begins the iterative process by simulating the initial throw of the three dice represented by the variables blue, green, and red. The sum of the random process is assigned to the variable total that is cons'ed onto the-list. Upon subsequent iterations of the loop, we simulate the toss of die only if the variable counter has certain values that correspond to the entries in Table 13.8.1. Note that green changes when the count is divisible by 2 and blue changes when the count is divisible by 4, so these conditions are used to determine when to "roll" the green and blue dice. (For the divisibility test, we compare the *remainder* of division – using the % operator – to zero.)

Example 13.8.1: one-over-f.sal

```
define function 1-over-f(number)
  loop
    with the-list
    for counter from 0 below number
    for blue = random(5) then
                #?(counter % 4 = 0,
                   random(5), blue)
    for green = random(5) then
                #?(counter % 2 = 0,
                   random(5), green)
    for red = random(5)
    for total = blue + green + red
    set the-list @= total
    finally return the-list
  end
```

We can easily apply our function to generate a list of notes based on the 1/f algorithm. Example 13.8.2 creates a pattern generator by calling the SAL function 1-over-f inside a score generator. The note index, sg:count, indexes into the pitch list to obtain the pitch for each note.

Example 13.8.2: one-over-f-music.sal

```
begin
  with pitches = 1-over-f(10),
       dur-pattern = make-cycle(
                        list(q, q, i, i, q))
  exec score-gen(save: quote(1-over-f-music),
                 score-len: length(pitches),
                 pitch: 40 + nth(sg:count,
                                 pitches),
                 vel: 10,
                 ioi: 0.3 * next(dur-pattern))
end
```

13.9 Suggested Listening

Gloriette for John Cage for mechanical organ was composed by Heinrich Taube in 1993. The piece is a tribute to the composer John Cage, who died in 1992. As Heinrich Taube states, "In keeping with the late composer's interest in chance music, this work was composed using an algorithmic chance process in which the likelihood of the musical notes C-A-G-E being played gradually increases over the course of the work, the composer's name slowly emerges out of the harmonic background of G dorian" (Taube, 1993).

Entropy for computer-controlled piano by Christopher Dobrian (Dobrian, 1991) explores the perception of randomness and order (entropy and negentropy) in musical structure, and demonstrates the use of stochastic methods not only as a model for the distribution of sounds in time, but also as a method for variation of a harmonic "order." The composing algorithm takes as its input a description of some beginning and ending characteristics of a musical phrase, and outputs the note information necessary to realize a continuous transformation from the beginning to the ending state. The algorithm composes melodic phrases of any length by calculating arrays of instantaneous probabilities, and incrementing toward the ending point and repeating the process.

13.10 Suggested Reading

The chapter "Xmusic and Algorithmic Composition" in *The Nyquist Reference Manual* discusses pattern generators, score generation, and score manipulation functions in great detail. The section "Random Number Generators" discusses a variety of functions that generate random numbers with different probability distributions.

Karlheinz Essl's tribute to Anton Webern is based on a twelve-tone row from Webern's last work. Essl then uses the tone row as the basis for an algorithm that randomly generates carillon chimes in real time (http://www.essl.at/works/webernuhrwerk/download.html).

Chapter 14 Hierarchical and Recursive Musical Structure

Most programs are hierarchical. We have already seen many examples of nested expressions and function calls. Complex programming problems should always be decomposed hierarchically into understandable units that can be implemented as functions. Music is often hierarchical. We can decompose traditional music into movements, sections, voices, phrases, chords, and notes. Musical structures can be reflected in software structures of algorithmic compositions. In this chapter, we look at some of the issues of moving from "flat" musical structures to hierarchical and recursive ones.

14.1 Structure from Nested Patterns

Pattern generators can be nested hierarchically to create interesting musical structure. In this section, we present a very simple rhythm generator based on nested patterns. Rhythmic patterns can be perceived only if there is repetition involved. Interestingly, almost any rhythmic pattern becomes interesting (or at least salient) when it is repeated. Thus, to make a rhythmic pattern, we only need to create a sequence of rhythmic intervals and then repeat them.

An interesting way to generate a rhythmic pattern is to divide a time span into equal intervals and flip a coin to decide whether each interval will contain a sound or not. We can model this as a simple random pattern: make-random({#t #f}). Example 14.1.1 uses make-random with a for: to keyword parameter to make a rhythmic pattern of length 12.

Example 14.1.1: Rhythmic pattern generation

```
SAL> set rp = make-random({#t #f}, for: 12)
SAL> print next(rp, #t)
{#f #t #t #f #f #f #t #f #f #t #t #f}
```

If we were to play this pattern once, it would not really sound like a pattern since every element is random. However, if we use make-copier to repeat periods, they become recognizable and suddenly sound very rhythmic. Example 14.1.2 uses make-copier to repeat each pattern twice, and a loop prints 6 periods of patterns.

Example 14.1.2: make-copier repeats patterns

```
SAL> set cp = make-copier(rp, repeat: 2)
SAL> loop repeat 6 print next(cp, t) end
{#t  #f  #f  #f  #f  #t  #f  #f  #t  #t  #f  #t}
{#t  #f  #f  #f  #f  #t  #f  #f  #t  #t  #f  #t}

{#t  #t  #t  #t  #t  #f  #f  #t  #f  #f  #f  #t}
{#t  #t  #t  #t  #t  #f  #f  #t  #f  #f  #f  #t}

{#f  #t  #t  #t  #f  #t  #f  #t  #t  #f  #f  #t}
{#f  #t  #t  #t  #f  #t  #f  #t  #t  #f  #f  #t}
```

In this example, a blank line was inserted manually between groups to illustrate that that the pattern changes every two periods of length 12. Using these ideas, we can make a random, rhythmic drum machine. We will use bass drum, snare, and cymbal samples (included in Nyquist), each with a different pattern. The patterns will be 8 time intervals each and the patterns will change every 4 repetitions.

In Example 14.1.3, one-drum generates a score for one of the drum sounds, using copies of periods as described above. The drummer function calls one-drum three times for the bass drum, snare, and cymbal scores, and merges them. The drum sounds themselves are loaded from files, e.g. kit/snare-1.wav contains a stereo snare drum sound. The drumsound function appends the file name to a path obtained from the global variable *plight-drum-path* and loads the file using s-read. The *plight-drum-path* is set by loading "../demos/plight/drum.lsp", which is part of the Nyquist software distribution.

Experiment with this program. There is no need to make all of the patterns the same length. Other sounds can be used. Try latin percussion sounds or record your voice. The patterns generated here tend to have "anchor points" where the listener feels a downbeat, but since all choices are random, these "anchor points" might not be at the beginning of the cycle. Think about what cues indicate the beginning of a repeating pattern. Modify the program to either generate patterns that seem to begin on the first beat, or rotate patterns generated by make-random so that a good candidate for the first beat is in the first-beat position.

Chapter 14 · Hierarchical and Recursive Musical Structure

Example 14.1.3: drummer.sal

```
load "../demos/plight/drum.lsp"

define function one-drum(
                name, beats, copies, phrases, ioi)
  begin
    with rp = make-random({#t #f}, for: beats),
         cp = make-copier(rp, repeat: copies),
         score
    return score-gen(
            name: name,
            score-len: beats * copies * phrases,
            pitch: #?(next(cp), 60, nil),
            vel: real-random(60, 120),
            ioi: ioi)
  end

define function drumsound(file, vel)
  return s-read(strcat(*plight-drum-path*, file)) *
         (vel / 120)

define function bd(vel: 100) ; bass drum
  return drumsound("kit/kick-1.wav", vel)
define function sn(vel: 100) ; snare
  return drumsound("kit/snare-1.wav", vel)
define function cy(vel: 100) ; cymbal
  return drumsound("kit/20-ride-1.wav", vel)

define function drummer(ioi, phrases)
  begin
    return timed-seq(score-merge(
            one-drum(quote(bd), 8, 4, phrases, ioi),
            one-drum(quote(sn), 8, 4, phrases, ioi),
            one-drum(quote(cy), 8, 4, phrases, ioi)))
  end

play drummer(0.15, 4)
```

14.2 Hierarchy in Scores

Here is a "toy" problem that illustrates both a conceptual approach to music composition and some programming solutions. The problem is, given a score, to harmonize C4 and E4 with a C major triad and harmonize D4 with a G7 chord. This is a "toy" problem in the sense that, while simple, it represents a whole class of programs where a score contains an abstract representation of the music. The score must somehow be "refined" into a more completely specified composition.

One simple approach is to use score-apply to transform notes. Recall that, by convention, the pitch: attribute of a score event can contain a number for a single note or a list of numbers for a chord. We can replace C4, D4, and E4 pitches with chords to achieve our goal, as shown in Example 14.2.1. In this example, score-apply uses add-harmony to check every note and replace pitches as described. The final score is saved in harm-out.

Example 14.2.1: harmonize.sal

```
; build a test score
begin
  with pitches =
        list(A3, B3, C4, D4, E4, F4, G4, A4),
      pitch-pattern = make-line(pitches)
  exec score-gen(save: quote(harm-in),
              score-len: length( pitches),
              pitch: next(pitch-pattern),
              vel: 100, ioi: 1)
end ;; global harm-in is now initialized

define function add-harmony(time, dur, expr)
  begin
    with pitch =
          expr-get-attr(expr, keyword(pitch))
    if member(pitch, list(c4, e4)) then
      return list(time, dur,
                expr-set-attr(expr, keyword(pitch),
                      list(pitch, c3, e3, g3)))
    else
      begin
        if pitch = d4 then
          return list(time, dur,
                expr-set-attr(expr, keyword(pitch),
                      list(d4, b2, d3, f3, g3)))
        else return list(time, dur, expr)
      end
  end

set harm-out = score-apply(harm-in,
                    quote(add-harmony))
```

While this technique is fairly simple, it can only be used to turn notes into chords. What if the new notes do not occur at the same time? One approach is based on the fact that to play a score, SAL evaluates expressions. We can change the name of the function from note (the default) to a custom function that generates multiple notes. This is illustrated in Example 14.2.2. The first step is to use score-voice to change the score events to call harmonize instead of note. score-voice takes a score and a list of substitutions. Here, there is just one substitution: a list that specifies a change from note to harmonize. The next step is to define harmonize to synthesize chords where appropriate. We will learn more about using Nyquist to define new synthesis methods later, but the code for harmonize should be fairly readable based on your knowledge of SAL and the embedded comments.

Example 14.2.2: harmonize-2.sal

```
set harm-out = score-voice(harm-in,
                           {{note harmonize}})

define function harmonize(pitch: 60, vel: 100)
  begin
    if member(pitch, list(c4, e4)) then
      return sum(
        ; synthesize and mix the sounds
        ; use @ to delay entrances of sounds,
        ; creating a C-major arpeggio
        note(pitch: c3, vel: vel) @ 0,
        note(pitch: e3, vel: vel) @ 0.05,
        note(pitch: g3, vel: vel) @ 0.1,
        note(pitch: pitch, vel: vel) @ 0.15)
    else
      begin
        if pitch = d4 then
          return sum(
            note(pitch: b2, vel: vel) @ 0,
            note(pitch: d3, vel: vel) @ 0.05,
            note(pitch: f3, vel: vel) @ 0.1,
            note(pitch: g3, vel: vel) @ 0.15,
            note(pitch: pitch, vel: vel) @ 0.2)
        else
          return note(pitch: pitch, vel: vel)
      end
  end

exec score-play(harm-out)
```

Notice that this example does not create a new score; it only expands the score into arpeggiated chords when the score is played. If you save the score to a MIDI file and play it, for example, you will not hear the chords because they are not explicitly represented. This may be a feature (you can avoid clutter in the score; you can experiment with different renderings of chords without changing the score) or a problem (you cannot see or edit the details in a MIDI editor; you cannot transpose the chords using score operations).

Now, let our goal be to generate a new score where the harmony is represented as new notes. For this task, we will use score-apply to iterate over the events in the score. Each event will be handled by appending notes to a list, forming a new score

Example 14.2.3 begins by initializing harm-out to nil. This is the list that will contain the new score. Next, add-note is defined to provide a convenient way to add a note to harm-out. Most of the work is done by harmonize, a function that takes a time, duration, and expression. It extracts the pitch: and vel: attributes from the expression and tests the pitch for the three cases: the note can be harmonized with a C-major triad, a G7 chord, or just played as is. The appropriate notes are added to the score using add-note. score-apply iterates over the input score, harm-in, applying the harmonize function to each note. harmonize returns well-formed events as expected by score-apply. However, the value returned by score-apply is ignored. The real value of interest is harm-out, which has accumulated all the original notes plus the chord notes. To finish the processing, harm-out is sorted into time order.

Notice in this example that the arpeggios *precede* the note they harmonize. One of the advantages of working with scores is that time can "run backwards," allowing notes to cause events to occur earlier as well as later. This is not possible using synthesis methods as in Example 14.2.2 (although one could delay everything *but* the arpeggios to achieve a similar effect).

Example 14.2.3 hints at a more general method of creating scores. While it is often convenient to use score-gen, which is basically a loop, to construct scores, it is also possible to construct scores explicitly and directly from list functions. In this example, there was really no need to construct the harm-in score. We could have more easily just called harmonize from a loop, as shown in Example 14.2.4.

Chapter 14 · Hierarchical and Recursive Musical Structure

Example 14.2.3: harmonize-3.sal

```
set harm-out = nil ;; new score to accumulate events

define function add-note(time, dur, pitch, vel)
  begin
    set harm-out @= list(time, dur,
                         list(quote(note),
                              keyword(pitch), pitch,
                              keyword(vel), vel))
  end

define function harmonize(time, dur, expr)
  begin
    with pitch = expr-get-attr(
                           expr, keyword(pitch), 60),
         vel = expr-get-attr(expr, keyword(vel), 100)
    if member(pitch, list(c4, e4)) then
      begin
        exec add-note(time - 0.15, dur, c3, vel)
        exec add-note(time - 0.10, dur, e3, vel)
        exec add-note(time - 0.05, dur, g3, vel)
        exec add-note(time, dur, pitch, vel)
      end
    else
      begin
        if pitch = d4 then
          begin
            exec add-note(time - 0.20, dur, b2, vel)
            exec add-note(time - 0.15, dur, d3, vel)
            exec add-note(time - 0.10, dur, f3, vel)
            exec add-note(time - 0.05, dur, g3, vel)
            exec add-note(time, dur, pitch, vel)
          end
        else
          exec add-note(time, dur, pitch, vel)
      end
    return list(time, dur, expr)
  end

exec score-apply(harm-in, quote(harmonize))
set harm-out = score-sort(harm-out)
```

Example 14.2.4 uses loop to iterate through the list of pitches, calling harmonize once for each one. The loop also increments the time variable so that notes are arranged sequentially in time.

Example 14.2.4: harmonize-4.sal

```
define variable harm-out ;; new score
; assume add-note is defined (Example 14.2.3)
; assume harmonize is defined (Example 14.2.3)
loop
  for p in list(A3, B3, C4, D4, E4, F4, G4, A4)
  for time from 0
  exec harmonize(time, 1,
                  list(quote(note),
                       keyword(pitch), p,
                       keyword(vel), 100))
  finally set harm-out = score-sort(harm-out)
end
```

14.3   Encapsulation

Encapsulation is the act of placing one thing inside another. In programming, encapsulation means to place the details of a computation or data inside a function, effectively "hiding" them from other parts of the program. This separation of concerns is critical when programs start to become large and complicated. Ideally, programs should be modular, allowing sections to be modified or replaced without impacting the whole program. In contrast, without encapsulation, a small program change can have consequences throughout the program. This would make the program difficult to understand, debug, and modify.

To illustrate encapsulation, we will write a function that generates a sequence of notes with a given start time, tempo, and transposition. The function, named notes, is shown in Example 14.3.1. Following the definition of notes, a loop is used to call notes many times with increasing times, tempi, and transpositions, creating a cascade of sequences.

Previously, our scores generated with score-gen started at zero, but notice here that score-gen is nested inside a call to score-shift that shifts the score in time by the value of the time parameter. The tempo parameter is really a time scale factor that is multiplied by the durations. The expression exp(i / −6.0) calculates the tempo parameters, which get exponentially smaller as i increases. Thus, the tempo increases each time by a small factor. Notice also how the scores returned by notes are accumulated into the variable *score*. You can play the result by calling exec score-play(*score*).

Example 14.3.1: encapsulation.sal

```
define variable *score*
define function notes(start, tempo, transpose)
  begin
    with pitch-pat =
           make-heap(list(C4, D4, DS4, F4, FS4,
                          GS4, A4, B4, C5)),
         dur-pat =
           make-heap(list(s, s, s, sd, sd, sd,
                          i, i, id, id, qd))
    return score-shift(
             score-gen(score-len: 9,
               pitch: transpose + next(pitch-pat),
               ioi: tempo * next(dur-pat)),
             start)
  end

set *score* = nil
loop
  for i from 0 below 6
  set *score* =
        score-merge(*score*,
          notes(2 * i, exp(i / -6.0), i * 5))
end
```

Experiment with this program. Try using make-cycle instead of make-heap for pitch-pat. Modify the program so that new instances of notes enter closer together in time. Modify the program so that there is less change in tempo with each instance of notes. Decide what you think would make the music sound more interesting, design changes to achieve your goal, implement the changes, and test the results.

Example 14.3.2 is inspired by a fractal called the Sierpinski triangle and based on a musical version by Rick Taube. This example demonstrates recursive encapsulation in the creation of a musical fractal. The music is constructed in layers. The first layer is just a single note. The second layer consists of three notes that span the duration of the note in the first layer, and these notes are transposed by 0, 11, and 6 semitones. The third layer takes each of the second layer notes, divides the duration by 3, and transposes by 0, 11, and 6 semitones. Each additional layer continues to subdivide and transpose notes of the previous layer.

To implement this algorithm, we encapsulate the operation of subdividing and transposing using a function. The function calls itself recursively to realize successive layers.

Example 14.3.2: sierpinski.sal

```
define function sierpinski(dur, pitch, layer, tim)
  begin
    with score =
           list(list(tim, dur,
                     list(quote(note),
                          keyword(pitch), pitch,
                          keyword(vel), 100))),
         transpose-pat
    if layer > 1 then
      begin
        set transpose-pat = make-cycle({0 11 6})
        set dur = dur / 3.0
        loop
          for i from 0 below 3
            set score =
                score-merge(score,
                  sierpinski(dur,
                      pitch + next(transpose-pat),
                      layer - 1, tim + i * dur))
      end
    end
    return score
  end

exec score-play(sierpinski(20, c1, 6, 0))
```

14.4   Compositional Environments

Quite often, the output of an algorithm does not result in the creation of an entire composition. Higher-level compositional environments such as MIDI sequencers or multi-track digital audio workstations may be used to edit, process, or assemble the output of your algorithms. Post processing of the output of compositional algorithms implies that these algorithms themselves are a part of a whole. For this reason, the composer must carefully think about the formal structure of a composition and how the output of an algorithm relates to the composition as a whole.

Algorithms that output MIDI data may be positioned onto the tracks of a MIDI sequencer. By positioning the data in a time-domain representation, the composer can readily experiment with the placement of events in time and the density of those events. A MIDI sequencer allows for graphical editing of MIDI data so small changes to the output of an algorithm are simplified.

Figure 14.4.1 shows an example of the output of two algorithms positioned in the time-domain representation of a MIDI sequencer.

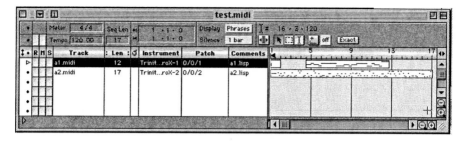

Figure 14.4.1: A MIDI sequencer display

Because SAL can output MIDI data from scores (using score-write-smf) as well as audio (using score-play), the composer may wish to assemble a composition using a digital audio workstation that works with both MIDI and audio. Similar to Figure 14.4.1, the user-interface of a digital audio workstation generally uses a time-domain representation of audio and MIDI allowing the composer great freedom in the organization of musical events.

14.5 Suggested Listening

The second movement of *American Miniatures* by David A. Jaffe uses a drum pattern derived from Congolese music, combined with an algorithmic drum improvisation. The latter was done by systematically performing random perturbations on the drum pattern, with the perturbations becoming denser and denser, along with an increase in tempo. The output of this program, written in Common Music, was a Music Kit scorefile that was used to drive the Music Kit "mixsounds" program. Each "note" in the file was an individual drum sample (Jaffe, 1992).

Eulogy by Mary Simoni integrates processed speech and algorithmic processes to create a tribute commemorating the funeral Mass of her father. Csound was used to process the speech written and spoken by her siblings. Common Music was used to generate a recitative-like accompaniment to the processed speech. The composition was assembled using a MIDI sequencer that supports digital audio (Simoni, 1997).

Stelios Manousakis has written a thesis and music based on Lindenmayer Systems (or L-Systems), which use rules to recursively construct fractal-like shapes or sounds from the micro- to the macro-scale. (L-System music is conceptually similar in many ways to the Sierpinski triangle example in this chapter.) Some of Manousakis's music can be heard online at http://www.modularbrains.net/.

Chapter 15   Composing Sonic Microstructure and Macrostructure

Throughout the previous chapters, we have assumed that scores and notes form an interface between the world of the composer, who creates the scores and notes, and the world of the synthesizer, which turns note specifications into sounds. Common music practice, MIDI, and even most music synthesis languages promote this idea. In this chapter, however, we will dig below the note level to explore the possibilities of pattern generation and algorithmic composition at microscopic levels of sonic detail.

So far, we have relied upon built-in functions, especially note, in Nyquist to perform scores. We will have to learn more about Nyquist's synthesis capabilities in order to explore further. The next section contains a much-abbreviated introduction to Nyquist as a synthesis language.

After learning about sound synthesis in Nyquist, Section 15.2 presents a general function for sound synthesis using pattern generators for sound control, and Section 15.3 explains how to encapsulate synthesis algorithms so they can be invoked from a Nyquist score.

One of the most important elements of music is the evolution of various qualities over time. These include dynamics, tempo, pitch register, harmonic tension, and many others. One of the attractions of algorithmic composition is that one can specify high-level trends and trajectories, leaving the details to be worked out automatically. When the first results are not satisfying, one can modify the high-level specification rather than tediously rewriting many notes. Section 15.4 shows how you can use high-level controls to guide pattern generators.

Algorithmic composition is particularly interesting for work at the level in between traditional notes and traditional musical sound. It would be humanly impossible to perform sounds with elaborate "micro-structure," but computers allow us to approach the synthesis of tones with the same mindset we bring to composition. The GENDY programs by Xenakis and colleagues (1992) are influential and pioneering work. Sergio Luque surveys this work and expands the concept in his thesis (2006). *Microsound* by Curtis Roads (2004) explores "granular" sound, which refers to sounds and textures created by combining many short sound events, usually lasting from 10 to 100 ms.

15.1 Sound Synthesis in Nyquist

We have written programs that deal with numbers, lists, and symbols. Nyquist can also compute *sounds*. A sound in Nyquist is basically a function of time that returns a floating point number. Each sound has a starting time, ending time (they are not infinite), a sample rate, and some other properties. Nyquist has many functions that return or manipulate sounds. For example pluck(g4, 3.0) returns a plucked-string sound with pitch G4 and a duration of 3 seconds.

play is a special command that evaluates an expression and plays the resulting sound. Try evaluating play pluck(g4, 3.0). Typically, sounds are constructed by combining many of the built-in functions in Nyquist. In Example 15.1.1, we multiply our plucked string sound by a low-frequency sinusoid to make a fluttering effect. The "*" operator multiplies two sounds together. The lfo function takes two inputs—a frequency and a duration.

The play command prints some information as it works. The first line says that the sound is being saved to the file nyquist-temp.wav. If you want to keep a sound produced by Nyquist, a simple way is to just copy or rename this file so that Nyquist will not overwrite it with a new sound. The next line displays sample counts as the sound is computed and played. These numbers print about once for every second of sound. When the computation completes, play prints the total number of samples computed (132300) and some information about normalization. Normalization is the process of adjusting the overall sound level to avoid distortion. The last thing printed is the return value of play, which is the peak amplitude of the sound. If things are working normally, this should be about 0.9. Otherwise, you might want to consult the Nyquist manual about normalization options.

Example 15.1.1: A tone with rapid amplitude modulation

```
SAL> play pluck(g4, 3.0) * lfo(6, 3.0)
Saving sound file to ./nyquist-temp.wav
 44880   88740
total samples: 132300
AutoNorm: peak was 0.899999,
      peak after normalization was 0.9,
      new normalization factor is 1
0.899999
```

Figure 15.1.1 illustrates the output of pluck, the output of lfo, and the output of mult (the "*" operator) to give a better idea of what is going on in this computation. The figure shows only the first 1.5

seconds where the amplitude of pluck is relatively high. Notice how at each point in time, the *amplitude*, or height of the product signal, is the product of the amplitude of the signal returned by pluck and the amplitude of the signal returned by lfo. Thus, "*" performs ordinary multiplication, but at every point in time.

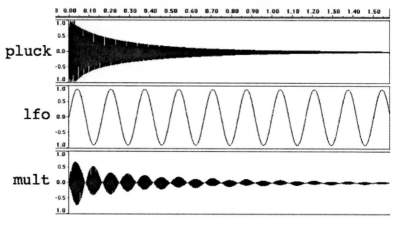

Figure 15.1.1: The intermediate results returned by pluck, lfo, and mult functions

Nyquist sounds can be "spliced" together in sequence using the seq form. seq takes any number of expressions as inputs, evaluates them sequentially, and returns a single sound. Example 15.1.2 illustrates how seq can be used to play a sequence of pluck sounds.

Example 15.1.2: Using seq

```
play seq(pluck(c4, 0.3), pluck(d4, 0.3),
         pluck(b4, 0.3), pluck(d5, 2))
```

Another very useful Nyquist function is pwl, short for "piece-wise linear." This function computes a sound based on a series of *breakpoints*, which give values of the sound at designated times. The value of the function is linearly interpolated between these values. pwl is not useful for describing audio directly; instead, it offers a general way to describe time-varying parameters.

pwl functions are implicitly 0 at time 0. The first two inputs are the time and value of the first breakpoint. The second two inputs are the time and value of the second breakpoint, and so on. The last breakpoint is specified by a time only—the value is implicitly zero. In Nyquist, you can use the s-plot function to display a graph of any sound, including the output of pwl functions. Figure 15.1.2 contains images of the plot output for two pwl functions used in Example 15.1.3. These plots have been annotated to show the connection between inputs and the result.

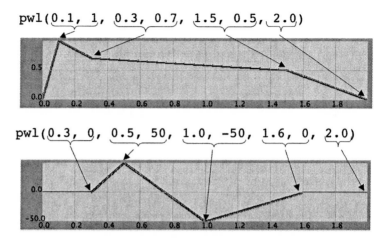

Figure 15.1.2: Graphs of two pwl control functions

Another way to create pwl functions is using the Nyquist IDE envelope editor. You can start this editor by clicking the EnvEdit button. Details can be found in the on-line Nyquist manual accessed using the Help menu. In this book, we will limit ourselves to text-based specifications of pwl functions which can be edited directly as parts of programs.

In Example 15.1.3, pwl functions control the amplitude and frequency of an oscillator implemented by fmosc. The output of fmosc is multiplied by the first pwl function to shape the overall amplitude. The fmosc function also takes two inputs that control frequency. The first is a base pitch specified as a MIDI pitch number. The second input (returned by the pwl function) is a sound that gives a frequency deviation in *Hertz* (oscillations per second). Listen to the sound while studying the graphs of the pwl control functions in Figure 15.1.2.

Example 15.1.3: Using pwl

```
play pwl(0.1, 1, 0.3, 0.7, 1.5, 0.5, 2.0) *
     fmosc(c4, pwl(0.3, 0, 0.5, 50, 1.0, -50,
                   1.6, 0, 2.0))
```

While these examples present only a small fraction of the functions and capabilities of Nyquist, they should at least introduce how

Nyquist performs sound synthesis: functions return sounds that serve as both audio signals and time-varying controls, these sounds are passed as inputs to other functions that perform further processing, and finally a resulting sound is passed to play, which saves the sound as a sound file and also plays it.

15.2 A Pattern-Driven Sound Generator

pwl is a very general function for control, but it can be very tedious to construct elaborate control functions. What would happen if we could construct pwl-like controls using pattern generators? This is not too difficult in Nyquist, but it requires some detailed knowledge of Nyquist functions. Rather than spend a chapter or two presenting all the required background knowledge, we will present two "ready-made" functions and refer the reader to the Nyquist documentation for the details. We will use these functions without further modification, so a detailed understanding of how they work will not be necessary.

The first function, pat-ctrl, constructs a control function (which is a Nyquist sound) from segments where the duration and amplitude of each segment are obtained from patterns. Consider the code and plot in Figure 15.2.1. There are two cycle patterns. The first is used to compute segment durations, which are 0.1, 0.2, 0.1, 0.2, ... The second computes the amplitude or height of the segments, which are 0, 1, 2, 0, 1, 2, ... Since any pattern generators can be passed to pat-ctrl, it becomes a very powerful control mechanism.

```
pat-ctrl(make-cycle({0.1 0.2}),  ;duration
         make-cycle({0 1 2}))     ;amplitude
```

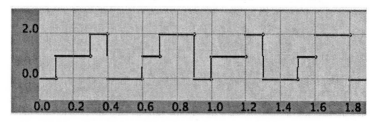

Figure 15.2.1: Output from pat-ctrl with simple patterns as input

The implementation of pat-ctrl is quite compact. The idea is to use the Nyquist seq form and to observe that the desired sound can be described recursively: "a pat-ctrl is the first segment followed by a pat-ctrl." The segment is generated using another Nyquist function, const, which takes, conveniently, a value and a duration as inputs. The definition is given in Example 15.2.1:

Example 15.2.1: pat-ctrl.sal

```
define function pat-ctrl(durpat, valpat)
  return seq(const(next(valpat), next(durpat)),
             pat-ctrl(durpat, valpat))
```

To use pat-ctrl, we need a way to turn a time-varying signal into sound. We could listen to pat-ctrl directly, but instead we will use it to control the frequency of an oscillator. To keep things simple, we will not control amplitude. Example 15.2.2 shows the implementation of pat-fm, which is based on the synthesis technique of frequency modulation, or FM. The overall pitch is controlled by the pitch input which is added to the pitch offsets returned by valpat. The overall duration of pat-fm is controlled by the dur input which is used to construct a pwl amplitude control for hzosc.

Example 15.2.2: pat-fm.sal

```
define function pat-fm(
                    durpat, valpat, pitch, dur)
  begin
    with hz = step-to-hz(
                    pitch + pat-ctrl(durpat, valpat))
    return pwl(0.01, 1, dur - 0.1, 1, dur) *
           hzosc(hz + 4.0 * hz * hzosc(hz))
  end
```

The best way to understand pat-fm is with simple examples. Example 15.2.3 uses pat-fm and a cycle pattern generator to play a C-major scale. The duration pattern input is just 0.2, so every "note" is 0.2 seconds long.

Example 15.2.3: pat-fm-scale.sal

```
play pat-fm(0.2,
            make-cycle({0 2 4 5 7 9 11 12}),
            c4, 4.8)
```

Now consider the slight variation in Example 15.2.4, where the duration pattern produces a random stream of very small durations (from 2 to 4 milliseconds). In this example, the "notes" or pitch offsets are so short, they blend to form a timbre rather than distinct pitches.

Example 15.2.4: pat-fm-fast.sal

```
play pat-fm(make-random({0.002 0.004 0.006}),
            make-cycle({0 2 4 5 7 9 11 12}),
            c4, 4.8)
```

Continuing to experiment, we can make very elaborate patterns, still producing very short durations. The resulting sounds blur the distinction between timbre and melody. Example 15.2.5 illustrates this approach, and endless variations of this example can be created by changing input values.

Example 15.2.5: pat-fm-complex.sal

```
set durpat =
        make-product(
          make-copier(
            make-random({0.005 0.01 0.02 0.0025},
                        for: 1),
            repeat: 10),
          1.0)

set valpat =
        make-sum(
          make-copier( ; long-term changes
            make-accumulate(
              make-random(
                {-4 0 1 2 3 {-24 weight: 0.06}}),
                for: 1, min: -20, :max 20),
            repeat: make-product(
                    make-random({1 2 3}),
                    20)),
          ; short-term changes for make-sum:
          make-heap({0 3 5 6 7 9}))

play pat-fm(durpat, valpat, c4, 40)
```

The durations are controlled by durpat. The outermost pattern is a product of a copier pattern and a number (1.0). This makes it easy to scale all durations, just by changing one number. The copier pattern makes 10 copies (using the repeat: keyword parameter) of each period returned by the random pattern. Since the default is to return periods of 4 random numbers, the for: input of make-random is set to 1 so that each period contains just one random number. Thus the output might be .01 .01 .01 .01 .01 .01 .01 .01 .01 .01 .02 .02 .02 .02 .02 .02 .02 .02 .02 .02 followed by more random numbers in groups of 10.

The pitch offsets are controlled by valpat, which is the sum of a complex pattern and a heap pattern. The heap chooses items from the

Chapter 15 · Composing Sonic Microstructure and Macrostructure set {0, 3, 5, 6, 7, 9}. If this set were used alone, the output would be a turbulent sound concentrated in a narrow pitch range of 9 semitones. To give more variation over time, the first input to make-sum (labeled with the comment "long-term changes") produces a relatively slowly varying pitch offset that is added to the heap pattern. To make this offset vary slowly, make-copier is used to copy every value for 10, 20, or 30 times using the repeat: keyword. Although we could just say repeat: 20 to consistently repeat everything 20 times, the code selects a repeat count randomly from the list {1 2 3}, and multiplies it by 20. Thus, you can change one number (20) to get more or fewer repetitions, and you can change the list {1 2 3} to get more or less variation in the repetition counts. The long-term offsets are computed by make-accumulate, which effectively produces a random walk by summing integers returned by make-random. Most of the choices for make-random are small offsets (−4, 0, 1, 2, and 3), but there is also a jump of −24 with a very small weight. The idea is that the long-term pitch offset tends to drift upward over time in small steps, with an occasional retreat when −4 is chosen. However, the long-term offset will occasionally jump downward by two octaves (−24 semitones). You can hear these events quite clearly in the audio output. To prevent the accumulate pattern from getting too high or too low, output values are restricted using min: and max: keywords.

You should experiment with Example 15.2.5 by changing numbers to hear their effect. Take out the max: and min: restrictions on make-accumulate to hear what happens when the pitch is allowed to drift randomly without limit. Adjust the overall durations to be much shorter and much longer, and listen to the results. Even when pitches last only milliseconds, the offsets labeled "short-term changes" have an effect. Try a whole-tone scale {0 2 4 6 8 10}, octaves {0 12 24}, a major triad {0 4 7}, and other pitch sets and listen for the differences.

15.3 Nyquist Sounds and Scores

The previous example suggests that elaborate patterns could be used to specify entire compositions. While this is true, it might become very tedious. It might make more sense to write scores to determine structure at a higher level. If desired, scores might even be created using patterns and other compositional algorithms. In either case, it is necessary to invoke instances of functions such as pat-fm from a score. That is the topic of this section.

Scores contain expressions that are evaluated by XLISP. These expressions must satisfy three properties:

1. The expression must return a sound.
2. The expression must be a function call with only keyword parameters.
3. The expression must synthesize sound according to the Nyquist environment that specifies when a sound should start and how long it should last.

pat-fm satisfies only the first requirement, so we will write a new function that satisfies all three properties and calls pat-fm to do the actual work. Notice that even though the sound expression is evaluated by XLISP and uses Lisp syntax, the expression can call a function written in SAL, so we can continue working with SAL.

Since we are writing a new function, we can decide what input parameters to use. There are no right or wrong choices, but obviously you should choose parameters that change from one instance to the next in the score, and you need not bother making parameters for values that always remain the same. We will control pat-fm with the following parameters:

- grain-dur: – the relative duration of the "notes" within a sound. This will be a scale factor with a nominal value of 1.
- spread: – the maximum amount of the long-term pitch deviation above and below the base frequency, nominally 20.
- pitch: – the base frequency for both long-term and short-term deviations, nominally 60.
- fixed-dur: – if true, all durations are the same. If false, durations are picked at random and repeated 10 times as in Example 15.2.5.
- vel: – an overall loudness control, nominally 100.

Example 15.3.1 presents a new function, pat-fm-note that can be called from a score. Notice that all parameters are declared as keyword parameters. durpat and valpat are now declared locally in a with clause. This is important in case there is more than one copy of pat-fm-note invoked from a score—each will have its own local copy of durpat and valpat. grain-dur becomes the multiplier in make-product to scale durations. fixed-dur is used to select a list of durations for make-random—either (0.01), where 0.01 is the only choice, or {0.005 0.01 0.02 0.0025}, where there are 4 choices. The spread and pitch inputs are passed to pat-fm. The vel input is used to scale the output of pat-fm.

The third requirement of a score expression is that it follows the time and duration specified in the Nyquist environment, which is a set of implicit parameters to every sound synthesis function that controls time, duration, and other properties. In many cases, sound synthesis functions automatically use these parameters and "do the right thing," but in this case, we need to add some explicit control. First, pat-fm is embedded in a stretch-abs form – this "turns off" any implicit time stretching within the execution of pat-fm, which has its own duration control. Second, in the with, we capture the requested duration by calling get-duration(1.0). The result is saved in duration and passed on to pat-fm. Details of the Nyquist environment and transformations are covered in the Nyquist documentation.

Example 15.3.1: pat-fm-note.sal

```
define function pat-fm-note(grain-dur: 1.0,
                spread: 20, pitch: c4,
                fixed-dur: nil, vel: 100)
  begin
    with durpat =
          make-product(
            make-copier(
              make-random(
                #?(fixed-dur, {0.01},
                   {0.005 0.01 0.02 0.0025}),
                for: 1),
              repeat: 10),
            grain-dur),
         valpat =
           make-sum(
             make-copier( ; long-term changes
               make-accumulate(
                 make-random(
                   {-4 0 1 2 3 {-24 :weight 0.06}}),
                 for: 1, min: - spread, max: spread),
               repeat: make-product(
                       make-random({1 2 3}), 20)),
             ; short-term changes for make-sum
             make-heap({0 3 5 6 7 9})),
         duration = get-duration(1.0)
      return stretch-abs(1.0,
               vel * 0.01 * pat-fm(durpat, valpat,
                               pitch, duration))
  end
```

Now we are ready to call pat-fm-note from a score. Example 15.3.2 uses an entirely hand-written score to invoke four instances of pat-fm-note that overlap in time. Each instance but the last is generally higher in pitch and has shorter grain durations than the one before.

Notice that this score is constructed using braces, which implicitly quote the list elements. This is one case where using keywords (e.g. grain-dur:) as symbols is allowed. SAL translates them automatically into the Lisp form with a preceding colon (e.g. :grain-dur), which is just what we need here. It might be surprising that we can use pitch symbols (e.g. c3). Recall that these are global variables that normally contain MIDI pitch numbers, e.g. c3 is 48. The reason we can pass the *symbol* c3 after the pitch: keyword rather than the *value* of c3 is that the entire sound expression will be evaluated by XLISP to produce a sound. At that time, c3 will be evaluated to obtain 48, and this numerical value will be passed to pat-fm-note. As always, numbers evaluate to themselves, so numerical inputs are unaltered by evaluation.

Example 15.3.2: pat-fm-score.sal

```
exec score-play(
   {{ 0 30 {pat-fm-note grain-dur: 8 spread: 1
                        pitch: c3 fixed-dur: t
                        vel: 50}}
    {10 20 {pat-fm-note grain-dur: 3 spread: 10
                        pitch: c4 vel: 75}}
    {15 18 {pat-fm-note grain-dur: 1 :spread: 20
                        pitch: c5}}
    {20 13 {pat-fm-note grain-dur: 1 spread: 10
                        grain-dur: 20 pitch: c1}}})
```

Another option is to generate scores using score-gen or other techniques, using algorithmic composition methods to arrange instances of pat-fm-note. Hint: use name: quote(pat-fm-note) in score-gen to invoke pat-fm-note (most of our previous examples omitted name: and used the default function name note).

15.4 Nyquist Sounds and Global Control Functions

Scores offer one way to specify high-level structure in music, but they have the limitation that every event in the score generates a new instance of some sound generator. What if the sound is supposed to evolve according to some continuously varying parameters? In this section, we will see how to make pat-fm track a pitch trajectory specified by a pwl function. We will also see how a pwl function can be used to guide pitch selection in score-gen.

In Example 15.2.5, we used a fairly elaborate pattern based on a random walk to create an overall pitch trajectory for pat-fm. In Example 15.4.1, the value of a pwl function is used instead. The variable pitch-contour holds this value, which is of type sound. Recall that sounds are just signals that can represent any value that changes over time. This sound is a slowly changing one created with pwl to represent a slowly varying base pitch. Figure 15.4.1 shows a graph of pitch-contour that was produced with the command exec s-plot(pitch-contour, 22, 1000). (The two optional inputs say to plot 22 seconds of the sound and to plot 1000 points – more than enough to get one point per pixel in the display. Without the duration (22), the plot will show only the beginning of the long signal.)

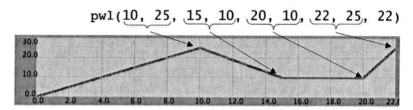

Figure 15.4.1: Plot of pitch-contour

Our goal is to incorporate values from pitch-contour into pattern generation; thus we need a way to access a sound at a particular time point to obtain a number. The built-in function sref accomplishes this task, and to simplify the code, we define a SAL function, get-pitch, that returns this value. sref takes two inputs: a sound to be accessed, and a time offset. Here, the time offset is zero because we want the *current* time. For anyone with programming experience, the notion of *current time* may seem unusual. Nyquist maintains a notion of time when it computes sounds, and we will soon see that get-pitch is called in the context of computing a sound, so get-pitch will automatically move through pitch-contour, producing a sequence of changing pitch values that follow the plan spelled out by the pwl breakpoints.

Example 15.4.1 shows the definition of pitch-contour and get-pitch and introduces a new type of pattern constructor. The make-eval pattern evaluates an expression whenever the pattern needs to generate a value. The expression must be a Lisp expression, not a SAL expression. Recall that sound expressions in scores are also Lisp expressions, so we have already seen how to write a function call: just put the function name (a symbol) as the first element of a list, and place any inputs in the list after the function name. In this case, there are no inputs, so the list contains only the function name. The expression to make the pattern is make-eval({get-pitch}). To test your understanding, explain the meaning of the following (incorrect) expressions: make-eval(get-pitch), make-eval(quote(get-pitch)), make-eval(list(get-pitch)). In Example 15.4.1, you can see that the "long term" pitch changes generated by a random walk in Example 15.2.5 are replaced by the make-eval pattern that accesses pitch-contour. You can hear the general pitch contour following the pwl function, rising by 25, falling to 10 and holding steady for 10 seconds, and finally rising back to 25.

Example 15.4.1: pwl-pat-fm.sal

```
define variable pitch-contour =
        pwl(10, 25, 15, 10, 20, 10, 22, 25, 22)
define function get-pitch()
   return sref(pitch-contour, 0)

define function pwl-pat-fm()
   begin
     with durpat =
            make-product(
              make-copier(
                make-random(
                  {0.005 0.01 0.02 0.0025},
                  for: 1),
                repeat: 10),
              1),
          valpat =
            make-sum(
              make-copier( ; long-term changes
                make-eval({get-pitch}),
                repeat: make-product(
                          make-random({1 2 3}), 20)),
              ; short-term changes for make-sum
              make-heap({0 3 5 6 7}))
     return pat-fm(durpat, valpat, c4, 22)
   end

play pwl-pat-fm()
```

In this example, pitch-contour functions as a score. More control functions can be added to govern the evolution of other parameters such as grain duration. Note how small changes to pitch-contour can make significant changes to this little composition. In the next section, we will see how Nyquist control functions can be used to guide score generation.

15.5 Scores and Global Control Functions

Composers often think in terms of overall melodic contour and other large-scale structures. Nyquist control functions, specified using pwl or other means, can guide the computation of note parameters within score-gen.

In Example 15.5.1, pitch is calculated by using sref to look up the current value of pitch-contour. The second input of sref is sg:start, the start time of the note. The observant reader may well ask: Why specify sg:start here when we specified 0 in Example 15.4.1? A full explanation is rather involved, but basically, the input is a relative offset from the *current time* of signal evaluation. In Example 15.4.1, sref is invoked during a signal computation, whereas Example 15.5.1 calls sref before computing any signals, so there the current time is always 0 and we need to offset this by sg:start.

Continuing with Example 15.5.1, the value returned by sref is added to c4. In addition, even-numbered notes are transposed down 5 semitones. Finally, truncate is applied to the pitch value to make it an integer. There is nothing that requires integer pitch numbers, and it is possible at this point to return whole tones, quarter tones, or even map the pitch to the nearest note in a diatonic scale.

In this example, the duration (dur:) of each note is slightly shorter than the inter-onset time (ioi:), and the velocity (vel:) is 100.

Example 15.5.1: pwl-score.sal

```
begin
  with pitch-contour = pwl(10, 25, 15, 10,
                           20, 10, 22, 25, 22),
       ioi-pattern = make-heap({0.2 0.3 0.4})
  exec score-gen(save: quote(pwl-score),
         score-dur: 22,
         pitch: truncate(
                  c4 +
                  sref(pitch-contour,
                       sg:start) +
                  #if(oddp(sg:count), 0, -5)),
         ioi: next(ioi-pattern),
         dur: sg:ioi - 0.1,
         vel: 100)
end
```

Listen to this example, and try some variations by editing the breakpoints that determine pitch-contour. Also, try taking out the truncate function.

15.6 Further Explorations

This chapter only scratches the surface of the possibilities of combining continuous functions and signal processing techniques with discrete event sequences and algorithmic composition techniques. We have seen how patterns and algorithmic composition techniques can control minute details of sound synthesis. We have also seen how signals (sounds) can control or direct large-scale musical forms. But these are just an introduction.

On the synthesis front, algorithmic composition can also be used to select digital audio effects, waveforms, and many other details of sound generation. Since Nyquist is a sound synthesis system as well as a composition system, it offers many ways to easily explore connections between algorithmic decision making and sound synthesis.

To control larger forms, the pwl function is just one way to compute a control function. Other functions, such as lfo (the low-frequency oscillator), can be used, and there are many opportunities for manipulating control functions with filters and other effects. The Nyquist IDE also includes a function editor that can be used to edit control functions using a graphical interface. Finally, it should be pointed out that Nyquist can extract control signals from audio data. Built-in functions such as rms for amplitude analysis, yin for pitch analysis, and snd-fft for spectral analysis offer a way to "recycle" music data and even non-music audio in interesting ways.

15.7 Suggested Listening

Iannis Xenakis used his GENDY-N program to create *S.709* (1992), an influential work where audio waveforms are constructed algorithmically. This piece is recorded on the CD titled *Electronic Music.*

Christopher Ariza factored form, ostinati, and texture into an algorithm where the user sets inputs such as hexachord, octave displacements, MIDI assignments, and more. The result is the composition *guido's windchime* (http://www.flexatone.net/cgi-bin/py/flexNet/software/flexatone.cgi?stateNext=1&id=guido&count=0).

Chapter 16 Extended Examples

One of the difficulties of writing about programming of any kind is that realistic examples are simply too big and full of uninteresting detail for ordinary reading. Consequently, we, as authors, try to distill examples down to their essential elements and hope the reader will understand how to apply these elements in larger, more realistic contexts. In this chapter, we will present "real" examples in the hope that seeing larger programs will help to clarify the *process* of algorithmic composition and prepare the reader to work beyond the "toy" examples seen so far.

The first program describes the development of a piece of music by Roger Dannenberg for the soundtrack of a multimedia science show on tissue engineering. The second program is based on the work of Edwin Shao, who developed algorithms for converting text to music as an undergraduate class project at Carnegie Mellon University.

16.1 Jellyfish Music Example

This is a personal account of a compositional process, so I will use the first person for my description. My task was to create the entire soundtrack for a multimedia show on tissue engineering that was designed for presentation in a planetarium. (Although planetaria are designed to project star fields and teach the public about astronomy, they are usually equipped with multiple image projectors, multichannel sound diffusion, and automated control, making them ideal for multimedia presentations of all kinds.) I will describe the music for one short scene that included beautiful images of jellyfish. There is a voice-over that runs throughout the scene, so one challenge was to coordinate the music with the voice, working with it rather than competing with it. I used algorithmic composition mainly so that I could adjust the structure, harmony, and durations without extensive rewriting. That way, if the music, voice, and images did not work well together, I could make changes rather easily.

This music was originally created in Nyquist before the pattern generator library (xm.lsp) was available. I have attempted to recreate the development process using the methods and software described in this book.

I began by improvising[1] at a synthesizer keyboard. I found a simple texture that sounded promising, created from a few note choices under each hand. I observed that I was mainly alternating left and right hands and avoiding note repetitions in either hand. For example, if the left hand played an F, it would typically be followed by a note in the right hand, and that would likely be followed by a note in the left hand that was *not* an F.

This led to a more formal description of a generative algorithm: Start with two sets of pitches named *lh* and *rh*. Construct a melody as a sequence of pitches, where each pitch is chosen as follows: First, select a set (either *lh* or *rh*). Favor the set that has been selected fewer times in the past. Next, select a pitch from the set. Do not choose the same pitch that was selected last time, and avoid pitches that have been selected recently.

This description is practically calling for pattern generators. Selecting a set (*lh* or *rh*) can be accomplished with weighted random selection, and pitch selection can use a heap pattern. Let's create a simple test and listen to the results:

Example 16.1.1: jellyfish-1.sal

```
define function j1(
        beatdur, notes, lh-heap, rh-heap, notedur)
    begin
    with lh-pat = make-heap(lh-heap, for: 1),
         rh-pat = make-heap(rh-heap, for: 1),
         p-pat = make-random(list(lh-pat,
                                      rh-pat))
        return score-gen(score-len: notes,
                    save: quote(j1-score),
                    dur: notedur, ioi: beatdur,
                    vel: real-random(70, 120),
                    pitch: next(p-pat))
    end

exec score-play(j1(0.35, 20, list(g3, ef4, f4),
            list(g4, bf4, c5, d5), 0.5))
```

Example 16.1.1 uses make-heap to select from left-hand and right-hand pitch sets, and make-random is used to select which hand will play the next pitch. Note that for: 1 is used with make-heap; otherwise, after make-random selected a hand, the hand pattern would be called to play all of its pitches before selecting the next

---

[1] Given my keyboard skills, "noodling" might be a better term.

hand to play. Using for: 1 tells the hands to play periods of length 1, so a new hand is selected after each pitch.

Listening to this example, the piano sound is rather bare. I spent a lot of time creating synthetic instruments for this music, and we will address some of the orchestration issues later. For now, the other problem is that this example does not fully meet the specification we started with. In particular, you might hear some repeated notes. This happens when the same hand is chosen twice in succession *and* the hand exhausts its set of pitches with the first note *and* after replenishing the set, the heap pattern happens to randomly choose the note that was played previously. It is not too likely, but it does happen.

The heap pattern offers an option (max: 1) to disallow repetitions like this, but the reality is that you will always run into situations where the desired behavior is not built in. Your choices are either to compromise or write programs to do what you want. I chose to add a little program complexity. This enabled me, in addition to eliminating repetitions, to weight the choice of hand based on how many times notes had been played by that hand. (I am not sure this part really matters, but this is how the music was conceived and implemented.)

The new solution uses heap patterns, but they are called explicitly so that I can throw out repeated notes. This makes it hard to use a random pattern to select the next hand that plays, so the weights and selection are also explicit in the code.

In Example 16.1.2, variables are defined to retain pattern generators (lh-pat and rh-pat), the number of pitches generated from each pattern (lh-cnt and rh-cnt), and the previous pitch generated from each pattern (lh-prev and rh-prev). Ideally, these should be declared in a begin-end block, making them local to one function, but in this case, the variables must retain their values between calls to select-pitch, so they must be globals. The select-pitch function uses lh-cnt and rh-cnt to make a weighted selection that favors the hand used the least so far. For example, if lh-cnt and rh-cnt are 3 and 4, respectively, then lhw and rhw will be 16 and 25, so lhw / (lhw + rhw) is about 0.39. The random number from rrandom() is between zero and one, so it has a 39% chance of picking the right hand and a 61% chance of picking the left hand.

Once a hand is picked, a loop generates pitches from the heap pattern (lh-pat or rh-pat) until the pitch does not match the previous pitch (lh-prev or rh-prev). This will take at most two iterations; then the selected pitch is returned.

Example 16.1.2: jellyfish-2.sal

```
define variable
    lh-heap = list(g3, ef4, f4),
    rh-heap = list(g4, bf4, c5, d5),
    lh-pat = make-heap(lh-heap, for: 1),
    rh-pat = make-heap(rh-heap, for: 1),
    lh-cnt = 0, ; how many previous lh?
    rh-cnt = 0, ; how many previous rh?
    lh-prev, rh-prev ; remember prev pitches
; choose left or right hand,
; generate non-duplicate pitch
define function select-pitch()
  begin
  with lhw = 1 + lh-cnt * lh-cnt,
       rhw = 1 + rh-cnt * rh-cnt ; weights
       ; favor the hand used the least so far
  if rrandom() > float(lhw) / (lhw + rhw)
  then
    begin ; use left hand
      set lh-cnt += 1 ; increment use count
      ; generate left-hand pitch until it's
      ; not a duplicate
      loop
        for pitch = next(lh-pat)
        while pitch = lh-prev
        finally
          begin ; remember selection
            set lh-prev = pitch
            return pitch
          end
      end
    end
  else ; use right hand
    begin ; just like the left-hand code
      set rh-cnt += 1 ; increment use count
      loop
        for pitch = next(rh-pat)
        while pitch = rh-prev
        finally
          begin ; remember the selection
            set rh-prev = pitch
            return pitch
          end
      end
    end
  end
```

```
define function j2(beatdur, notes, notedur)
  begin
    return score-gen(score-len: notes,
                     save: quote(j1-score),
                     dur: notedur, ioi: beatdur,
                     vel: real-random(70, 120),
                     pitch: select-pitch())
  end

exec score-play(j2(0.35, 20, 0.5))
```

The function j2 builds a score, calling select-pitch to generate each pitch. The composition so far seems boring after a short time, so I decided to change pitch sets. This part of the work is not algorithmic. I made a list of times where a change in harmony would complement the script. The scripted narration was already recorded when I started work, so I could write down exact times of phrases. Example 16.1.3 has my notes on timing and phrases from the script.

Example 16.1.3: Excerpt from jellyfish-3.sal

```
;; start at 251.5 "bones and a skeleton"
;; 263 "thank goodness simple fractures"
;; 269 "these are ancient drawings"
;; 280 "this simple form of engineering..."
;; 289 "what about this horribly ..."
;; 301 "remedy"
;; 305 "of course"
;; 312 "basically"
;; 319 "a scaffold"
;; 334 "make new bone?"
;; 344 "scientists"
;; 351 "...naturally." end
```

Based on these timings and the mood of the script, I composed pitch sets at the keyboard. These pitch sets became inputs to function calls that generated scores. The technical difficulty here is that the duration of each section does not necessarily span a whole number of notes, so I could not simply generate sections and splice them together. Instead, I needed a way to generate notes until *approximately* the desired time, then start generating the next section where the previous one left off. (An alternative method would be to work out all the times in terms of exact beats, but that would make it difficult to change tempos at a later time.) In this case, the problem determined the program structure. I would simply write a function that generates notes from the current time until approximately the desired end time. Then I would call this function many times with different input values to build the piece from beginning to end. This approach is similar to the one used in Example 14.3.1 (encapsulation.sal).

Example 16.1.4 is the result of this approach. The main function, j3, calls j-sect once for each section of music. j-sect is similar to j2 in Example 16.1.2 except that it stores the computed score in the local variable section and appends it to *score*. Thus, repeated calls to j-sect build a complete score.

One potential problem with this score is that, because independent sections are spliced together, the last note of one section could be repeated at the beginning of the next section. Fortunately, this never happens because the lh-prev and rh-prev variables remember the previous pitch across calls to j-sect. In other cases, the Nyquist function score-adjacent-events might be useful to do some local adjustments of pitches or other parameters (see Example 4.5.14).

Example 16.1.4: Code from jellyfish-3.sal

```
;; uses variable definitions and select-pitch
;; definition from Example 16.1.2
define function j-sect(
            start, dur, beatdur, lh-heap, rh-heap)
  begin
    with notes = (start + dur - *time*) / beatdur,
         section ; result score for this section
    ;; reset some variables used by select-pitch:
    set lh-pat = make-heap(lh-heap, for: 1)
    set rh-pat = make-heap(rh-heap, for: 1)
    set lh-cnt = 0 ; how many previous lh selections?
    set rh-cnt = 0 ; how many previous rh selections?
    set notes = 2 * round(notes / 2) ; even # of nts
    set section = score-gen(score-len: notes,
                        begin: *time*,
                        ioi: beatdur,
                        vel: real-random(70, 120),
                        pitch: select-pitch())
    ;; merge new notes with previous ones in *score*:
    set *score*  = score-merge(*score*, section)
    ;; update time so next section follows this one
    set *time* += notes * beatdur
  end


define variable *score* = nil, *time* = 251.5
```

```
define function j3()
  begin
    ;;              start  dur beatdur  lh-heap/rh-heap
    exec j-sect(251.5, 11.5, 0.44, {g3 ef4 f4},
                                   {g4 bf4 c5 d5})
    exec j-sect(263  ,  6 , 0.38, {f3 df4 ef4},
                                   {f4 af4 c5})
    exec j-sect(269  , 11 , 0.33, {fs3 ds4 e4},
                                   {g4 af4 df5})
    exec j-sect(280  ,  9 , 0.33, {bf2 af3},
                                   {d4 gf4 af4 bf4})
    exec j-sect(289  , 12 , 0.36, {ef3 c4 df4},
                                   {ef4 af4 bf4 df5})
    exec j-sect(301  ,  4 , 0.33, {f3 c4},
                                   {f4 g4 bf4 c4})
    exec j-sect(305  ,  7 , 0.33, {cs3 b3},
                                   {fs4 cs5 e5})
    exec j-sect(312  ,  7 , 0.33, {cs3 b3},
                                   {e4 fs4 b4} )
    exec j-sect(319  , 15 , 0.33, {bf3 af3},
                                   {ef4 f4 bf4 c5})
    exec j-sect(334  , 10 , 0.36, {ef3 af3 df4},
                                   {f4 af4 bf4 c5})
    exec j-sect(344  , 10 , 0.40, {bf3 f3 c4},
                                   {af4 bf4 f5 g5})
  end

exec j3()
exec score-play(score-shift(*score*, -251.0))
```

16.2 Orchestration

Now that the pitch and rhythm are taken care of, we can turn our attention to timbre. Originally, I thought I might use one instrument sound (but not the piano) for this little piece, but at some point decided I wanted to change the orchestration when I changed pitch sets. This can be implemented simply by passing the orchestration information to the function that generates each section.

In Example 16.2.1 you can see that j-sect from Example 16.1.4 has been renamed to j-orch, and a new parameter, instr, has been added. The value of instr is a symbol that names a synthesis function. The line "name: instr" tells score-gen to use the value of instr as the function name for each score event. j-orch is called from within j4, which provides synthesis function (instrument) names for each section. The synthesis functions are defined in orchestra.sal.

To finish the piece, I added some reverberation and chorus effects, as shown below in Example 16.2.2. (Some further processing was done with audio and video editing software to add the voice-over, refine the levels to make all the narration intelligible, etc.) Describing things from the innermost expression outward, the function jrender uses timed-seq to synthesize the score. A few seconds of silence are appended to allow for reverb decay. (The seq function joins the result of timed-seq with silence generated by s-rest.) Then jrender applies chorus and reverb. The output of the reverb is saved to the file jellyfish.wav using s-save. Unlike play or score-play, the function s-save does not use the "autonorm" facility to automatically scale the output amplitude of a sound. If the level is too low, the sound will be hard to hear, but if the level is too high, the sound will be clipped to lie within the maximum values of +1 and −1, causing distortion of the desired waveforms. In this example, we multiply the output of my-reverb by 1, so in fact, no scaling was necessary. How do we know? The value returned by s-save is the maximum sample value. The format function prints a message with this peak value returned by s-save. If the value is in a good range, say, between 0.5 and 1, then the scale factor is fine. If not, you should edit the scale factor and try again.

Example 16.2.1: Excerpts from jellyfish-4.sal

```
load "orchestra" ;; definitions of instruments
define function j-orch(
        start, dur, beatdur, lh-heap, rh-heap, instr)
    begin
    with notes = (start + dur - *time*) / beatdur,
         section ; result score for this section
    ;; reset some variables used by select-pitch:
    set lh-pat = make-heap(lh-heap, for: 1)
    set rh-pat = make-heap(rh-heap, for: 1)
    set lh-cnt = 0 ; how many previous lh selections?
    set rh-cnt = 0 ; how many previous rh selections?
    set notes = 2 * round(notes / 2) ; even # of nts
    display "j-orch", instr
    set section = score-gen(score-len: notes,
                    name: instr, begin: *time*,
                    ioi: beatdur,
                    vel: real-random(70, 120),
                    pitch: select-pitch())
    exec score-print(section)
    ;; merge new notes with previous ones in *score*:
    set *score* = score-merge(*score*, section)
    ;; update time so next section follows this one
    set *time* += notes * beatdur
    end
```

```
define variable *score* = nil, *time* = 251.5
define function j4()
  begin
    ;;            start  dur  beatdur lh-heap/rh-heap
    exec j-orch(251.5, 11.5, 0.44, {g3 ef4 f4},
                {g4 bf4 c5 d5}, quote(sine-bell))
    exec j-orch(263  , 6  , 0.38, {f3 df4 ef4},
                {f4 af4 c5}, quote(j1-note))
    exec j-orch(269  , 11 , 0.33, {fs3 ds4 e4},
                {g4 af4 df5}, quote(ting-tone))
    exec j-orch(280  , 9  , 0.33, {bf2 af3},
                {d4 gf4 af4 bf4}, quote(ting-pluck))
    exec j-orch(289  , 12 , 0.36, {ef3 c4 df4},
                {ef4 af4 bf4 df5},
                quote(ting-pluck-mellow))
    exec j-orch(301  , 4  , 0.33, {f3 c4},
                {f4 g4 bf4 c4},
                quote(flutey-tingy-pno))
    exec j-orch(305  , 7  , 0.33, {cs3 b3},
                {fs4 cs5 e5},
                quote(flutey-tingy))
    exec j-orch(312  , 7  , 0.33, {cs3 b3},
                {e4 fs4 b4}, quote(ting-tone-del))
    exec j-orch(319  , 15 , 0.33, {bf3 af3},
                {ef4 f4 bf4 c5}, quote(ting-pluck))
    exec j-orch(334  , 10 , 0.36, {ef3 af3 df4},
                {f4 af4 bf4 c5}, quote(ting-pluck-del))
    exec j-orch(344  , 10 , 0.40, {bf3 f3 c4},
                {af4 bf4 f5 g5}, quote(k-sound))
  end

exec j4()
```

The function play-file plays the file. By using s-save followed by play-file, we can compute scores of any complexity and play them back smoothly, even if the computer cannot compute the sound in real-time.

Example 16.2.2: Excerpt from jellyfish-4.sal

```
;; MY-REVERB -- reverb effect
;;    mixes dry signal with reverberated signal
define function my-reverb(snd, rt, depth)
  return (1 - depth) * snd +
         depth * reverb(snd, rt)

define function jrender(score)
  exec format(#t, "PEAK: ~A~%",
         s-save(1.0 * my-reverb(
                       stereo-chorus(
                         seq(timed-seq(score),
                             s-rest(3.0))),
                       1.5, 0.1),
                ny:all, "jellyfish.wav"))

exec jrender(score-shift(*score*, -251.0))

exec play-file("jellyfish.wav")
```

16.3 Text to Music

Music is often referred to as a language (Minsky, 1981a, 1981b) and there are many parallels. The idea of translation from text to music is quite natural to the algorithmic musician. In fact, one of the first instances of algorithmic composition is a method of translating text to pitches in *Micrologus* by Guido d'Arezzo around 1025.

The example here is based on a program by Edwin Shao. The basic idea of this program is to map each letter of a text string to a pitch, forming a pitch sequence. To assure "reasonable" pitches, the program relies on instrument descriptions that give a range of integers that can be used to indicate pitch. Each instrument can have a unique range, and it is up to the instrument to convert from an integer in this range to an actual pitch. A list of three values is used to represent an instrument. Rather than access these values using generic functions such as first, second, and third, mnemonic access functions are defined (see Example 16.3.1) to make the program more readable. instr-make is defined to create an instrument description from three parameters.

Example 16.3.1: Instrument structure excerpt from wordmusic.sal

```
;; INSTR structure represents instruments as a
;; list: (name lowest highest)
;; These are accessor functions. Use them so
;; that your code is not dependent upon the
;; exact list layout:
;;
define function instr-name(instr)
  return first(instr)
define function instr-lowest(instr)
  return second(instr)
define function instr-highest (instr)
  return third(instr)
define function instr-make(
                          name, lowest, highest)
  return list(name, lowest, highest)
```

The program will convert characters of text to integers (details will follow) and then map these integers into the range of an instrument. The function map-pitch performs this task by using % (the remainder operator), relying on the property that n % range is a number between 0 and range-1.

Example 16.3.2: map-pitch excerpt from wordmusic.sal

```
;; MAP-PITCH -- translate input number into
;; instrument range
define function map-pitch(n, instr)
  return n % (instr-highest(instr) -
             instr-lowest(instr)) +
         instr-lowest(instr)
```

The basic algorithm is as follows: starting with a text string, translate each character of text to an integer using the char-code function. Then use map-pitch to generate a pitch in the range of the desired instrument. A note is generated for each character.

To make things more interesting, the duration of each note is determined by a variable that is updated when certain punctuation characters are encountered.

Another aspect of the program is instrument selection. The text is divided into paragraphs, where two adjacent newline characters indicate a paragraph. An instrument is selected for each paragraph from a list of instruments. Instrument selection is based on the length of the paragraph, using the remainder of the length divided by the number of instruments to index into the instrument list.

We are now ready to look at the code for the wordmusic program. The algorithm is broken into two functions. Example 16.3.3 shows the first one, wordmusic, which takes input text as a single string, and a list of instruments. It returns a score.

wordmusic uses a loop to find and translate paragraphs in text. Initially, score is empty (nil) and text is the complete text to be translated. Each iteration of the while loop removes a paragraph from text and appends the translated paragraph to score. The test in the while loop causes the loop to exit when text is the empty string (in other words the last paragraph has been removed).

Example 16.3.3: Wordmusic excerpt from wordmusic.sal

```
define function wordmusic(text, translations)
  begin with i, ;index of paragraph boundary
             score, paragraph
    loop ; iterate through paragraphs of text
    while length(text) > 0
    ; find end of paragraph:
    set i = string-search("\n\n", text))
    display "wordmusic", i, text
    if null(i) then
       ; not found, so go to end of text
       set i = length(text)
    else ; found. include newlines in count
       set i += 2
    ; i is now the length of the first
    ; paragraph. Extract it here:
    set paragraph = subseq(text, 0, i)
    set text = subseq(text, i) ; remove it
    set score = score-append(score,
                  paragraphmusic(paragraph,
                                 translations))
    finally return score
  end
end
```

To find a paragraph, string-search finds the first location of two newlines (a newline is written as "\n"; the backslash is called an *escape character* and is used as a prefix to change the interpretation of "n" from "n" to newline). If a match is not found, string-search returns nil. This case is tested by the if command. If the search results in nil, the index i is set to the length of the entire text. In other words, we treat the remaining text as a final paragraph. On the other hand, if two newlines are found, we increment the index i by 2 so that the newlines are included in the paragraph. Next, subseq is used to copy the first i characters of text into paragraph. This has no effect on the text string, so the next expression takes the remaining text starting at location i and assigns it to text, effectively removing the first i characters. Finally, paragraphmusic is used to compute a score from paragraph (which saved the characters removed from text), and the result is appended to score, which accumulates all the notes.

Example 16.3.4 shows the definition of paragraphmusic, which is based on score-gen. Most of the code is in the function new-dur-pause and deals with the computation of dur and pause from (1) the current character, represented as a string of length one, and (2) the previous values of dur and pause passed in as a list of the two values. A chain of if-then-else commands checks for a match to the special characters, including period, comma, question mark, exclamation point, colon, semicolon, space, and newline. When a special character is matched, dur and pause are updated. Notice that string comparison must use the string-equal function rather than "=". (The "~=" operator would also work.) Other characters are ignored, which means that dur will hold until the next special character changes it. To keep dur positive, it is constrained to be at least 0.025 (seconds). At the end of new-dur-pause, dur and pause are packed into a list and returned. This is a programming trick that allows us to return more than one value from a function.

In paragraphmusic, the length of the score is the length of the text. The instrument is selected by taking the remainder (% operator) of the text length divided by the number of instruments: length(translations). The pre: keyword is used in score-gen to call new-dur-pause. To extract a one character string from the paragraph, we use subseq, a built-in function. Notice how sg:count, which counts the number of notes computed so far, is used to select the character. For pitch, we use map-pitch, defined in Example 16.3.2, which requires a number and an instrument description. The number used is the internal (ASCII) code used to represent the current character.

A *character* is an XLISP data type we have not used so far and which is not really supported by SAL. For example, you can write #\A in in XLISP to indicate the character "A," but this is not a valid SAL expression. Nevertheless, SAL does not prevent you from calling any XLISP function. We use char to access a character in the paragraph string, and char-code to extract the integer representation of that character: char-code(char(paragraph, sg:count)) returns an integer that we pass to map-pitch.

Example 16.3.4: paragraphmusic excerpt from wordmusic.sal

```
;; convert a one-character string to a
;;    duration and pause
define function new-dur-pause(c, dur-pause)
  begin
    with dur = first(dur-pause),
         pause = 0 ; default is no pause
    if string-equal(c, ".") then
      begin
        set dur -= 0.1
        set pause = 1
      end
    else
      if string-equal(c, ",") then
        begin
          set dur -= 0.05
          set pause = 0.5
        end
      else
        if string-equal(c,"?") then
          begin
            set dur += 0.35
            set pause = 1
          end
        else
          if string-equal(c, "!") then
            begin
              set dur -= 0.3
              set pause = 0.3
            end
          else
            if string-equal(c, ":") |
               string-equal(c, ";") then
              begin
                set dur -= 0.1
                set pause = 0.1
              end
            else
              if string-equal(c, " ") then
                set pause = 0.1
              else
                if string-equal(c, "\n") then
                  begin
                    set dur -= 0.05
                    set pause = .25
                  end
    ; else default is previous dur and no pause
    ; make sure dur is now greater than zero
    set dur = max(dur, 0.025)
    return list(dur, pause)
  end
```

```
        define function paragraphmusic(paragraph,
                                       translations)
    begin
      with len = length(paragraph),
           ;; get index into instruments
           i = len % length(translations),
           ;; get the ith instrument
           instr = nth(i, translations),
           ;; initial beat period and pause
           dur-pause = {0.3 0},
           ;; character from paragraph
           c
      return score-gen(
           score-len: len,
           pre: setf(dur-pause,
                     new-dur-pause(
                       subseq(paragraph, sg:count,
                                         sg:count + 1),
                       dur-pause)),
           name: instr-name(instr),
           pitch: map-pitch(
                     char-code(char(paragraph,
                                    sg:count)),
                     instr),
           dur: first(dur-pause),
           ioi: first(dur-pause) +
                second(dur-pause))
    end
```

Finally, we are ready to generate some music. We define render-words in Example 16.3.5 to convert text to sound using wordmusic.

After computing a score, Example 16.3.5 uses timed-seq to synthesize it. Some reverberation is added. Note again the use of seq to append some silence before passing the sound to the reverb function. Also note the result is scaled by 0.5 to avoid audio clipping (in this case, the synthesized score exceeds the maximum sample value of 1, so scaling is necessary before saving the sound samples).

The text passed to render-words extends over multiple lines. It is acceptable for quoted strings to span many lines, but you must be careful to close the string with a double-quote character. Also, any embedded double-quote characters must be *escaped* by prefixing them with a back-slash character. (See the word "gong" in the example.) What would happen if the double-quotes were not escaped?

render-words uses the global variable translations, which must be a list of instrument descriptors. This variable is set when the file instruments.sal is loaded. Each instrument descriptor is created by calling instr-make, and translations is just a list of these descriptors. Details can be found in instruments.sal.

Example 16.3.5: Excerpt from wordmusic.sal

```
define function render-words(text)
  begin
    with snd = timed-seq(
                 wordmusic(text, translations))
    return 0.5 * snd +
           0.1 * reverb(seq(snd, s-rest(5)),
                        2.0)
  end

define variable *peak*
set *peak* = s-save(render-words(
"This is some text.

How will it sound? Hopefully, it will
be interesting.

Isn't \"gong\" noticed by this program?

define function paragraphmusic(paragraph,
                               translations)
  begin
    with len = length(paragraph),
         ;; get index into instruments
         i = len % length(translations),
         ;; get the ith instrument
         instr = nth(i, translations),
         ;; initial beat period and pause
         dur-pause = {0.3 0},
         ;; character from paragraph
         c
    ...
  end

Hacker Haiku:
  Three things are certain:
  Death, taxes, and lost data.
  Guess which has occurred.
"), ny:all, "wordmusic.wav")

display "finished rendering sound", *peak*

exec play-file("wordmusic.wav")
```

Try rendering different text strings. You might want to modify the program to read text from a file. There are many elaborations possible, for example to control dynamics. You might want to invent your own algorithms for text-to-music translation. Other instrument sounds can be incorporated, using instruments.sal as a guide.

16.4   Suggested Listening

Emma Speaks by Mary Simoni and Jason Marchant explores the application of Augmented Transition Networks to the development of form in choreography and multimedia. Choreography and dance by Emma Cotter were captured on video and edited such that the video post processing introduced another layer of choreography. Music was composed for the edited video using Common Music (refer to example on accompanying electronic media) (Simoni & Marchant, 1998).

Chapter 17 Epilogue

Algorithmic composition is important because it offers new ways of thinking about the organization of sound that we call music. In principle, algorithmic composition cannot create anything that we could not create by traditional methods, but that is like saying that a composer, in principle, could write out the ones and zeros of a digital audio recording. In practice, algorithmic composition allows us to explore new kinds of music. The very idea that music can be generated by automated processes is the beginning of many philosophical and aesthetic discussions about the nature of art, beauty, creativity, and humanity.

We have seen many techniques of algorithmic composition. In nearly every case, the main feature of the algorithm is that music is abstracted from the detailed sound or note level to some *model* of music. Examples include patterns from pattern generators, graph models, and transformations of "natural" data such as text into parameters of music. The importance of models is that they shift the focus of composition from notes or sound events to higher-level structure and control.

A characteristic of algorithmic composition is that, often, the composer has only a vague idea about how the output will sound. However, because the process of music generation is highly automated, the composer can adjust parameters and algorithmic details again and again to gradually improve the work.

Another characteristic of algorithmic composition is the surprise one gets when algorithmic details interact in unexpected ways or when computed sounds do not match what was intended or imagined. Even program "bugs" can turn out to be useful. This constant surprise can inspire us and lead to creative discoveries that might never occur while working at a piano keyboard or with pencil and manuscript paper. It is too easy to fall back on what we know and what we have learned.

Algorithmic composition is hard work. If you think automation will make life easy or simple, you will probably be disappointed with the whole approach. If you read this book, you may also feel that the secret of algorithmic composition has been withheld. How can these simple techniques result in anything profound and beautiful? Where are the really good algorithms? The answer is that good results can be achieved from simple means, but it takes careful listening and lots of experimentation. You should not expect to pick up some already-written algorithm, plug in a few numbers, and walk away with a masterpiece. As with any kind of music making, algorithmic composition requires practice to build skill and experience. On the other hand, it should be encouraging that algorithmic composition *does not* require advanced programming techniques, artificial intelligence, machine learning, or a sophisticated knowledge of digital signal processing.

In the future, algorithmic composition seems to be a perfect match for interactive technologies including games, cell phones, web sites, and personal music players. Not only do these devices have the computer power needed to generate music algorithmically, but they create a context in which it makes sense for music to change and adapt to the state of the world or the state of the user. We expect to see algorithmic composition become more common as composers explore new application areas.

We hope that readers will now feel empowered and ready to pursue their own creative musical directions. Seek inspiration from the natural world, from society, and even from technology. Use your ear and your imagination to evaluate your work, and do not be afraid to work hard to make programs that behave the way you want. Trying only the easy things is the path to mediocrity. Also, do not be afraid to throw away work and start over (but always save a backup copy) when the behavior is disappointing. Eventually, you will hit upon a procedure that holds promise, and after many iterations of refinement and evaluation, you will develop something remarkable.

Algorithmic compositions rarely sound like "conventional music" or successfully imitate a known style. However, it is often possible to incorporate some of the theory or characteristics of existing musical forms. Probably the most interesting outcome occurs when algorithmic compositions suggest a new musical form, structure, and inner organization that could not have been imagined or completed without the help of a computer. This is the ultimate attraction: to create music that takes us beyond what we know and even beyond what we could have imagined.

Appendix   SAL Commands and Functions

The following lists summarize commands and functions used in this book. For details on command syntax and a complete list of functions, see the *Nyquist Reference Manual*. In some cases optional or keyword parameters are not mentioned here to simplify the presentation.

Commands

> begin-end – execute a sequence of commands.
> define variable – declare and initialize a variable.
> define function – declare and define a function.
> display – print variable names and values.
> if-then-else – conditionally evaluate commands.
> load – evaluate the commands in a file.
> loop-end – iteratively evaluate commands.
> play – play a sound.
> print – print the values of expressions to the output window.
> return – return a value to the function calling expression.
> set – associate or bind a variable to the value of an expression.
> with – declare local variables.

Functions

List Functions

length(*list*) – length of a list or string.
first(*list*), car(*list*) – first element of a list.
second(*list*) – second element of a list.
third(*list*) – third element of a list.
fourth(*list*) – fourth element of a list.
rest(*list*), cdr(*list*) – remainder of list after the first element.
nth(*n, list*) – get list element at position *n*.
nthcdr(*n, list*) – get remainder of list starting at position *n*.
reverse(*list*) – reverse the order of *list*.
cons(*head, list*) – construct a list of *head* followed by *list*.
list(*e1, e2, ...*) – construct a list from elements.
append(*list1, list2, ...*) – construct a new list by concatenating lists.
member(*expr, list*) – search for *expr* in *list*.

assoc(*expr, alist*) – look up *expr* in an association list.
intersection(*list1, list2*) – set intersection, treating lists as sets.
union(*list1, list2*) – set union, treating lists as sets.
set-difference(*list1, list2*) – set difference, treating lists as sets.
subsetp(*list1, list2*) – is *list1* a subset of *list2*?
mapcar(*function, list1*) – apply *function* to each element of *list.*

Math Functions

(See Table 3.3.1 for a list of operators)
round(*x*) – round *x* to an integer.
truncate(*x*) – round *x* down to an integer.
abs(*x*) – absolute value of *x.*
min(*x, y, ...*) – minimum value of inputs.
max(*x, y, ...*) – maximum value of inputs.
interpolate(*x, x1, y1, x2, y2*) – linear interpolation.
random(*i*) – random integer from 0 to i–1.
rrandom() – random float (real) from 0 to 1.
real-random(*x, y*) – random float (real) from *x* to *y.*

Pattern Functions

(See Table 5.3.1 for a list of pattern generators.)
next(*expr*) – get the next item from a pattern object.

Predicate (Test) Functions

atom(*x*) – is *x* an atom?
endp(*x*) – is *x* the end of a list (nil)?
evenp(*x*) – is *x* even?
floatp(*x*) – is *x* a float (real, floating point, flonum)?
integerp(*x*) – is *x* an integer?
listp(*x*) – is *x* a list?
minusp(*x*) – is *x* negative?
null(*x*) – is *x* nil?
numberp(*x*) – is *x* a number?
oddp(*x*) – is *x* odd?
plusp(*x*) – is *x* positive?
symbolp(*x*) – is *x* a symbol?
zerop(*x*) – is *x* zero?

Quoting Functions

quote(*s*) – returns expression (or symbol) *s* without evaluation.
keyword(*s*) – convert (unevaluated) symbol *s* to a keyword.

Score Functions

timed-seq(*score*) – render *score* returning a sound.

score-adjacent-events(*score, function*) – apply function to events.
score-append(*score1, score2, ...*) – append scores.
score-apply(*score1, function*) – apply function to each event.
score-filter-length(*score, cutoff*) – remove notes playing past *cutoff*.
score-get-begin(*score*) – get the begin time.
score-get-end(*score*) – get the end time.
score-index-of(*score, function*) – find first note satisfying *function*.
score-last-index-of(*score, function*) – last note satisfying *function*.
score-merge(*score1, score2, ...*) – create score combining all notes.
score-play(*score*) – render a score to sound and play it.
score-randomize-start(*score, amt*) – perturb note start times.
score-read-smf(*filename*) – read standard MIDI file into a score.
score-repeat(*score, n*) – repeat a score *n* times.
score-scale(*score, keyword, x*) – scale each *keyword*'s value by *x*.
score-select(*score, function*) – select notes that satisfy *function*.
score-set-begin(*score, time*) – set *score* beginning to *time*.
score-set-end(*score, time*) – set *score* ending to *time*.
score-sort(*score*) – sort events in *score* into time order.
score-sustain(*score, x*) – scale each note duration by *x*.
score-transpose(*score, keyword, x*) – add *x* to each *keyword* value.
score-voice(*score, list*) – replace event functions according to *list*.
score-write-smf(*score, filename*) – write *score* to MIDI file.

event-time(*note*) – get the time of *note*.
event-set-time(*note, time*) – change start *time* of *note*.
event-dur(*note*) – get the duration of *note*.
event-set-dur(*note, dur*) – change *duration* of *note*.
event-expression(*note*) – get the expression from *note*.
event-set-expression(*note, expr*) – change *expression* of *note*.
event-has-attr(*note, attribute*) – does the *note* have *attribute*?
event-get-attr(*note, attribute, default*) – get *attribute* from *note*.
event-set-attr(*note, attribute, value*) – set *attribute* of *note* to *value*.

expr-has-attr(*expression, attribute*) – test if *expression* has *attribute*.
expr-get-attr(*expression, attribute, default*) – get value of *attribute*.
expr-set-attr(*expression, attribute, value*) – set *attribute* to *value*.

Sound Functions

const(*x, duration*) – generate a constant amplitude *x* for *duration*.
fmosc(*pitch, modulation*) – generate an FM sound.
hzosc(*frequency*) – generate a sine with variable frequency (in Hz).
note(pitch: *pitch*, dur: *duration*) – generate a generic sound.
piano-note-2(*pitch, dynamic*) – generate a piano sound.

pwl(*t1, l1, t2, l2,..., tn*) – piecewise linear control function.
pluck(*pitch, duration*) – generate a plucked string sound.
reverb(*snd, time*) – reverberate *snd* with a given reverberation *time*.
s-plot(*sound, dur, samples*) – plot *sound* in a Nyquist IDE window.
s-rest(*duration*) – generate silence with a given *duration*.
seq(*expr1, expr2, ...*) – construct sound sequentially.

String and Character Functions

strcat(*s1, s2, ...*) – concatenate strings.
string-equal(*s1, s2*) – test strings for equality (case-sensitive).
string-search(*pattern, string*) – find *pattern* in *string*.
subseq(*string, start, end*) – extract a subsequence of *string*.
char(*string, index*) – extract one character from a *string*.
char-code(*character*) – get integer code for *character*.
format(*output, format, x, y, z, ...*) – print values using *format* string.
#print(*expr*) – functional form of print command.
#display(*string, expr1, expr2,...*) – functional form of display.

System Functions

setdir(*string*) – set and return the current directory (folder).
open(*filepathstring*) – open a text file for input.
open(*filepathstring*, direction: :output) – open file for output.
read() – read user input.
read(*file*) – read from an opened file.
close(*file*) – close an opened file.

Bibliography

Adorno, Theodor. 1980. *Philosophy of Modern Music*. New York, NY: The Seabury Press.

Aiken, Jim. 1996. The Limitations of EMI. *Computer Music Journal* 20 (3): 5–7.

Allen, John. *Anatomy of Lisp*. New York: McGraw Hill, 1978.

Ames, Charles. 1987. Automated Composition in Retrospect: 1956–1986. *Leonardo* 20 (2): 169–186.

Ames, Charles. 1989. The Markov Process as a Compositional Model: A Survey and Tutorial. *Leonardo* 22 (2): 175–187.

Ames, Charles. 1995. Thresholds of Confidence: An Analysis of Statistical Methods for Composition, Part I: Theory. *Leonardo Music Journal* 5: 33–38.

Ames, Charles. 1996. Thresholds of Confidence: An Analysis of Statistical Methods for Composition, Part 2: Applications. *Leonardo Music Journal* 6: 21–26.

Apel, Willi. 1979. *Harvard Dictionary of Music*. Cambridge, MA: The Belknap Press of Harvard University Press.

Ariza, Chris. 2005a. *An Open Design for Computer-Aided Algorithmic Music Composition: athenaCL* [Ph.D. Thesis]. New York: New York University. (Also available from www.dissertation.com.)

Ariza, Chris. 2005b. The Xenakis Sieve as Object: A New Model and a Complete Implementation. *Computer Music Journal* 29 (2): 40–60.

Ariza, Chris. 2007. Automata Bending: Applications of Dynamic Mutation and Dynamic Rules in Modular One-Dimensional Cellular Automata. *Computer Music Journal* 31 (1): 29–49.

Assayag, Gerard, Camilo Rueda, Mikael Laurson, Carlos Agon, and Olivier Delerue. 1999. Computer-Assisted Composition at IRCAM: From Patchwork to Open Music. *Computer Music Journal* 23 (3): 59–72.

Bach, J. S. 1752. *Die Kunst der Fuge*. Edited by Carl Czerny. New York, NY: C. F. Peters Corporation.

Berg, Paul. 1996. Abstracting the Future: The Search for Musical Constructs. *Computer Music Journal* 20 (3): 24–27.

Berg, Paul. 2008. *Using the AC Toolbox: A Tutorial.* The Hague: Institute of Sonology. (Available from www.koncon.nl/ACToolbox/files/AC_Toolbox_Tutorial.pdf.)

Boulanger, Richard Charles. 1999. *The Csound Book: Perspectives in Software Synthesis, Sound Design, Signal Processing, and Programming.* Cambridge, MA: The MIT Press.

Boynton, Lee, Pierre Lavoie, Yan Orlarney, Carnillo Rueda, and David Wessel. 1986. MIDI-Lisp, a Lisp-Based Music Programming Environment for the Macintosh. In *Proceedings of the 1986 International Computer Music Conference.* San Franciso, CA: The International Computer Music Association.

Brindle, Reginald Smith. 1969. *Serial Composition.* London, England: Oxford University Press.

Brooks, Stephen and Brian J. Ross. 1996. Automated Composition from Computer Models of Biological Behavior. *Leonardo Music Journal* 6: 27–31.

Brown, Andrew R. and Andrew Sorensen. 2009. Interacting with Generative Music through Live Coding. *Contemporary Music Review* 28 (1): 17–29.

Bukofzer, Manfred F. 1947. *Music in the Baroque Era.* New York, NY: W. W. Norton & Company, Inc.

Chadabe, Joel. 1997. *Electric Sound: The Past and Promise of Electronic Music.* Upper Saddle River, NJ: Prentice-Hall, Inc.

Collins, Nick. 2009. Musical Form and Algorithmic Composition. *Contemporary Music Review* 28 (1): 103–114.

Cope, David. 1991. *Computers and Musical Style.* Edited by John Strawn. 6 vols. Vol. 6, The Computer Music and Digital Audio Series. Madison, WI: A-R Editions.

Dannenberg, Roger B. 1989. The Canon Score Language. *Computer Music Journal* 13 (1): 47–56.

Dannenberg, Roger B. 1997. Machine Tongues XIX: Nyquist, a Language for Composition and Sound Synthesis. *Computer Music Journal* 21 (3): 50–60.

Dannenberg, Roger B. *Nyquist* [Web page]. SourceForge, 2005 [cited July 6, 2012]. Available from http://nyquist.sourceforge.net/.

Dewdney, Alexander K. 1985. Computer Recreations. *Scientific American*, August 1985, 16–24.

Dodge, Charles. 1988. Profile: A Musical Fractal. *Computer Music Journal* 12 (3): 10–14.

Dodge, Charles and Curtis Bahn. 1986. Musical Fractals. *Byte* 11 (6): 185–196.

Dodge, Charles and Thomas Jerse. 1997. *Computer Music: Synthesis, Composition, and Performance*. 2nd ed. New York, NY: Schirmer Books.

Döbereiner, Luc. 2008a. CompScheme: A Language for Composition and Stochastic Synthesis. In *Proceedings of the Sound and Music Computing Conference '08* (SMC '08), Berlin [cited July 6, 2012]. Available from http://www.doebereiner.org/texts.html.

Döbereiner, Luc. 2008b. *Structuring Symbolic Spaces— Programming Languages and Composition Systems in Computer Music* [Bachelor's thesis]. The Hague: Institute of Sonology [cited July 6, 2012]. Available from http://www.sonology.org/NL/ thesis-pdf/structuring%20symbolic%20spaces.pdf.

Ebciouglu, K. 1992. An Expert System for Harmonizing Chorales in the Style of J. S. Bach. In *Understanding Music with AI*. Menlo Park, CA: AAAI Press.

Ernst, David. 1977. *The Evolution of Electronic Music*. New York, NY: Schirmer Books.

Finer, Jem, Janna Levin, Kodwo Eshun, Christine Wertheim, and Margaret Wertheim. 2003. *Longplayer*. London: Artangel.

Forte, Allen. 1973. *The Structure of Atonal Music*. New Haven, CT: Yale University Press.

Gardner, Martin. 1986. White and Brown Music, Fractal Curves and 1/f Fluctuations. *Scientific American* 238: 16–32.

Grout, Donald Jay. 1973. *A History of Western Music*. Revised ed. New York, NY: W. W. Norton & Company, Inc.

Hiller, Lejaren and Leonard Isaacson. 1959. *Experimental Music*. New York, NY: McGraw-Hill, Inc.

Hiller, Lejaren. 1970. Music Composed with Computers–A Historical Survey. In *The Computer and Music*, edited by H. Lincoln. Ithaca, NY: Cornell University Press.

Hoppin, Richard H. 1978. *Medieval Music*. New York, NY: W. W. Norton and Company.

Hudak, Paul. 2000. *Haskore* [Web page, cited July 6, 2012].
Available from http://www.haskell.org/haskellwiki/Haskore.

International MIDI Association (IMA). 1983. *MIDI Musical
Instrument Digital Interface Specification 1.0*. Los Angeles, CA:
International MIDI Association.

Jones, Kevin. 1989. Generative Models in Computer-Assisted
Musical Composition. *Contemporary Music Review* 3 (1): 177–
196.

Kao, Edward P.C. 1997. *An Introduction to Stochastic Processes*.
Belmont, CA: Wadsworth Publishing Company.

Keene, Sonya E. 1989. *Object-Oriented Programming in Common
LISP*. Reading, MA: Addison-Wesley Publishing Company.

Knuth, Donald E. 1973. *The Art of Computer Programming, Vol. 1:
Fundamental Algorithms*. Reading, MA: Addison-Wesley, Inc.

Koenig, Gottfried M. 1987. Genesis of Form in Technically
Conditioned Environments. *Interface* 16 (3).

Kretz, Johannes. 2006. Navigation of Structured Material in "Second
Horizon" for Piano and Orchestra. In Carlos Agon (Ed.), *The OM
Composer*. Paris: IRCAM Centre Pompidou, 107–124.

Lansky, Paul. 1990. *Cmix*. Princeton, NJ: Godfrey Winham
Laboratory, Princeton University.

Laurson, M. and J. Duthen. 1989. Patchwork, a Graphical Language
in Pre-Form. In *Proceedings of the 1989 International Computer
Music Conference*. San Francisco, CA: International Computer
Music Association.

Loy, Gareth. 1989. Composing with Computers—A Survey of Some
Compositional Formalisms and Music Programming Languages.
In *Current Directions in Computer Music Research*, edited by
Max Mathews and John Pierce. Cambridge, MA: The MIT Press.

Luque, Sergio. 2006. *Stochastic Synthesis: Origins and Extensions*
[Master's Thesis]. The Hague: Institute of Sonology [cited July 6,
2012]. Available from http://www.sergioluque.com/thesis.
html.

Lutz, Mark. 2007. *Learning Python*. 3rd edition. Sebastopol, CA:
O'Reilly.

Machlis, Joseph. 1961. *Introduction to Contemporary Music*. 2nd
edition. New York, NY: W. W. Norton & Company.

Malt, Mikhail. 1993. *Patchwork Introduction*. Paris: IRCAM.

Mandelbrojt, Jacques, Marcel Frémiot, and Roger F. Malina. 1999. Introduction: The Aesthetic Status of Technological Art. *Leonardo* 32 (3): 211–215.

Manousakis, Stelios. 2006. *Musical L-systems* [Master's Thesis]. The Hague: Institute of Sonology [cited July 6, 2012]. Available from http://www.modularbrains.net/research.html.

McAlpine, Kenneth, Eduardo Miranda, and Stuart Hoggar. 1999. Making Music with Algorithms: A Case Study System. *Computer Music Journal* 23 (2): 19–30.

McLuhan, Marshall. 1964. *Understanding Media*. New York, NY: McGraw-Hill.

Minsky, Marvin. 1981a. Music, Mind, and Meaning. *Computer Music Journal* 5 (3): 28–44.

Minsky, Marvin. 1981b. Music, Mind and Meaning. In *Music, Mind and Brain: The Neuropsychology of Music*, edited by Manfred Clynes. New York, NY: Plenum.

Moore, F. Richard. 1990. *Elements of Computer Music*. Englewood Cliffs, NJ: Prentice-Hall.

Purse, Bill. 2005. *The Finale Primer: Mastering the Art of Music Notation with Finale*. San Francisco: Backbeat Books.

Rahn, John. 1990. The Lisp Kernel: A Portable Software Environment for Composition. *Computer Music Journal* 14 (4): 42–58.

Roads, Curtis. 1996. *The Computer Music Tutorial*. Cambridge, MA: The MIT Press.

Roads, Curtis. 2004. *Microsound*. Cambridge, MA: The MIT Press.

Rodet, Xavier and Piere Cointe. 1984. FORMES: Composition and Scheduling of Processes. *Computer Music Journal* 8 (3): 32–50.

Rothstein, Joseph. 1992. *MIDI: A Comprehensive Introduction*. 2nd ed. Madison, WI: A-R Editions, Inc.

Rowe, Robert. 1994. *Interactive Music Systems*. Cambridge, MA: The MIT Press.

Rudolph, Thomas and Vincent Leonard. 2007. *Sibelius: A Comprehensive Guide to Sibelius Music Notation Software*. Milwaukee: Hal Leonard.

Salzman, Eric. 1974. *Twentieth-Century Music: An Introduction*. 2nd ed. Prentice Hall History of Music Series. Englewood Cliffs, NJ: Prentice-Hall, Inc.

Schottstaedt, William. 1989. Automatic Counterpoint. In *Current Directions in Computer Music Research*, edited by Max Mathews and John Pierce. Cambridge, MA: The MIT Press.

Schottstaedt, William. 1991. *Common Lisp Music*. Palo Alto, CA: Center for Computer Research in Music and Acoustics, Stanford University.

Seay, Albert. 1975. *Music in the Medieval World*. Edited by H. W. Hitchcock. 2nd ed. Prentice-Hall History of Music Series. Englewood Cliffs, NJ: Prentice-Hall, Inc.

Simoni, Mary, Benjamin Broening, Christopher Rozell, Colin Meek, and Gregory H. Wakefield. 1999. A Theoretical Framework for Electro-Acoustic Music. In *Proceedings of the 1999 International Computer Music Conference*. San Francisco, CA: International Computer Music Association.

Sorensen, A. 2005. Impromptu: An Interactive Programming Environment for Composition and Performance. In *Proceedings of the Australasian Computer Music Conference 2005*. Andrew R. Brown and Timothy Opie, eds. Brisbane: ACMA, 149–153.

Spiegel, Laurie. 1981. Manipulations of Musical Patterns. In *Proceedings of the Symposium on Small Computers in the Arts*, 19–22.

Spiegel, Laurie. 1996. That Was Then—This Is Now. *Computer Music Journal* 20 (1): 42–45.

Steele, Guy L. 1990. *Common LISP—The Language*. 2nd ed. Bedford, MA: Digital Press.

Taube, Heinrich. 1989. *Common Music Documentation* [html].

Taube, Heinrich. 1991. Common Music: A Music Composition Language in Common Lisp and CLOS. *Computer Music Journal* 15 (2): 21–32.

Taube, Heinrich. 1993. Stella: Persistent Score Representation and Score Editing in Common Music. *Computer Music Journal* 17 (4): 38–50.

Taube, Heinrich. 1995. An Object-Oriented Representation for Musical Pattern Definition. *New Music Research* 24 (2): 121–129.

Taube, Heinrich. 1996. Higher-Order Compositional Modeling. In *Proceedings of the 1996 International Conference on Musical Cognition and Perception*. Montreal.

Taube, Heinrich. 1997. An Introduction to Common Music. *Computer Music Journal* 21 (1): 29–34.

Taube, Heinrich. 2004. *Notes from the Metalevel: An Introduction to Algorithmic Music Composition.* New York: Taylor & Francis.

Taube, Heinrich. 2005. *SAL* [Web page]. SourceForge, 2000 [cited July 6, 2012]. Available from http://commonmusic.sourceforge.net/cm2/doc/dict/index.html.

tENTATIVELY, a cONVENIENCE. 2009. *HiTEC (Histrionic Thought Experiment Collective) "Systems Management."* Pittsburgh: Encyclopedia Destructica.

Todd, Peter M. 1989. A Connectionist Approach to Algorithmic Composition. *Computer Music Journal* 13 (4): 27–43.

Tonality Systems. 1993. *Symbolic Composer.* West Yorkshire: Tonality Systems.

Touretzky, David S. 1990. *Common LISP: A Gentle Introduction to Symbolic Computation.* Redwood City, CA: The Benjamin/Cummings Publishing Company, Inc.

Voss, Richard F. and John Clarke. 1978. 1/f Noise in Music: Music from 1/f Noise. *Journal of the Acoustical Society of America* 63 (1): 258.

Wang, G. and P. Cook. 2003. ChucK: A Concurrent, On-the-Fly Audio Programming Language. In *Proceedings of the 2003 International Computer Music Conference.* San Francisco: International Computer Music Association, 217–225.

Winkler, Todd. 2001. *Composing Interactive Music: Techniques and Ideas Using Max.* Cambridge, MA: MIT Press.

Winston, Patrick Henry and Berthold Klaus Paul Horn. 1989. *LISP.* 3rd ed. Reading, MA: Addison-Wesley Publishing Company.

Xenakis, Iannis. 1971. *Formalized Music.* Bloomington, IN: Indiana University Press.

Xenakis, Iannis. 1992. *Formalized Music.* Revised ed. New York, NY: Pendragon Press.

Discography

Bach, J.S. *Musical Offering*. LL 1181 London.

Bach, J.S. *The Art of the Fugue*. ML 5738 Columbia.

Berg, Alban. *Lyric Suite*. LM-2531 RCA Victor.

Cage, John. *HPSCHD*. H 71224 Nonesuch.

Cage, John. *Concert for Piano and Orchestra / Atlas Eclipticalis.* WER6216-2. Wergo.

de Vitry, Phillipe. *Garrit gallus – In nova fert*. 77095-2-RC Deutsche Harmonia Mundi.

Degazio, Bruno. *On Growth and Form*. San Francisco, CA: ICMC92: The International Computer Music Association.

Dobrian, Christopher. 1991. *Entropy* for computer-controlled piano. Artful Devices, Music for Piano and Computers, EMF 2000.

Dodge, Charles. *Profile*. 450-73 Neuma Records.

Furman, Pablo. *Matices Coincidentes*. Los Angeles, CA: The Society of Electro-Acoustic Music in the United States.

Haas, Jeffrey. *Keyed Up,* mvmt. III. Los Angeles, CA: The Society for Electro-Acoustic Music in the United States.

Hiller, Lejaren. *The ILLIAC Suite*. HS 25053 Heliodor.

Jaffe, David. 1992. *American Miniatures*, mvmt. II—*After the Battle of Bull Run*. Berkeley, CA: Well-Tempered Productions.

Kimura, Mari. 1992. *"U" (The Cormorant)*. San Francisco, CA: ICMC92: The International Computer Music Association.

Lansky, Paul. *Late August*. San Francisco, CA: New Albion Records.

Mozart, Wolfgang Amadeus. *Musikalisches Würfelspiel*. 422-545-2 Philips.

Simoni, Mary. *Eulogy*. San Francisco, CA: Leonardo.

Simoni, Mary and Jason Marchant. 1998. *Emma Speaks*. San Francisco, CA: The International Computer Music Association. CD-ROM.

Stockhausen, Karlheinz. *Klavierstück/Piano Pieces IX-XI*. CD 310 009 H1 Koch Schwann Musica Mundi.

Taube, Heinrich. *Gloriette for John Cage.* San Francisco, CA: ICMC94: The International Computer Music Association.

Xenakis, Iannis. *Amorsima-Morsima.* S36560 Angel.

Xenakis, Iannis. *Strategie, Jeu pour deux orchestres.* VCD 47253 Varese Sarabande.

Xenakis, Iannis. *Electronic Music.* EM102. EMF Media.

Discography

Index

global, 82
local, 82
Vitry, Phillipe de, 7, 8, 15
Voss, Richard F., 183

Wagner, Richard, 10
Webern, Anton, 10, 13, 186
well-formed list, 17
while clausxse in loop, 155
Wieciek, Joe, 2

Winston, Patrick Henry, 5
with command, 85

Xenakis, Iannis, 12, 13, 15, 212, 242
XLISP, 2

Z correspondents, 110
zerop, 31
Z-related sets, 110